WITHDRAWN

Writing 22

The publication of this book was largely made possible by a grant from the National Endowment for the Arts in Washington, D.C., a federal agency created by an Act of Congress in 1965.

By Robert Creeley

ROBERT CREELEY

A Quick Graph

Collected Notes & Essays

Edited by Donald Allen

Four Seasons Foundation
San Francisco: 1970

Grateful acknowledgment is made to the following publications
in which some of this material first appeared:
*A Nosegay in Black, Agenda, Artisan, Arts Magazine,
Big Table, Black Mountain Review, Contact* (Toronto),
*Elizabeth, First Person, The Floating Bear, The Free
Lance, Goad, Harper's Bazaar, The Humanist,
The Lugano Review, Montevallo Review, The Nation, New
Mexico Quarterly, Nomad, Origin, Outburst, The
Outsider, Poetry, The Sparrow, Work, Yale Literary
Review,* and *Yugen.*

Acknowledgment is also made to the following publishers
for having first printed some of the material here collected:
The Bobbs-Merrill Co., Inc.; Brandon House; Calder
& Boyars Ltd.; The Divers Press; Doubleday & Co., Inc.;
Alice Garver (*Togetherness*); Jargon Press; The Jewish
Museum (*Recent American Sculpture*); The National
Council of Teachers of English (*Poems for Young
Readers*); New Directions; Penguin Books Ltd.; and Charles
Scribner's Sons.

Library of Congress Catalog Card Number: 67-30650

Cover photograph by Ellie Dorfman

The Writing Series is edited by Donald Allen and published
by Four Seasons Foundation
Distributed by Book People, 2010 Seventh Street,
Berkeley, California 94710

Contents

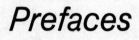

Prefaces

The Gold Diggers

HAD I LIVED some years ago, I think I would have been a moralist, i.e., one who lays down, so to speak, rules of behavior with no small amount of self-satisfaction. But the writer isn't allowed that function anymore, or no man can take the job on very happily, being aware (as he must be) of what precisely that will make him.

So there is left this other area, still the short story or really the tale, and all that can be made of it. Whereas the novel is a continuum, of necessity, chapter to chapter, the story can escape some of that obligation, and function exactly in terms of whatever emotion best can serve it.

The story has no time finally. Or it hasn't here. Its shape, if form can be so thought of, is a sphere, an egg of obdurate kind. The only possible reason for its existence is that it has, in itself, the fact of reality and the pressure. There, in short, is its form — no matter how random and broken that will seem. The old assumptions of beginning and end — those very neat assertions — have fallen way completely in a place where the only actuality is life, the only end (never realised) death, and the only value, what love one can manage.

It is impossible to think otherwise, or at least I have found it so. I begin where I can, and end when I see the whole thing returning. Perhaps that is an obsession. These people, and what happens to them here, have never been completely my decision — because if you once say something, it will lead you to say more than you had meant to.

As the man responsible, I wanted to say what I thought was true, and make that the fact. It has led me to impossible things at times. I was not obliged, certainly, to say anything, but that argument never made sense to me.

1954

All That Is Lovely in Men

THESE POEMS MAKE use of a variety of materials, else of course they do not exist — not enough. Line-wise, the most complementary sense I have found is that of musicians like Charlie Parker and Miles Davis. I am interested in how that is done, how 'time' there is held to a measure peculiarly an evidence (a hand) of the emotion which prompts (drives) the poem in the first place. If this seems hopeful, let me point to the 'line' of Miles Davis' chorus in "But Not For Me" — Bach is no different, but the time is. There I think we must do it for ourselves. We must, as Dr. Williams insists, find a 'measure' (a scale) — and I am, here, interested in the attempt to do this, also.

Otherwise, I have been called a 'domestic' poet, which celebration Robert Graves somewhere suggests is the death of the Muse altogether. But such is my 'world,' like they say — what space I can recognize — and with no confinement of anything whatsoever. At one time it must have been, a woman was this insistence, i.e., a fact in herself so variable her very presence was a wonder. Well, now where is she? I think I have been there now and again — simply there. A poet, call him what you will, knows his Muse, 'domestic drudge' or not. To hell with it. Let each man save himself as best he can.

1955

The Whip & For Love

WHEREVER IT IS one stumbles (to get to wherever) at least some way will exist, so to speak, as and when a man takes this or that step — for which, god bless him. Insofar as these poems are such places, always they were ones stumbled into: warmth for a night perhaps, the misdirected intention come right; and too, a sudden instance of love, and the being loved, wherewith a man also contrives a world (of his own mind).

It seems to me, now, that I know less of these poems than will a reader, at least the reader for whom — if I write for anyone — I have written. How much I should like to please! It is a constant concern.

That is, however, hopeful and pompous, and not altogether true. I write poems because it pleases me, very much — I think that is true. In any case, we live as we can, each day another — there is no use in counting. Nor more, say, to live than what there is, to live. I want the poem as close to this fact as I can bring it; or it, me.

January 26, 1957

A Form of Women

SOMEWHERE IN HIS *The White Goddess,* Robert Graves calls
up the Irish saying — that it is death to mock a poet, to love
a poet, to be a poet. For the ill-mannered and poor in heart,
these recommendations will be specious; but for the pre-
cariously situate, such sayings will indicate much warmth
and possibility (albeit a little faded at this time). One will
want to know the how, and also the where, of these sadly
dispossessed men. It will be the burden of these poems (in
part) to provide clues to the answering of these things.

Not having spoken — my uncle said, still waters run deep
— until I was fourteen, I then developed a habit which has
lasted me beyond other equally emotional attachments. I
have lost women, so to speak, and perhaps the children
which were theirs also. I have rarely lost my voice, however;
but it has been much altered by circumstance, from time to
time, like the donkey braying in the woods. Having such a
sound to make, it is hard to decide where it should best
occur.

But the sound occurs no matter. The first poem in this
book is for my oldest son, David — in no real hope that he
will 'understand' it, but that the forms from which it is contrived will follow him in his own life as they have in mine.

1959

The Island

A SUSPICIOUSLY SIMPLE sense of life is that it is, in any one man, conclusive. Oh, for *him* — of course; but for this world I wonder, or rather think it is only in the relationships men manage, that they live at all. People try with an increasing despair to live, and to come to something, some place, or person. They want an island in which the world will be at last a place circumscribed by visible horizons. They want to love free of a continuity of roads, and other places. This island is, finally, not real, however tangible it once seemed to me. I have found that time, even if it will not offer much more than a place to die in, nonetheless carries one on, away from this or any other island. The people, too, are gone.

1963

Words

THINGS CONTINUE, but my sense is that I have, at best, simply taken place with that fact. I see no progress in time or any other such situation. So it is that what I feel, in the world, is the one thing I know myself to be, for that instant. I will never know myself otherwise.

Intentions are the variability of all these feelings, moments of that possibility. How can I ever assume that they must come to this or that substance? I am trying to say that what I think to say is of no help to me – and yet insist on my seriousness, which is a sense of my nature I would like to admire.

Words will not say anything more than they do, and my various purposes will not understand them more than what they say.

1967

One

Notes for a New Prose

> *"Language is not reality but*
> *another of the* instruments *by*
> *which man engages reality ..."*

IT IS, CERTAINLY, reasonable to comment that Joyce's earlier work presents no such divergence from normality as does, now, even the mention of his name. There is, to be got at, a straight line of impact, search, through the early work, the poems, the play (which is all 'idea') to the fact of *Ulysses* and then, *Finnegans Wake*. It is useless to avoid it, or to mistake its point. Which must be: it is not the content which is changed. It is the extension of the content into form that has been tempered, made strong.

To go back. We had been led to believe that connotation was this: the suggestions of 'meaning' beyond the supposedly exact, denotative meaning which custom of usage had put upon the phrase or word in question. Then, by way of the opening created by 'associational' content of phrase, gesture, practice, ways, in short, METHOD — connotation became meaning versus meaning, became the fight for sense, in shorthand. (Some call this 'symbol ...') "It isn't what the words mean. It's what they mean to you ..."

Just so, with Joyce. That is, the possible suggestions (which can now be called: manifestations) of sense (which was about to become: value) became the criteria for an ultimate 'sense' (though no millennium). Because this was done with language, or, more strictly, within the words themselves, there we took our sight, a bead on: what might be up. Wrong from the start, since it was not words for the sake of words, but, for the sake of what content, possible, might shape them, into sense. Taken as such, Joyce is the craftsman, casting about for a model, for the model — what is in the head. Not to make himself, but to make, what is in himself.

Form is the extension of content. This was the first rule.

2

> "*A man must create himself, if he is an artist, instrument also IN ORDER THAT his work be not expression but illumination . . .*"

Possible arguments for the supposition that poetry is, now, more able than prose, or more able to make itself an extension of the present context, this life, etc., have first to do with the fact of its ability, (1) to compress, and (2) to project supposition, as fact. In prose, the lean toward a 'solution' or a stasis of idea most usually marks the book as a failure; I mean, insofar as a writer of prose is willing to give space to this fixing of idea as the logical 'end' of movement, etc., just so far we usually won't go along with him. And I would figure that we are right. But we deny him, even so, the way out of it, this fix, or what could get him beyond these 'logics.' Take the idea of a man running alongside a train, taking notes yet. He would be about it, what is now expected — while the poet, at home, can project this iron monster to any place which may please him. It is, then, that we are still confused by the idea of 'reality' in prose. We do not as yet get the basic fact, that reality is just that which is believed, just as long as it is, believed. Poets are more used to this thing: reality as variants round the center, or, simply, what has been left us.

So how could a prose catch up? Difficult to make the competition actual. It isn't. Elsewhere, it had been pointed out that "poetry insists upon or suggests a quite different 'Universe': a universe of reciprocal relations . . ." The swing of idea, in stasis — is still poetry. But prose is the *projection* of ideas, in time. This does not mean that the projection must be an 'actual' one, date by date, etc. The word is law, is the creator, and what it can do, is what any prose can do. There is nothing more real, in essence, about a possible prose than there is about any possible poetry. The ordering of *conjecture* will remain as 'real' as the ordering of fact, given the right hand.

More to the point, to note the difference, again, between poetry and prose, one of the differences, since there are others as well. Poetry, as the formulation of content, in stasis; prose, as the formulation of content, in a progression, like that of time. This is a simple way of putting it. But sufficient to show that while poetry depends on the *flux contained,* held within the form, in stasis, prose may intend such a limiting but cannot justify one. It has no beginning or end. It has only the length it happens to have. "Might be continued . . ." Just here is the key to its possible reach, that, in spite of itself, it has to continue, keep going — cannot stop.

So, in some sense, the usual idea of beginning and end have put upon prose an order alien to its nature. This is not to imply a 'necessary chaos.' It means only that it is, by nature, against conclusions — or is (as nature is) intent only on its present. It is the breaking out, of context, of form, and down or back, always to the progression, enforced by the nature of its content, and so determined.

It has neither beginning nor end.

3

> *"Are we not automatic, to think
> that because prose — and — the
> — novel did, since the 18th, &
> conspicuously, in the 19th, &
> dyingly, in the 20th, do a major
> job, that it need now be fruit-
> ful?"*

As soon as the novel, as soon as prose, generally, supposed
for itself, a context other than what it might, on each occasion make, it had done itself the greatest possible disservice.
And this is not to be mistaken. We can note, perhaps, that
while poetry may have combined itself in several, to mean,
one thing worked in the hands of several men, at certain
times with success, prose has never been effectual so taken,
as a job, or so treated. I can remember the notes that Kafka
had written about his attempt to write a novel with Brod —
or the more amusing attempts of Dylan Thomas, etc. Certainly, the novelist hates his neighbor, hates him for writing,
to begin with, and hates him doubly, for writing prose. Perhaps this a false lead. It matters little except that it can
clear the sense of the necessary singleness of the man who
writes prose. And that any constriction, is too much.

The suggestion that record-making can now be taken as
one of the major jobs of those that make prose is wrong only
in its supposition that there exists any occupation for prose,
prior to its coming. It is wrong in the same way that posit-
ing any 'frame' for prose is wrong. Prose is a plausible
and profitable instrument for making records. But stories?
Novels? One wonders if it is to the point to set them an end
before they have demonstrated their own. "As Rousset, e.g.,
wrote *L'Univers Concentrationnaire* (*not Les Jours de
Notre Morte*) — and, over a weekend, because he figured

to die the next week of the Causes; or Martin-Chauffier, who has been a novelist, & who chose in *L'Homme et la Bête*, to tell not even what he had heard others say (the last vestige of the novelist!) but only & precisely what had happened to him; vide Joe Gould ..."

Joe Gould's HISTORY. One wonders. Or, who put him to such work? Joe Gould.

Pointless to argue such a thing. It is not that prose cannot be put to such work, that it hasn't that capability, that it couldn't deal with that end of things. Rather, like nothing else, it must be new. And if, say, tradition concerns itself with these frames, then prose has no tradition. None whatsoever. It should demand that it has none. More than we, or they, may have spoken.

It could be, has been, the collection of ideas. And nothing better, for such documentation. But records? It was the fact of its perspective, that made what it gave, of such, reliable. That it is without, frame. What makes it reliable. That it owns to no master, that it can't. Its terminals, ends, are fictitious. Someone dies. "It was the end of THAT period ..." But continual, that it repeats, goes over and under, around. Has form, frame, only as it is such a going. As someone had said of Stendhal — it all fell into exact place, exact.

It stands by itself.

4

> "*The reason why, at this juncture of time, one fights so hard for prose, is, that it enables him to get in, to go by, that head of his, to let it play over his things, outside objects ...*"

To go back to Joyce. To that mistaking we have made of him; and you may document this for yourselves or look to find who has made of those books something beyond the man who may have written them. Oddly enough, the most exact criticism of these things appeared at the same time that the books themselves did. At least, that first interest prevented the fatal preoccupations with the 'purpose,' of Joyce, with his own use, as symbol. At least for a time.

Speaking of James, Pound had written that the logic of the pieces the former had written for the *Yellow Book* group was that need to push beyond the curve, in order to establish it. So, generally, position is established in prose, and intention. Hence, this idea of the assumed obliquity, itself a way of placing something, in the context. Is prose roundabout? It's not that question which should be asked. Any way could be the right one. What is got to, what is placed, would be the better thing to be asking, after it's done.

Again — de Gourmont's sentence, ". . . *d'écrire franchement ce qu'ils pensent — seul plaisir d'un écrivain* . . ." And could it be less, granting it must be more?

A new prose . . . Better to think of this, only, as what may now come. I think we can hang on to those who have left us something strong enough to carry over into this time. Prose cannot exist free of its ability to apply; it can't be faked. So it would be that Stendhal can still give us the sense, or one sense, of the order, the 'form,' not to be taken as the form of poetry, nor as we come back to it, that more basic form of prose. There is the fact that the more correct translation of Dostoevsky's *Notes from Underground* must be — "Notes from Under the Floor," or, "Out from the Cracks Like Any Roach."

Perhaps it will still be necessary to point to the fact that, while poetry will be the clear, the fact of the head, prose will be the coming, and going. Around. It is there that it can hit, beyond poetry. It is not a matter of better, or worse. There is no competition. The drift, in prose, and the way, of the swing, the reach — we have the necessary evidence, or I must believe we have.

> I am very old today, the sky is grey,
> I am not very well.
> Nothing can prevent madness.
> As an honourable man who abhors exagger-
> ation, I do not know what to do . . .

We begin, or end, there.

[*Origin*, No. 2, 1951]

A Note on the Objective

WHETHER from an altogether 'scientific' attitude, or from some wish to disassociate, only, by way of the surface of language, one idea from another, *objectivity* has become the apparent trademark of the careful mind. Common use would put upon this *objectivity* the air of the cool head, that is, one capable of confronting divers phenomena in their own particulars, rather than as extensions of one's own senses. It was this battle, between the *objective* and the *subjective,* then, which had replaced the looser and more worn fight between classicism and romanticism.

But intentions, as is usual, belie results. Or are belied by them. Because, however actual an intention may be, however well considered, reasoned, etc., its result is not to be found prior to that act which effects it, and altogether useless to assume the intended victory before it's come to pass. In this case, *objectivity* is, in intention, the prime aspect of a method which plans to deal with the 'things around' as characters in themselves, having as their first claim on the attention, their own actuality. In matters of poetry, it amounts to the wish to transmit, free of imprecise 'feeling,' the nature of 'that' which has moved one to write in the first place. As such, this wish intends as complete a break as possible with the *subjective.*

In effect, this break is not actual, since the writing comes to 1) using this 'that' as a character for use (as content in the poem); and 2) using 'that' as an impetus for the act of writing itself — simply what's pushing. In short, while the first is concerned with abstracting the experience as *objective* data, the second is equally concerned with keeping it as *subjective* impulse. And pointless to comment: it's a fight.

A useless fight. However right it may be to damn the use of the *subjective* method as an excuse for emotional claptrap, it's apt to push us away from any understanding of the *subjective* in a more basic character, i.e., "belonging to, or of, or due to, the consciousness . . ." Impossible to write anything, lacking this relation of its content to oneself. Put another way: things have to come in before they can go out.

Perhaps best to junk both terms, or at least to understand this necessary balance, one with the other. We can't stand outside our content and at the same time we can't eat it like an apple, etc. And perhaps, finally, more to the point than either of these two stances is that one which maintains: a man and his objects must both be presences in this field of force we call a poem.

[*Goad*, Summer 1951]

How to Write a Novel

THE RULES have been obvious enough — mainly the injunction to hold to 'character and action,' and one novelist, of at least some reputation, has said he was constitutionally in favor of 'plot.' But it means very little.

Otherwise, one can go back to even the hackneyed examples. *"The Life and Opinions of Tristram Shandy, Gent...* appeared on the 1st of January 1760." A simple fact; and from that time, hence, like they say, at least one major evidence, against the above rote, was there to be dealt with.

I am speaking, in short, of *time* — of what that is in a prose narrative, and of what it has done there. As frame, as the main means to a coherent order.

It is certainly very attractive. That is, it is a line, a very solid one, for the hoisting up of anything which may interest the novelist; his characters, etc., his apprehension of 'the meaning of life,' etc. And, more than that, what other continuum is possible; how else effect a reasonable series, how project, by language, the incident reality, say that it is there, and prove it?

At least that, for a clear sense of the problem. By some means or other, this demanded, a man must make of his narrative a cohesion of the things there occurring, must give them demonstrable relation. Which is order of a kind; and we've gone wrong, only, in believing it to be of one kind, no other to be admitted.

Beyond humor, *Tristram Shandy* is the narrative of one man's attentions, of what they found to fasten on. That is a defensible comment — there is very clear writing in this book.

"The lines were very natural — for they were nothing at all to the purpose, says *Slawkenbergius*, and 'tis a pity there were no more of them; but whether it was the Seig. *Diego* was slow in composing verses — or the hostler quick in saddling mules — is not averred . . ."

Go at it another way. Take it as your own headache, and think, then, if what counts is that the day goes by, etc., etc.; or that something in it, precisely in, was of interest, and that made it all otherwise. This is the contrary — if one can fasten on there.

Similarly, one thing leads to another — with or without *time*. An instant is a precise formulation, even of a universe. It doesn't finally matter much whether it lead to another; it has its own logic. Or say, perhaps better, that there are two ways of evoking a reality: that it has place in *time*, or that it is existent in *space*. There is some choice between them, at least for the novelist.

"Early in 1880, in spite of a well-founded suspicion as to the advisability of perpetuating that race which has the sanction of the Lord and the disapproval of the people . . ." Whereas this present table, with the typewriter on it, two books, milk bottle, is something else again. Or clearly a different *field*. It is that sense I am intent on making clear.

To write of one is not to write of the other. There is the escape of *time*, that escape which *time* affords; so that the man dies, too soon, or the book ends.

What else. ("Is this a fit time, said my father to himself, to talk of PENSIONS and GRENADIERS?")

The divers techniques used to confront *time*, in the long narrative, are ultimately makeshift; they solve very little.

Flashback, recall by certain of the characters, juxtaposition (too simply) of 'time' sequences — none of much use. Because, to be in that passage, to make that the sequence (that the days go by), is a definite commitment, and not to be dodged easily.

But put the weight on the other sense, of things shifting, among themselves — and *time* there to be a qualification among many — it is a release.

A release, immediately, of the very things themselves — not gratuitously, since relation is aimed at — why they all keep together. And to the extent that *time* bears on that, all right, i.e., all right to make use of it. But not as the main line.

The present novel* is attack on this ground. Clearly. Unequivocally aimed at that, to break *time* back to a use which isn't crippling. It is of very great interest.

[*New Mexico Quarterly*, Summer 1952]

*John Hawkes: *The Beetle Leg*.

To Define

THE PROCESS OF DEFINITION is the intent of the poem, or is to that sense — "Peace comes of communication." Poetry stands in no need of any sympathy, or even goodwill. One acts from bottom, the root is the purpose quite beyond any kindness.

A poetry can act on this: "A poem is energy transferred from where the poet got it (he will have some several causations), by way of the poem itself to, all the way over to, the reader." One breaks the line of aesthetics, or that outcrop of a general division of knowledge. A sense of the KINETIC impells recognition of force. Force is, and therefore stays.

The means of a poetry are, perhaps, related to Pound's sense of the *increment of association;* usage coheres value. Tradition is an aspect of what anyone is now thinking — not what someone once thought. We make with what we have, and in this way anything is worth looking at. A tradition becomes inept when it blocks the necessary conclusion; it says we have felt nothing, it implies others have felt more.

A poetry denies its end in any *descriptive* act, I mean any act which leaves the attention outside the poem. Our anger cannot exist usefully without its objects, but a description of them is also a perpetuation. There is that confusion — one wants the thing to act on, and yet hates it. *Description* does nothing, it includes the object — it neither hates nor loves.

If one can junk these things, of the content which relates

23

only to denial, the negative, the impact of dissolution — act otherwise, on other things. There is no country. Speech is an assertion of one man, by one man. "Therefore each speech having its own character the poetry it engenders will be peculiar to that speech also in its own intrinsic form."

[*Nine American Poets, Artisan* (Liverpool: 1953)]

A Note on Poetry

. . . OLSON'S NOTION of the poem as a *field* at once clears us from the usual sense of progression, i.e., that we have a line, building forward perhaps to 'climax,' and then relaxing to an 'end.' For example, seeing a poem as a *field*, a high energy construct, we assume a sense that points to one basic means of coherence: a relevant and actual tension between the divers parts present, to come to (in this sense *only*) what we call the 'whole.'

This is then clear: a poem will be a *thing* of parts, in such relation, that the tension created between them will effect an actual coherence in form.

That does not say anything yet about line, or imagery, or anything else. It allows those components, possible, to be then defined.

(Before getting on — to see this exactly. That I *can* say, for example:

> my blood is
> (the tree of
> silence, bleak in
> the dawn.

That is bad poetry not because it is *formally* bad; it is bad because all nouns used are general, do not sufficiently define themselves in context. But you see the point — that if these nouns were hard clear things, full — in that sense — a tension

could then be actual, and some segment of 'poetry' would
also be present.

No poet can ride past Pound's dicta re the generalities;
almost to say, take an hour off and read that part again,
"dim fields of peace" or something. *No poetry*, if it doesn't
get that.)

When Williams beats on the sonnet, and he has done it I
think brilliantly — he is hitting at a usage which denies
form *now*. In short — that implies we ourselves are incapable — as our predecessors were of course *not* — of invention, of finding in the direct context of what we know, where
we are, an exact means to form — which will be the direct
issue of such contact. The sonnet says, in short, we must
talk, if you want, with another man's mouth, in the peculiar
demands of that 'mouth,' and can't have our own.

To the contrary — any man who will listen to his own
speech, to the way any words come from himself, can find
the character of his own language. In this sense: "Therefore
each speech having its own character the poetry it engenders will be peculiar to that speech also in its own intrinsic
form." It is by no means a general prescription if one takes
that as *fact,* and acts accordingly, i.e., does go to that sense
of his own speech — and builds there.

When Olson speaks of *breath*, he is speaking of an exact
thing — a thing which can be defined, say, physiologically,
and whose influence on the rhythm patterns of our speech
can't be pushed off. When a man breaks a line like this:

> What can you see
> Out there?

the $64 question is why, and one is almost brought to offer
that for an answer — if he had it.

At least it has no relation to the breath, or the breathing,
quite actually, of any man. One tries it this way & that — and
can't say it as *written*.

One wants to write the poem, put it, as ultimately one would say it; the page is his means, *not* his end. If we grant that poetry must be relegated, finally, to what the eye can read, then we have no poetry — or we have to define our intentions all over again. We have at best what Stevens puts: "There is, however, a usage with respect to form as though it were a derivative of plastic shape."

Otherwise, one works in, to the page, as where he can score, in a literal sense, the language of his poem; he wants that as his means, the structure of his words *on the page,* in the sense that their spatial positions there will allow a reader to *read* them, with his own *voice,* to that end the poet is after — i.e., the poem in its full impact of *speech.*

This is why *line* is a problem, an immense one. We let it dictate to us — bend us into a formal structure not at all our own, as words would otherwise find their relations. We let it block the actual impulse.

Simply — one say sees a fire, a big one, flames all over hell, and shouts, fire. And maybe wants help, of course wants it, yells, for god sake, hurry, etc. Or whatever. Take, as literal problem — how write it, on the page, so that the emotion, of the language, will be *form*-ally declared by the spatial relations of the words — or better, by how the words come, in what order, in what relation. Can he write it:

> fire, fire, for god sake
> hurry, etc., etc., etc.

What *is* the progression called for, how hold in, keep in, multiple emotions at hand.

Breath anyhow is one means to solution, I think it is the *only* means. How does the breath 'say' it. And getting that — then how best indicate what that tells us, on the page. To switch it then, to the poem:

     but out there, on that dirt, in front, directly
     before your eyes, more, yr existence:
death, the
possibility of same, the certitude
right there in front of yr
eyes, god damn yr
eyes
this bull and this man (these men) can
kill
one another

         ("This" by Charles Olson)

  That, in short, is the fact — what then happens. Against
the strictures of the 'formal' pattern, one comes to the actually written, and written for an actual speech. The emotion
literal in the poem becomes literal in its transmission; the
breath, for which the emotion is dominant, makes the relevant positions — so *listened* to.

  Another aspect is, *"Dichten: Condensare,"* i.e., what Bunting found in the German-Italian dictionary. If one can say
it in five words, and there is no good reason to say it in ten —
he says it in five. The demands of the usual patterned 'form'
have also increased verbiage — and a man adds a word to
fill out a line he shouldn't have bothered with in the first
place.

  Ultimately, in the poem, language becomes the word, in
relation to the whole complex of its impulse — of what stands
behind it.

  One can't write about *content* because that is singularly
each man's own business. I.e., that is what the reader is for —
to say whether or not he has been affected. In that last, call
it, job — one can hardly respect such 'judgment' if it makes
no attempt to understand. Sometime he may want a like understanding — or perhaps he does already.

A poetry in any sense 'new' has its own problems, of understanding. It would be best to read without stopping at this
line or that, i.e., not reading against oneself, or the poem.
That is no pleasure for anyone. At the same time understanding is a complex process, i.e., I understand 'love' to the extent
that I experience it. This is relevant to the poem.

"Only the most absolute sincerity under heaven can effect
any change."

[From a letter to the editor.
Contact (Toronto), No. 6, 1953]

A Dilemma

WHY PEOPLE DON'T go out and get better jobs, or finally come
to some sense of themselves which might allow a more profitable exploitation . . . On the one hand, there are too many
people — you cannot kill them all, you cannot find a logic
quite sufficient to do this. And if they will not die quickly
enough with sickness, or tiredness, old age and the like,
then at least they can be confined to those places where
one will not have to, simply, consider them.

A logic is fashioned like this, a logic of impenetrable
worthiness. It follows that, between a man and his wife,
there must be constantly some means whereby she can
spit on him — and he, likewise, on her. Love, at best, will
become a question of sensation. And on good days she will
sigh, "my lover . . . ," and on bad days she will spit, "my
lover . . . ," etc. He will live in a room. With luck, someone
will buy him, i.e., someone also bought, and so with means,
will buy him — which is the hierarchy of how to live,
literally. To make money — at the first, enough to live on,
by which I mean, to eat with, to be clothed with, and then,
very soon, also to allow that better stance, to be 'better'
clothed, and so on.

But some people, if they are still 'people,' have been
removed from this by war, by 'depression' areas, by many
things finally, in terms of which they are neither very interesting nor important. And let me make very clear that
this is *not* a question of any bitterness or sentimentality or

whatever. Some people cannot 'live' anymore. There is neither reason for them to nor room nor means nor values, nor any of those things by which others, certainly more fortunate, may still claim 'significance.' And by much the same token, it is a little hysterical to feel our own securities are endangered by the specific reality of something like the hydrogen bomb, i.e., suppose one were to install, say, plumbing in a house, a toilet and all that, and then the toilet is flushed, and, all things being equal — can it be a surprise, or even the point, that (of course!) the toilet flushed?

Heretofore our dangers have been of two kinds, the one (big) metaphoric, and the other (contained) literal. So that to trip on a stone, then, meant, a) we stubbed a toe (literal) and b) this pain was token of the possibility of all pain, accident, and what might happen (metaphoric). Now enough is accomplished to make an end to that, i.e., we can have the two as one. We can all die at one time.

Which is not, really, a relief. It might be, just as for some people any death not now too painful, not too long, might be. What is there for an alternative except the dreary love too often exercised as it is. Belief — in what. And so on. Dead people already, at best.

I am sorry myself not to care anymore, or not to care for much beyond one or two things. That, say, to love anyone becomes more impossible. "I did love . . . ," one says, etc. I still want to, etc. Perhaps against the distortion, lying, deceit, viciousness, horror, cruelty, and all that, it will still be possible to make that most minimal of defenses — at least the knowledge that there might be others likewise confronted.

[*Black Mountain Review*, Autumn 1954]

A Note

I BELIEVE IN A poetry determined by the language of which it is made. (Williams: "Therefore each speech having its own character the poetry it engenders will be peculiar to that speech also in its own intrinsic form.") I look to words, and nothing else, for my own redemption either as man or poet. Pound, early in the century, teaches the tradition of "man-standing-by-his-word," the problem of *sincerity*, which is never as simple as it may be made to seem. The poet, of all men, has least cause and least excuse to pervert his language, since what he markets is so little in demand. He must find his living elsewhere. His aim must never be deflected by anterior commitment, even to those whom he loves. Words cannot serve responsibly as an apology for those who may wish to make them one.

I mean then *words* — as opposed to content. I care what the poem says, only as a poem — I am no longer interested in the exterior attitude to which the poem may well point, as signboard. That concern I have found it best to settle elsewhere. I will not be misled by the "niceness" of any sentiment, or its converse, malevolence. I do not think a poet is necessarily a nice man. I think the poem's morality is contained as a term of its structure, and is there to be determined and nowhere else. (Pound: "Prosody is the total articulation of the sound in a poem.") Only craft determines the morality of a poem.

Louis Zukofsky offers *A Test of Poetry* as "the range of

pleasure it offers as sight, sound, and intellection." I am pleased by that poem which makes use of myself and my intelligence, as a partner to its declaration. It does not matter what I am told — it matters, very much, how I am there used. Our world has been so delivered to the perversion of language (the word *qua* trick or persuader) that my own soul, such as I know it, comes to life in whatever clarities are offered to it. Poems allow me to go on living, and I am grateful for my life.

[*Nomad*, Winter-Spring 1960]

A Note on the Local

THE LOCAL IS NOT a place but a place in a given man — what part of it he has been compelled or else brought by love to give witness to in his own mind. And that is THE form, that is, the whole thing, as whole as it can get.

I think we will be fools to be embarrassed by it. We know the other neatness possible, the way of the neat pattern, and the dodging which it must call for. Grace has no part in that. At some point reached by us, sooner or later, there is no longer much else but ourselves, in the place given us. To make that present, and actual for other men, is not an embarrassment, but love.

[*First Person*, No. 1, 1961]

A Quick Graph

1. Recent BBC broadcasts of Pound interviews summarize the following:
   a) Writing: "You can't have a literature without curiosity. You cannot have a literature without *curiosity*. And when a writer's curiosity dies out, he is finished. You can do all the tricks you like, but without curiosity you get no literature with any life in it. . . . "
   b) Literacy: "A man has a right to have his ideas examined one at a time. . . . " (This parallels another comment made earlier, to the effect: literacy consists of the ability to recognize the same idea in different formulations. Both relate to Pound's insistence on the need to be able to dissociate ideas, i.e., to separate those living from those dead.)
2. Measure — which Dr. Williams continues to hammer at, as in a recent mimeographed sheet, "The American Idiom":
   "We must go forward uncertainly it may be, but courageously as we may. Be assured that measure in mathematics as in verse is unescapable, so in reply to the fixed foot of the ancient line including the Elizabethans we must have a reply: it is the variable foot which we are beginning to discover after Whitman's advent. . . . "
   One academic, Scully Bradley, some years ago made use of a shifting stress concept in an attempt to 'scan'

Whitman — prompted quite probably by the need to regularize common to such men; yet he showed understanding of the fact that the stress *may* be variable and yet cohesive in over-all effect. Too, he made the point of the 'rhyming' implicit in parallel or recurrent thought patterns (much as those used by Allen Ginsberg). Our ears tell us, certainly, that syllables may be grouped in a poem in such a way that they defy usual concepts of metric, and yet maintain a decided rhythm. In practice this has long been established. What does need revision is the old practice of 'phrasal' grouping, *qua* line, a loose solution tending to fall apart as the 'idea' the phrase implies exhausts itself and/or reaches its end. Poems of this sort read: The man sat down/ on the chair/ and lifted his foot/ into the air, etc. At no point should the rhythms *peculiar* to the given word, in the context it comes to *define,* be lost track of. *All* rhythm is specific. (Which in turn explains the boredom implicit in *generalized* iambics, etc.)

3. A sense of order — Louis Zukofsky defines one in his essay, "Poetry": *

"With respect to such action ["utterance," i.e., the movement of spoken words toward poetry] the specialized concern of the poet will be, first, its proper conduct — a concern to avoid clutter no matter how many details outside and in the head are ordered. This does not presume that the style will be the man, but rather that the order of his syllables will define his awareness of order. For his second and major aim is not to show himself but that order that of itself can speak to all men."

Kulchur, No. 8, 1962.

Or reading backwards:

> "The choice for science and poetry when symbols or words stop measuring is to stop speaking."

Such order proves as well "the contest any poet has with his art: working toward a perception that is his mind's peace," which Zukofsky has spoken of in *Bottom: on Shakespeare*.

4. Range — which can be variously characterized:

a) Zukofsky: "... the scientific definition of poetry can be based on nothing less than the world, the entire humanly known world."

b) Olson's *Maximus* has built from a like premise, with the corollary:

> He left him naked
> the man said, and
> nakedness
> is what one means
>
> that all start up
> to the eye and soul
> as though it had never
> happened before

c) It is equally Duncan's:

> that foot   informed
> by the weight of all things
> that can be elusive
> no more than a nearness to the mind
> of a single image

Range implies both what there is to deal with, and the wherewithal we can bring to that activity. Range describes the world in the limits of perception. It is the "field" in the old Pythagorean sense that "terms," as John Burnet says, are "boundary stones" and the place they so describe the "field" itself.

[*Floating Bear*, No. 2, 1961]

"Statement" for Paterson Society

A POEM IS A peculiar instance of language's uses, and goes well beyond the man writing — finally to the anonymity of any song. In this sense it may be that a poet works toward a final obliteration of himself, making that all the song — at last free of his own time and place. It is curious that this can be most true of that most personal, wherein the man leaves the environment of years and faces, to make his own the poem. But he can only do this, it seems to me, by the most scrupulous localism — because only the particular instance proves free in this way.

Again and again I find myself saved, in words — helped, allowed, returned to possibility and hope. In the dilemma of some literal context a way is found in the words which may speak of it.

Guatemala, January 31, 1961
[Floating Bear, No. 6, 1961]

Why Bother?

AN ART BEGINS prior to its conclusion — which is why there can be, with great use, an occasion offering that sense of means which conclusions per se deny. It can be put more simply. A magazine, not interested in being either the last word apropos some function, or taste, or simply a reflection of what is already 'valued' speciously or not — such a magazine may define the new possibility by being, quite literally, the place where it can be formulated.

No matter what becomes of it, art is local, local to a place and to a person, or group of persons, or just what's in the air despite how vague that sounds. It happens somewhere, not everywhere. When it does so happen everywhere, it has become a consequence of taste purely, a vogue or fashion, and/or what Pound calls 'style of the period,' and definition has given way to a reflection of a given effect.

No man can work free of the influence of those whom he may respect in his own art, and why 'originality' should imply, in any sense, that he should, is hard to follow. The light moves, so to speak, and those who see it have secured an 'originality' quite beyond that qualified by terms of personality or intent. In poetry, as in other arts, what is learned is first learned by the example, that is, by what exists in the art as a complex definition of possibilities: literally, this or that poem. Taste operates here as well, of course, but again Pound is relevant in that he said, damn your taste, I would like first to sharpen your perceptions, after which your taste can take care of itself.

May I submit that when the poem, or the opinion, or the taste, has come to that security of whatever large magazine — friendly or not — one may point to, then all has become primarily taste, an approval of taste, and that the actual work of definition which allowed taste its turn has gone?

A friend said once of his wife, that she said she wanted to be a singer, but what she really wanted to be was famous. One can be famous in many magazines, but not in those given to the definition of what a poem, right now, can be. There are no readers, and there are, even, few writers who will care to be bothered by what may be an attention alien to their own. Can you blame a German, French, English, poet for not caring specifically about what you face, here and now, as problems? But can you care for his, if all your mind is centered on the peculiar structure of that language given you, to effect, by its forms and its sounds, what it is, precisely, that you feel only as a poem? With nothing at all sentimental about it, and "Only the poem / only the made poem, to get said what must / be said . . ." as Williams writes all his life.

It is very possible that what one defines, as means, as possibilities, will prove only a temporary instance, a place soon effaced by other use, as when a whole city block is leveled to make a parking lot, or park. But that is the risk. One cannot avoid it, or do otherwise.

I believe in a magazine which is the specific issue of a few men, facing similar problems, places, things. They may, given ability, find the next step all must take if only because they are forced to take each such step with their own feet.

[*Tish*, September 14, 1962]

Introduction to The New Writing in the USA

NOTHING WILL FIT IF we assume a place for it. To attempt to classify writing before one has had the experience of its activity will be to misplace it altogether. What can be said is something itself particular — to senses of form, to the literal nature of living in a given place, to a world momently informed by what energies inhabit it.

1

The forties were a hostile time for the writers here included. The colleges and universities were dominant in their insistence upon an *idea* of form extrinsic to the given instance. Poems were equivalent to cars insofar as many could occur of similar pattern — although each was, of course, 'singular.' But it was this assumption of a *mold,* of a means that could be gained beyond the literal fact of the writing *here and now,* that had authority.

It is the more ironic to think of it, remembering the incredible pressure of *feeling* also present in these years — of all that did want 'to be said,' of so much confusion and pain wanting statement in its own terms. But again, it is Karl Shapiro's *Essay on Rime* (written in the South Pacific at a military base, "without access to books," in iambic pentameter) which is successful, and Auden is the measure of competence. In contrast Ezra Pound, H. D., William Carlos Williams (despite the token interest as *Paterson* begins to be published), Hart Crane, and especially Walt Whitman are largely disregarded.

The situation of prose I remember as much the same. Despite the apparent insistence of *digression* in the work of Joyce, Faulkner, Céline and others who are valued, there is nonetheless the attempt to shape all discussion of their 'form' to the context of an overt pattern, a symbolism, an explanation again anterior to the instance. In short, it is a period when criticism enjoys control of literary reference — so much so, that it can propose itself to be of primary value quite apart from its 'subjects.'

The sense of *form* which comes of this insistence is defined by Robert Duncan in an essay, "Ideas of the Meaning of Form":

Form, to the mind obsessed by convention, is significant insofar as it shows control. What has nor rime nor reason is a bogie that must be dismissed from the horizons of the mind. . . . Wherever the feeling of control is lost, the feeling of form is lost. The reality of the world and men's habits must be constricted to a realm — a court or a salon or a rationale — excluding whatever is feared. . . . Metaphor must be fumigated or avoided (thought of as displaying the author's fancy or wit) to rid the mind of the poetic where metaphor had led dangerously towards Paracelsus' universe of psychic correspondences, towards a life where men and things were beginning to mix and cross boundaries of knowledge. Poets, who had once had dreams and epiphanies, now admit only to devices and ornaments. Love, that had been a passion, had best be a sentiment or a sensible affection . . . . The struggle was to have ideas and not to let ideas have one. Taste, reason, rationality rule, and rule must be absolute and enlightened, because beyond lies the chiaroscuro in which forces co-operate and sympathies and aversions mingle. The glamor of this magic haunts all reasonable men today, surrounding them with, and then protecting them from, the darkness of possibilities that controls cannot manage, the world of thought and feeling in which we may participate but not dominate, where we are used by things even as we use them.

Confronting such *rule*, men were driven back upon the particulars of their own experience, the literal *things* of an immediate environment, wherewith to acknowledge the possibilities of their own lives. This alternative must now be familiar, but at that time there were few indeed to propose it. It is first found for me in Williams' introduction to *The Wedge* (1944):

Therefore each speech having its own character the poetry it engenders will be peculiar to that speech also in its own intrinsic form. . . . When a man makes a poem, makes it, mind you, he takes words as he finds them interrelated about him and composes them — without distortion which would mar their exact significances — into an intense expression of his perceptions and ardors that they may constitute a revelation in the speech that he uses. . . .

It is, in fact, a congruence of "the darkness of possibilities that control cannot manage" and that "revelation in the speech" that Williams emphasizes, which informs the first major work of Allen Ginsberg, *Howl*. He writes of its composition as follows:

By 1955 I wrote poetry adapted from prose seeds, journals, scratchings, arranged by phrasing or breath groups into little short-line patterns according to ideas of measure of American speech I'd picked up from W. C. Williams' imagist preoccupations. I suddenly turned aside in San Francisco, unemployment compensation leisure, to follow my romantic inspiration — Hebraic-Melvillean bardic breath. I thought I wouldn't write a *poem*, but just write what I wanted to without fear, let my imagination go, open secrecy, and scribble magic lines from my real mind — sum up my life — something I wouldn't be able to show anybody, writ for my own soul's ear and a few other golden ears. So the first line of *Howl.* . . .

It is relevant that he says, "I thought I wouldn't write a *poem,* but just write what I wanted to without fear . . . " — as does Duncan so emphasize that it was fear that felt "The reality of the world and men's habits must be constructed to a realm . . . excluding whatever is feared. . . . " The need becomes, then, literally:

> . . . to recreate the syntax and measure of poor human prose and stand before you speechless and intelligent and shaking with shame, rejected yet confessing out the soul to conform to the rhythm of thought in his naked and endless head,
> the madman bum and angel beat in Time, unknown, yet putting down here what might be left to say in time come after death,
> and rose reincarnate in the ghostly clothes of jazz in the goldhorn shadow of the band and blew the suffering of America's naked mind for love into an eli eli lamma lamma sabacthani saxophone cry that shivered the cities down to the last radio
> with the absolute heart of the poem of life butchered out of their bodies good to eat a thousand years.
>
>   (*Howl,* Part 1)

2

The usual critical vocabulary will not be of much use in trying to locate the character of writing we have now come to. If one depends on the dichotomy of *romantic* and *classical,* he is left with, too simply, an historical description, itself a remnant from an earlier 'period.'

The question becomes, *what is real* — and what is of that nature? The most severe argument we can offer against the 'value' of some thing or act, is that it is *not* real, that it has no given place in what our world has either chosen or been forced to admit. So it is the *condition* of reality which becomes our greatest concern — in which relation the following notes by Charles Olson are most useful:

> All things did come in again, in the 19th century. An idea shook loose, and energy and motion became as important a structure of things as that they are plural, and, by matter, mass. It was even shown that in the infinitely small the older concepts of space ceased to be valid at all. Quantity — the measurable and numerable — was suddenly as shafted in, to any thing, as it was also, as had been obvious, the striking character of the external world, that all things do extend out. Nothing was now inert fact, all things were there for feeling, to promote it, and be felt; and man, in the midst of it, knowing well how he was folded in, as well as how suddenly and strikingly he could extend himself, spring or, without even moving, go, to far, the farthest — he was suddenly possessed or repossessed of a character of being, a thing among things, which I shall call his physicality. It made a re-entry of or to the universe. Reality was without interruption, and we are still in the business of finding out how all action, and thought, have to be refounded. . . .
>
>   ("Equal, That Is, to the Real Itself")

This recognition had come primarily from scientific thinking, as it might be called — but its evidence in the way in which the world occurs in *Moby-Dick* (the object of Olson's discussion) is very striking. What happens to 'plot' or all such instance of 'category' — the assumption of action as *contained,* for example — when all is continuous, "when the discrete [isn't] any longer a good enough base for discourse...."? The sentence itself — as Fenollosa had proposed in *The Chinese Written Character as a Medium for Poetry,* and Olson reasserts — has become "an exchange of force" in no way a "completed thought," since such "completion" is impossible in the context of that *real* which Melville had apprehended, Olson notes, as "the absolute condition of present things..." Let it be stressed:

> [Melville] put it altogether accurately himself, in a single sentence of a letter to Hawthorne, written when he was writing *Moby-Dick* (1851): "By visible truth we mean the apprehension of the absolute condition of present things."

> (*Ibid.*)

The context so defined will include such present statement as this one taken from William Burroughs' *Naked Lunch:*

> There is only one thing a writer can write about: *what is in front of his senses at the moment of writing....* I am a recording instrument.... I do not presume to impose "story" "plot" "continuity",....

What has been criticized as a loss of coherence in contemporary American prose — specifically that of Burroughs and Kerouac — has been, rather, evidence of this character of the *real* with which we are involved. In "Kerouac's Sound" Warren Tallman makes a parallel distinction:

> In conventional fiction the narrative continuity is always clearly discernible. But it is impossible to create an absorbing narrative without at the same time enriching it with images, asides, themes and variations — impulses from within. It is evident that in much recent fiction — Joyce, Kafka, Virginia Woolf, and Faulkner are obvious

examples — the narrative line has tended to weaken, merge with, and be dominated by the sum of variations. Each narrative step in Faulkner's work is likely to provoke many sidewinding pages before a next narrative step is taken. More, a lot of Faulkner's power is to be found in the sidewindings. In brief, what happens in jazz when the melody merges with the improvisations and the improvisations dominate, has been happening in fiction for some time now.

Not only have the earlier senses of 'form' been rejected, but equally 'subject' as a conceptual focus or order has given place to the literal activity of the writing itself.

The objects which occur at every given moment of composition (of recognition, we can call it) are, can be, must be treated exactly as they do occur therein and not by any ideas or preconceptions from outside the poem, must be handled as a series of objects in field in such a way that a series of tensions (which they also are) are made to *hold*, and to hold exactly inside the content and the context of the poem which has forced itself, through the poet and them, into being.

(Charles Olson, *Projective Verse*)

But it is in the nature of the writing itself that this thinking finds its most active definition — as here in the final section of John Wieners' "A Poem for Painters":

. . . At last. I come to the last defense.

> My poems contain no
> wilde beestes, no
> lady of the lake, music
> of the spheres, or organ chants.

> Only the score of a man's
> struggle to stay with
> what is his own, what
> lies within him to do.
>
> Without which is nothing.
> And I come to this
> knowing the waste,
> leaving the rest up to love
> and its twisted faces,
> my hands claw out at
> only to draw back from the
> blood already running there.

3

Finally, there seems so much that might be said. The American condition has much to do with *place,* an active spatial term which differs in that way from what has been assumed its European equivalent. Space, as physical ground, not sky, I feel to be once again politically active — as it has always been for the American from the outset. It is useless, for example, to acknowledge the growing political weight of either Africa or China without seeing the literal measure these *places* effect in relation to all senses of the European continuum — in which the American takes its place, at least in part.

But more than that — since 'place' is not now more than activity — there is the queston of *all* terms of relationship, and of the possible continuities of that relationship in a *time* which is continuous and at all moments 'present' — else it never was.

The point seems that we cannot, as writers — or equally as readers — assume such content in our lives, that all presence is defined as a history of categorical orders. If the nature of the writing is to move in the field of its recognitions, the "open field" of Olson's *Projective Verse*, for example, then the nature of the life it *is* demands a possibility which no assumption can anticipate.

In such a situation the entity of oneself becomes more than a cultural 'program' and the attempt to recognize its potential has led to experiment with 'consciousness expanding' drugs such as mescaline, and writing which attempts to record such states, as Michael McClure's "Peyote Poem."

The impulse is also clear in attempts to rediscover the viable content of terms of life which precede the 'categorical' defined by Aristotle. One does not want to go 'back,' merely. But I feel it true, as Duncan writes, "We have come so far that all the old stories/ whisper once more ..." History, as 'progress,' seems quite dead.

Otherwise — *things* as they have taken place so consistently with us in this country are relevant, both as condition and as presence. They have been, always, a basic company, and they involve, with persistence, our uses of space. Further, I do not feel that Allen Ginsberg's insistent equation of states of feeling or being with so-called 'material' things is surreal and/or a dimension of reality less present in one of its aspects than in another. There is a persistent literalness in American writing — very much so in the tradition with which we are concerned — and it has never been easily 'symbolic.' "All the accumulations of life, that wear us out — clocks, bodies, consciousness, shoe, breasts — begotten sons — your Communism — 'Paranoia' into hospitals ..." is literal reality and literally apprehended. It is — as Denise Levertov notes from Jung for the title of one of her poems — that "everything that acts is actual," and the context may be a street in broad daylight where reality is just as pervasive 'as a dream' — in fact, *is* 'the dream' equally with consciousness.

One cannot describe it, so to speak. Either one acts in an equal sense — becomes the issue of a term 'as real as real can be' — or else there is really nothing to be said. Again, the writing here collected seems to me distinct in point of its distance from the usual habit of *description* — by which I mean that practice that wants to 'accompany' the *real* but which assumes itself as 'objectively' outside that context in some way. Certainly it is possible to minimize or otherwise distort one's concern in a given matter or relation. Yet one is either there or not, and being there, cannot assume some 'not being' so as to 'talk about it.'

I feel, however, that what I am trying to say here comes clearer in Edward Dorn's discussion of Olson's *Maximus Poems* (with their center in the town of Gloucester, Massachusetts):

> when the Place is brought forward fully in form conceived entirely by the activation of a man who is under its spell it is a resurrection for us and the investigation is not extractable. And it is then the only *real* thing. I am certain without ever having been there, I would be bored to sickness walking through Gloucester. Buildings as such are not important. The wash of the sea is not interesting in itself, that is luxuria, a degrading thing, people as they stand, must be created, it doesn't matter at all they have reflexes of their own, they are casual, they do more than you could hope to know, it is useful, it is a part of industry. It has an arrogance of intention. This is the significance of Olson's distrust of Thucydides and his care for Herodotus. It is the significance of Blake's "the practice of art is anti-christ." Which further means that if you are not capable of the non-functional striking of the World, you are not practicing art. Description, letting things lay, was reserved for not necessarily the doubtful, but the slothful, or the merely busy.

4

To tell the story, is all one can do. What accumulates as the tradition of a craft — its means, its sophistications — must each time be reapprehended, not for 'style.' Because as Louis Zukofsky has taken care to say, of poetry:

> This does not presume that the style will be the man, but rather that the order of his syllables will define his awareness of order. For his . . . major aim is not to show himself but that order that of itself can speak to all men.

> ("Poetry")

That undertaking most useful to writing as an art is, for me, the attempt to *sound* in the nature of the language those particulars of time and place of which one is a given instance, equally present. I find it here.

1965

"Poems are a complex"

POEMS ARE A complex, and exist by virtue of many things. First, they are a structure of sounds and rhythms which cohere to inform the reader (whether he listen aloud or in silence) with a recognition of their order. In this respect, I much agree with Louis Zukofsky's note of his own poetics, which, as he says, comprise a function having as lower limit speech, and upper limit music. Pound's note, that "Prosody is the articulation of the total sound of a poem," has equal relevance.

Since words are the material, and words have meanings in other senses, that fact also has pertinence. But I do not feel that *thing* in the language we call a poem has to do with a literal issue of semantic meaning. Yet that aspect of meaning is a material also, and clearly enters into the issue of image, or statement — or all such effects of something said.

I think for myself the primary term is that words can move in the measure of song, although I do not wish to confuse poetry with music. But in a poem I tend to hear whatever can be called its melody long before I have reached an understanding of all that it might mean.

Finally, I use several measures though never with much literal consciousness. Two further statements of Pound's long ago attracted me: "Only emotion endures ..." and "Nothing counts save the quality of the emotion...." I have used that sense with respect to all instances of writing, but

I would feel, as he, that poetry is that most fully charged with meaning. To that I would now add a recent emphasis of Olson's: "That which exists through itself is what is called meaning."

In other words, poems are not referential, or at least not importantly so. They have 'meaning' in that they do 'exist through themselves.' I have no very clear sense of where they may come from, but I have felt them most evident when least assumed. Lorca's "Theory and Function of the *Duende*" is interesting to me, although I would not so simply discredit either the Angel or the Muse to gain the "dark sounds" only. But I do feel poems to involve an occasion to which a man pays obedience, and which intentions alone never yield.

There are many ways indeed to say any of this, and I can't feel any one to be sufficient. I think I first felt a poem to be what might exist in words as primarily the fact of its own activity. Later, of course, I did see that poems might comment on many things, and reveal many attitudes and qualifications. Still, it was never what they said *about* things that interested me. I wanted the poem itself to exist and that could never be possible as long as some subject significantly elsewhere was involved. There had to be an independence derived from the very fact that words are *things* too. Poems gave me access to this fact more than any other possibility in language.

July 30, 1965
[*A Nosegay in Black*, Autumn 1966]

A Statement about the Poem "The Name"

MY OWN CENTERS OF feeling have much to do with my family
— literally my wife, and my three daughters. Feeling, or
perhaps best to call it *emotion,* is for me the most significant
content of a poem. I don't always or even often care what a
poem is talking *about,* but I do care very markedly about
the senses and the intensity of the emotion thus engendered.
This poem, then, was and is a way of feeling about the fact
of my daughter — a way of making that feeling evident for
a time when, perhaps, it will be a pleasure and reassurance
for her to know both how she came to be, and how then
that fact was felt. It is equally for all my daughters.

Too, I like the way this poem moves, in its lines, in the
way certain words pick up echoes of rhyme in others, sometimes very clearly, sometimes only as a shading. I like the
syncopation of the rhythms — most evident if you will make
a distinct pause (called a *terminal juncture!*) at the end of
each line, and will read the words relaxedly yet clearly, one
by one. I feel poetry as a complex of sounds and rhythms,
which move in a parallel to music. In fact, I believe it is
just this complex that makes poetry be the very singular
fact of words which it is.

[*Poems for Young Readers,* National Council
of Teachers of English, November 24-26, 1966]

Notes Apropos "Free Verse"

I THINK THE TERM "free verse" proves awkward just now in that it seems anchored in an opposition to a sense of traditional verse patterns, which are, because of their situation as history, more trusted. "Free" has such a width of associations — "free man," "free fall," "free prizes," etc. Too, it seems relevant that this sense of verse comes largely from American practice and that its primary figure is Whitman.

It nonetheless provokes a real situation. For example, Yvor Winters' tracking of "impulse" as informing principle in Emerson's discussions of poetry, as equally in Whitman's, and then in Crane's, cites the significance of this way of stating oneself in poetry as well as the historical range of its occasion. If one thinks of the literal root of the word verse, "a line, furrow, turning — *vertere*, to turn. . . . ," he will come to a sense of "free verse" as that instance of writing in poetry which "turns" upon an occasion intimate with, in fact, the issue of, its own nature rather than to an abstract decision of "form" taken from a prior instance.

The point is, simply enough, why does the "line" thus "turn" and what does inform it in that movement? Clearly to say that it is "free" or equally that it is "unfree" is to say nothing of much interest. I was impressed a few years ago, reading Joshua Whatmough's *Language*, to find him saying, as a linguist, that there was no explicit understanding as to why poetry "turns" in any instance at the precise moment it does — that is, no device of measure then defined could anticipate the precise articulations of this shifting in verse, no matter the verse be "traditional" or "free." Linguistics has, in other respects, qualified usefully the assumptions of traditional metrical systems in making evident the varying "weights" observable in "stress" (at least four in number) which had previously been dealt with in patterns which qualified syllables as "stressed" or "unstressed" — in short, a very imprecise and clumsy approximation of the activity.

I am myself hopeful that linguistic studies will bring to contemporary criticism a vocabulary and method more sensitive to the basic *activity* of poetry and less dependent upon assumed senses of literary style. Jacobsen's use of "contiguity" and "parallelism" as two primary modes of linguistic coherence interests me. Too, I would like to see a more viable attention paid to syntactical environment, to what I can call crudely "grammartology."

However, these are senses of things still far from my own experience in writing. So, briefly, as to that. I feel, as Robert Duncan put it, "a kind of readiness," much like that makes one feel like taking a walk, some imminence of occasion that has not as yet become literal. I have never, to my own recollection, anticipated the situation of my own writing in the sense of what I was about to say. It is certain enough that preoccupations recur — "themes," as Duncan has called them — but how these might gain statement as writing could not be proposed except as the literal writing then found means. I was struck by a comment Franz Kline once made: "If I paint what I know, I bore myself. If I paint what you know, I bore you. So I paint what I don't know. . . . " I write what I don't know. I feel the situation parallel to what Pollock suggests by his statement, "when I am in my painting. . . . " This, I feel, to be the condition Charles Olson defines in the key essay, "Projective Verse":

From the moment [a poet] ventures into FIELD COM-
POSITION — he puts himself in the open — he can go
by no track other than the one the poem under hand
declares, for itself. Thus he has to behave, and be, instant by instant, aware of some several forces just now
beginning to be examined. . . .

Pound notes Yeats' dependence upon "a chune in his
head" — and it is that equally, an ordering that is taking
place as one writes, which one follows much as he might
the melodic line of some song.

The simplest way I have found to make clear my own
sense of writing in this respect is to use the analogy of driv-
ing. The road, as it were, is creating itself momently in one's
attention to it, there, visibly, in front of the car. There is
no reason it should go on forever, and if one does so assume
it, it very often disappears all too actually. When Pound
says, "we must understand what is happening," one sense
of his meaning I take to be this necessary attention to what
is happening in the writing (the road) one is, in the sense
suggested, following. In that way there is nothing mindless
about the procedure. It is, rather, a respect for the possibilities of such attention that brings Allen Ginsberg to
say, "Mind is shapely." Mind, thus engaged, permits experience of "order" far more various and intensive than
habituated and programmed limits of its subtleties can
recognize.

I think each man writing will have some way, so to speak,
intimate with his own condition. That is, I feel there will
be an inherent condition for an ordering intimate to the
fact of himself as literal organism. Again, one of the several
virtues of Olson's "Projective Verse" was that of returning
to poetry its relation with *physiological* condition.

For my own part I feel a rhythmic possibility, an inherent periodicity in the weights and durations of words,

to occur in the first few words, or first line, or lines, of what it is I am writing. Because I am the man I am, and think in the patterns I do, I tend to posit intuitively a balance of *four*, a foursquare circumstance, be it walls of a room or legs of a table, that reassures me in the movement otherwise to be dealt with. I have, at times, made reference to my own interest when younger (and continuingly) in the music of Charlie Parker — an intensive variation on 'foursquare' patterns such as "I've Got Rhythm." Listening to him play, I found he lengthened the experience of time, or shortened it, gained a very subtle experience of 'weight,' all by some decision made within the context of what was called "improvisation" — but what I should rather call the experience of possibility within the limits of his materials (sounds and durations) and their environment (all that they had as what Pound calls "increment of association" but equally all they had as literal condition, their phenomenological fact). There is an interview with Dizzy Gillespie (in the *Paris Review*, No. 35) in which he speaks of rhythm particularly in a way I very much respect. If *time* is measure of *change*, our sense of it becomes what we can apprehend as significant condition of *change* — in poetry as well as in music.

In any case Williams showed me early on that rhythm was a very subtle experience, and that words might share equivalent duration even though "formally" they seemed in no way to do so. Pound said, "LISTEN to the sound that it makes," and Olson, in like emphasis, made it evident that we could only go "By ear."

Finally, there was and is the fact of, what it was one had to say — in Louis Zukofsky's sense, "Out of deep need. . . . " I never spoke easily and had to write, for the most part, just as adamantly. There is a section of Williams' "The Desert Music" which might be my own:

You seem quite normal. Can you tell me? Why
does one want to write a poem?

> Because it's there to be written.

Oh. A matter of inspiration then?

> Of necessity.

Oh. But what sets it off?

> I am that he whose brains
> are scattered
> aimlessly . . .

Why after all say any of this — but for some fear one is not
"doing it right" and isn't that, even, the occasion for such
argument as still can exist on the subject of "free verse,"
which is at best some "historical" label. Williams, at the
end of "The Desert Music," says all that anyone can:

> I *am* a poet! I
> am. I am. I am a poet, I reaffirmed, ashamed
> Now the music volleys through as in
> a lonely moment I hear it. Now it is all
> about me. The dance! The verb detaches itself
> seeking to become articulate
>
> And I could not help thinking
> of the wonders of the brain that
> hears that music and of our
> skill sometimes to record it.

December 11, 1966

[*Naked Poetry*, edited by Stephen Berg
and Robert Mezey, 1969]

"I'm given to write poems"

I'm *given* to write poems. I cannot anticipate their occasion. I have used all the intelligence that I can muster to follow the possibilities that the poem "underhand," as Olson would say, is declaring, but I cannot anticipate the necessary conclusions of the activity, nor can I judge in any sense, in moments of writing, the significance of that writing more than to recognize that it is being *permitted* to continue. I'm trying to say that, in writing, at least as I have experienced it, one is *in* the activity, and that fact itself is what I feel so deeply the significance of anything that we call poetry.

For some sense, then, of how it was I came to be involved with poetry, at the outset I was much more interested in *writing* apart from its designated modes, and perhaps I am characteristically American in that respect. To begin with, I was shy of the word "poet" and all its associations in a world I was then intimate with. It was not, in short, a fit attention for a young man raised in the New England manner, compact of Puritanically deprived senses of speech and sensuality. Life was real and life was earnest, and one had best get on with it. The insistent preoccupation with words did begin for me early, just that I did want so much to know what people were saying, and what, more precisely, they meant by it.

I think the most significant encounter for me as a young man trying to write was that found in the work of William

Carlos Williams. He engaged language at a level both familiar and active to my own senses, and made of his poems an intensively *emotional* perception, however evident his intelligence. Despite his insistence on his Mediterranean connections, so to speak, he was as Puritan as I — or Lawrence, or Thoreau or the Melville of *Pierre.*

Otherwise, the forties — the time in which I came of age — were complicated in many bitter ways indeed. Not the least of the problems then evident for someone trying to realize him or herself in the world was the confusion about the very nature of "literature" itself. Coming from New England, I felt awkwardness about books to begin with, because they were for me often instances of social mark or measure, even at times a privilege of intellectual order — just as Hardy speaks of them in *Jude the Obscure.* I was very shy about communicating my own commitments in reading, and yet I used books as a very real *place* to be. Not merely an escape from the world — the difficulty was how to get *into* it, not away — books proved a place very deeply open to me, at moments of reading, in a sense few others were ever to be.

Thinking of that, let me note kinship with another writer — Robert Duncan — who has played a very important role in my life, both as mentor, very often, and as one whom I feel to share with me this particular sense of world, and writing, and poetry, which I most deeply respect. In a collection of his called *The Opening of the Field*, significantly enough, the first poem begins:

OFTEN I AM PERMITTED TO RETURN TO A MEA-DOW
Then continues:

as if it were a scene made-up by the mind,
that is not mine, but is a made place,

that is mine, it is so near to the heart,
an eternal pasture folded in all thought
so that there is a hall therein

that is a made place, created by light
wherefrom the shadows that are forms fall.

This sense of a poem — that *place,* that *meadow* — has
echoes of so many things that are intimate to my own sense
of the reality experienced in writing. One would find that
field or "meadow" in Whitman also, and it would be equally
the sense of place I feel Allen Ginsberg many times to be
entering, to be speaking of or longing for. Charles Olson too
possesses its occasion in his sense of "open" verse or that
open field, as he insists upon it, in composition. I have found
it deeply in H.D.'s writing: "I go where I love and am
loved. . . . " And in Pound's "What thou lovest well remains, /
the rest is dross. . . . "

What thou lov'st well shall not be reft from thee
What thou lov'st well is thy true heritage
Whose world, or mine or theirs
                    or is it of none?
First came the seen, then thus the palpable
  Elysium, though it were in the halls of hell,
What thou lovest well is thy true heritage. . . .

All of these are, to my own mind, not only tokens but evidences of a place, a very distinct and definite *place,* that
poetry not only creates but itself issues from — and one in
writing is, as Duncan says, "permitted to return," to go
there, to be in that reality. There is a poem by Allen Ginsberg which has always moved me deeply. He calls it
simply "Song" and it is included in the first collection of his
poetry, *Howl.* The closing lines of this poem are:

yes, yes,
       that's what

I wanted,
> I always wanted,
I always wanted,
>> to return
> to the body
>> where I was born.

That body is the "field" and is equally the experience of
it. It is, then, to "return" not to oneself as some egocentric
center, but to experience oneself as *in* the world, thus,
through this agency or fact we call, variously, "poetry."

In the same passage quoted from Duncan, there is another
sense of much interest to me in the emphasis he puts upon
"made": "a scene," as he says, "made-up by the mind,/ that
is not mine, but is a made place,/ that is mine...." And
again, two lines following: "there is a hall therein/ that is
a made place...." This emphasis takes its occasion from
the sense of poet as maker, going back to the Greek root,
poiein, "to make."

One of the few books I've ever had that was stolen — not
by me, as it happened, but by a girl I persuaded to steal it
for me — was William Carlos Williams' *The Wedge*. It
proved *fire* of a very real order, and, for the record, was
subsequently stolen from me in turn when I was teaching at
Black Mountain in the mid-fifties. In 1944, when it was
first published and shortly after which I got hold of it, its
content was a revelation to me. In the preface Williams
makes this statement:

When a man makes a poem, makes it, mind you, he
takes words as he finds them interrelated about him and
composes them — without distortion which would mar
their exact significances — into an intense expression of
his perceptions and ardors that they may constitute a
revelation in the speech that he uses. It isn't what he

says that counts as a work of art, it's what he makes, with such intensity of perception that it lives with an intrinsic movement of its own to verify its authenticity.

I think this is very much the way Americans are given to speak — not in some dismay that they haven't another way to speak, but, rather, that they feel that they, perhaps more than any other group of people upon the earth at this moment, have had both to imagine and thereby to *make* that reality which they are then given to live in. It is as though they had to *realize* the world anew. They are, as Charles Olson says, "the last first people." Now, in contemporary fact, they are also the oldest issue of that imagination — even in some ways bitterly so, because they have thus inherited the world as not only a place to live in, but also as that reality for which they are responsible in every possible sense.

However, I would mistake my own experience of poetry if I were to propose it as something merely *intentional,* and what men may imagine, either as worlds or poems, is not simply a *purpose* either may satisfy. Williams also had no sense of patness in the making of a poem, or of a world — but felt, as he says in one of his own poems:

Be patient that I address you in a poem,
            there is no other
                        fit medium.
The mind
            lives there. It is uncertain,
                        can trick us and leave us
agonized. But for resources
            what can equal it?
                        There is nothing. We
should be lost
            without its wings to
                        fly off upon.

The mind is the cause of our distresses
           but of it we can build anew.
                         Oh something more than
it flies off to:
           a woman's world,
                         of crossed sticks, stopping
thought. A new world
           is only a new mind.
                         And the mind and the poem
are all apiece.

To put it simply indeed, it is not the intention to write that
matters, but that one *can* — that such a possibility *can* exist
in which the mind may make evident its resources apart
from the limits of intention and purpose.

In "The Desert Music" — for myself the loveliest form he
left us — Williams makes further qualification of the poem
in its peculiar and singular function of *making real:*

                         Only the poem
only the made poem, to get said what must
be said, not to copy nature, sticks
in our throats   .

The law? The law gives us nothing
but a corpse, wrapped in a dirty mantle.
The law is based on murder and confinement,
long delayed,
but this, following the insensate music,
is based on the dance:

                         an agony of self-realization
bound into a whole
by that which surrounds us   .

                              I cannot escape

I cannot vomit it up

Only the poem!

Only the made poem, the verb calls it
> into being.

Act becomes the primary issue of "verb," or *verbum,* a word.
"In the beginning was the Word" — and the word was the
reality of the imagination. The "music," which the poem's
title emphasizes and which becomes so central a content
in the poem's activity is that which vivifies, the *anima
mundi,* lifeness and/or life itself. Our response to it or what
it creates, its effects in the reality we are given, is the
"dance."

Now the music volleys through as in
a lonely moment I hear it. Now it is all
about me. The dance! The verb detaches itself
seeking to become articulate   .

Poems are very specific kinds of *dancing,* because language
is that possibility most specific to our condition as human
beings. But I do not speak easily of these things because I
feel, always, a timidity and confusion trying to isolate a
sense that can only be experienced in the literal fact of
the poem itself. It is as though I were trying to make actual
a sense of wetness apart from water itself.

It is possible, nonetheless, to continue now to use those
men I have used so much, to make evident what senses of
poetry have been for me insistent. In "Maximus, to Gloucester" Charles Olson gives measure of the occasion in a
way that informs my own:

He left him naked,
the man said, and
nakedness
is what one means

that all start up
to the eye and soul
as though it had never
happened before

My sense of his statment is this: in the fact of our lives we
are brought to primary situations, primary terms of experience — what they might have meant by "first things first"
but probably didn't. "Nakedness" is to stand manifestly in
one's own condition, in that necessary *freshness*, however
exposed, because all things are particular and reality itself
is the specific content of an instant's possibility. In poems
we realize, not in discursive or secondary manner, but with
this implicit and absolutely consequential fact of *firstness*,
terms of our own life, manifestations of that life which,
otherwise, are most awkwardly acknowledged. It is, again,
that "field" that Robert Duncan speaks of as being "permitted' to enter. First things. We arrive in poems at the
condition of life most viable and most primal in our own
lives.

I've said that I feel myself to be a poet who is *given* to
write. And I'm even awkward about using that designation,
that is, to call myself so, a poet — because I do not feel I
have that decision in it. Yet the complexity of the dilemma
seems to me a very real one. How shall we understand Williams' painfully marked insistence just before the close of
"The Desert Music":

> I *am* a poet! I
> am. I am. I am a poet, I reaffirmed, ashamed

In America, we are certainly not poets simply, nor much
of the time.

The saints of my own calendar are saints of this exposure,
beginning with Columbus and like men whose imagination
realized, *reified*, one might say, the world I live in. They

are Poe — who, as Williams makes clear, forced the *local* to yield him a world apart from the habits of English manner; Whitman — for the *permission* of life he insisted upon; Melville — the primary *imagination* of the isolation of our condition; Pound — who, like any Yankee, makes *intelligence* an invention of necessity; Hart Crane — whose "failure" regained the *possibility* of our response to what we are given to feel. It may well be that in the absence of such allusive society as European literature, in its own condition, has necessarily developed, that the American in contrast must so realize each specific thing of his own — "as though it had never/ happened before." I think of Williams' sharply contemptuous answer to the British English professor, met with in Seattle, Washington, of all places, who asked him after a reading, "where he got his language" — to which Williams replied, "Out of the mouths of Polish mothers" — meaning not Polish, but the harsh, crude, blocked "poor English" of those immigrant women he had as patients in his profession as a doctor. My "saints," then, are those men who defined for me an explicit possibility in the speech that I was given to use, who made the condition of being American not something chauvinistically national but the intimate fact of one life in one place at one time.

To speak then of the writing itself, which I can do only tentatively — just that I am persuaded by Heisenberg that "observation impedes function" — I have again much depended upon senses of procedure and examples (which are, of course, the point) given me by such men. In the forties there was so much talk *about* the poem, about levels of meaning, ambiguities, symbols, allusions. It was even felt that criticism itself would prove the most significant literary activity of the time.

Pound, in contrast, spoke of the literal condition of the writing, and it was he I used as guide — and continue to

now, twenty years later, because his advice proved facts
of perception as active to my mind now as when I first
came to them. For example, his quotation from Remy de
Gourmont, "Freely to write what one chooses is the sole
pleasure of a writer," continues for me the only actual
measure of the occasion I am aware of. He gave me the
experience of integrity as "Man standing by his word."
More, he spoke so clearly of the explicit situation of writing:

> In making a line of verse (and thence building the
> lines into passages) you have certain primal elements:
> That is to say, you have the various 'articulate
> sounds' of the language, of its alphabet, that is, and the
> various groups of letters in syllables.
> These syllables have differing weights and durations
>   A. original weights and durations
>   B. weights and durations that seem naturally im-
>   posed on them by the other syllable groups
>   around them.

> Those are the medium wherewith the poet cuts his
> design in TIME.

Against the arguments of taste and opinion which criticism
so largely depends upon, Pound called attention to the character of the activity:

> Rhythm is a form cut into TIME, as a design is de-
> termined SPACE. . . .
> LISTEN to the sound that it makes . . .

However, it is really Charles Olson I must thank for
whatever *freedom* I have as a poet, and I would value him
equally with Pound and Williams and those others I have
mentioned. *Freedom* has always been for me a difficult experience in that, when younger, I felt it had to propose

senses of experience and of the world I was necessarily *not* in possession of — something in that way one might escape to. I mistook, I think, the meaning of "freely to write what one chooses," which both de Gourmont and Pound may well have had in mind, because I took "freely" to mean "without significant limit" and "chooses" to be an act of will. I therefore was slow in realizing the nature of Olson's proposal, that "Limits / are what any of us / are inside of," just that I had taken such "limits" to be a frustration of possibility rather than the literal possibility they in fact must provoke. Despite Pound — or rather, because I could not hope to gain such means as he had — I had to find my own way, and at first I was completely ignorant of what it might be.

In consequence, what Olson made clear to me during the late forties and early fifties was of very great use. I am speaking of the *kind* of thinking that is evident in his essay, "Projective Verse," written during the same time. Let me quote an instance:

> The objects which occur at every given moment of composition (of recognition, we can call it) are, can be, must be treated exactly as they do occur therein and not by any ideas or preconceptions from outside the poem, must be handled as a series of objects in field in such a way that a series of tensions (which they also are) are made to *hold*, and to hold exactly inside the content and the context of the poem which has forced itself, through the poet and them, into being.

Not long ago, in conversation, Robert Duncan qualified his sense of *choice* as being *recognition*, that is, choice is significantly the act of recognition, and I believe it. What one "chooses" in writing is importantly of this nature, for me, and composition is the fact and effect of such activity. One isn't

putting things *into* poems, then, at least not as my own experience of writing informs me. There is never a "subject"
about which one constructs an activity called "poetry." Nor
can one, as Williams says, "copy nature," take from that
which is elsewise informed some felicitious appearance,
whether a rhyme or a so-called sentiment.

However best it might be put, what Olson made evident
to me was that writing could be an intensely specific revelation of one's own content, and of the world the fact of any
life must engage. It has nothing to do with "personalism" —
which, like personality, is a mirror or reflective image sense,
a cosmetic of intentions. To the contrary, what emerges in
the writing I most value is a content which cannot be anticipated, which "tells you what you don't know," which
you subvert, twist, or misrepresent only on peril of death.

What I have written I knew little of until I had written it.
If at times I have said that I enjoy what I write, I mean
that writing is for me the most viable and open condition
of possibility in the world. Things have happened there, as
they have happened nowhere else — and I am not speaking
of "make-believe," which, be it said, is "as real as real can
be." In poems I have both discovered and born testament
to my life in ways no other possibility has given me. Can
I *like* all that I may prove to be, or does it matter? Am I
merely living for my own approval? In writing it has seemed
to me that such small senses of existence were altogether
gone, and that, at last, the world "came true." Far from
being its limit or director, the wonder is that I have found
myself to be there also.

[Lecture delivered at the Literarisches Colloquium,
Berlin, January 1967; published in *Ein Gedicht und sein
Autor / Lyrik und Essay,* Herausgegeben und mit Ein-
leitungen versehen von Walter Höllerer (Berlin, 1967),
and in *Harper's Bazaar,* July 1967]

Two

Hart Crane and the Private Judgment

IN THE July 1932 issue of *Poetry* there is an essay by Allen Tate called "Hart Crane and the American Mind." Hart Crane had committed suicide on April 28, 1932. Tate's judgment certainly was affected by the fact, and by the friendship he had held for Crane, and yet the matter of his comments on Crane's life and value as a poet continues very much the same as what we deal with today, facing a like problem of judgment.

What Tate there gives to Crane is this: "Sometime in May, 1922, I received a letter from Hart Crane saying he liked a poem of mine which he had seen in the May number of *The Double Dealer*. It was my first printed poem, and Hart's letter was not only an introduction to him; it was the first communication I ever received from another writer.[1] In that same issue of *The Double Dealer* appeared some translations by him of Laforgue, which seemed to me very fine; I looked up previous numbers of the magazine, and found "Black Tamborine," an early poem that contained some of the characteristic features of this later and mature style. I had seen nothing like it in Anglo-American poetry. From that time until his death one could trace the development of a poetry which, though similar in some technical

[1] This letter is not in Weber's selection (*The Letters of Hart Crane* [New York: 1952]), but the one following (May 16, 1922) is to be found on p. 87.

respects to French Symbolism, is now a distinct contribution to American literature. It is a poetry that could have
been written only in this country and in this age."

Hart Crane has now become a kind of 'symbol,' for many,
of the irresponsible in poetry, the disordered intelligence
that creates a chaos only as a refuge from its own inabil-
ities. Mr. Grover Smith, for example, calls him "that pitiable
anarch . . . ," continuing "It should be patent to the student
of both [Crane's life and work], however, that Crane as
man and poet was grievously disordered, that the neurotic
irresponsibility of his private life and loves was directly
synchronous with the undisciplined fancy manifest in his
poetic images. Crane's inner world was a fluxion in which
neither personal relations nor traditional thought and utterance were coherent enough to form laws even for themselves."[2] This is, of course, a very personal judgment, and
one made completely as a contention — the only quotations
from the book in question are taken from Brom Weber's
introduction to *The Letters of Hart Crane*. Mr. Smith says,
of the letters themselves: "There is no concentration of alert
feelings; there is no style." But Mr. Tate had felt them to be
". . . always written in a pure and lucid prose . . ." Whatever
our own opinion may arrive at, at least we must see that we
can accept neither of these two given, until we have found
our own proof.

The 'failures,' 'mistakes,' 'flaws,' etc., of Hart Crane's
poetry have seemed to me intimate with the successes
equally demonstrable. I think that a reader must judge for
himself, at last, which quality is the more sustained. Crane

[2]Grover Smith, "On Poets and Poetry," *New Mexico Quarterly*,
Autumn 1953, p. 319. The article is an omnibus review, which may
explain the briefness of Smith's discussion of the Weber collection,
but hardly excuses the unsupported statements involved concerning
not only Crane's letters and poetry, but his "private life and loves"
as well. Cf. Weber's edition of *The Letters*, pp. 298 ff.

was 'disordered' to the extent that he conceived his responsibility as a poet to transcend even the obligations he felt as a man. Perhaps there is no direct proof of this fact, i.e., a statement unequivocally supporting it. But — "It is a new feeling, and a glorious one, to have one's inmost delicate intentions so fully recognized as your last letter to me attested. I can feel a calmness on the sidewalk — where before I felt a defiance only. And better than all — I am certain that a number of us at last have some kind of community of interest. And with this communion will come something better than a mere clique. It is a consciousness of something more vital than stylistic questions and 'taste,' it is vision, and a vision alone that not only America needs, but the whole world . . . What delights me almost beyond words is that my natural idiom . . . has reached and carried to you so completely the very blood and bone of me." [3]

The nature of this 'vision' concerned an alternative to the negativistic position which Eliot, and to a lesser degree (though ultimately even more final) Joyce, had provided for their work. The genius of both men made the position attractive almost 'per se' — at least the question of its implications does not seem to have been recognized at first by very many. But one of those who did, William Carlos Williams, speaks of it (in retrospect) as follows: "These were the years just before the great catastrophe to our letters — the appearance of T. S. Eliot's *The Waste Land.* There was heat in us, a core and a drive that was gathering headway upon the theme of a rediscovery of a primary impetus, the elementary principle of all art, in the local conditions. Our work staggered to a halt for a moment under the blast of

[3] Weber, *The Letters,* p. 127. Crane is 24 years old. Tate believes the conception of the 'idea' and 'leading symbolism' of *The Bridge* to date from the year following, i.e., "probably early in 1924."

Eliot's genius which gave the poem back to the academics. We did not know how to answer him."[4]

Hart Crane's answer was *The Bridge* — now discredited as a total poem, which is to say, a failure in terms of its literal writing, and the problems involved in that writing. But the conception? We know that the 'failure' in some sense caused Crane to doubt all of his abilities as a poet. Tate writes, "I think he knew that the framework of *The Bridge* was finally incoherent, and for that reason — as I have said — he could no longer believe in even his lyrical powers; he could not return to the early work and take it up from where he had left off." But Crane himself had written to Tate: ". . . perhaps it can serve as at least the function of a link connecting certain chains of the past to certain chains and tendencies of the future. In other words, a diagram or "process". . ."[5] It is here, I think, that the conception of the poem is most significantly stated, and since it has to do with problems of the 'scientific method' there is that reason for a brief digression.

Attitudes in the 'social sciences,' even as late as the twenties, continued to maintain that world view which held that a system of knowledge was extensible to a point where the world's ills might, reasonably, be done away with. Perhaps the attitudes were never quite so barely expressed, or even realized, but their content was nonetheless predicated on such a system of thought. Moreover, this way of thinking was involved in many of the other sciences, and was also, very clearly, the base idea or opinion held by many, many laymen.

[4] W. C. Williams, *Autobiography* (New York: 1951). It is relevant to point out the coincidence of materials in Williams' *In the American Grain* and Crane's *The Bridge*. Cf. Weber, *The Letters,* pp. 277-78.

[5] Weber, *The Letters,* p. 353. This is the letter of which Tate writes: "He had an extraordinary insight into the foundations of his work, and I think this judgment of it will never be refuted."

A recent book, *Modern Science and Modern Man,* by James B. Conant,[6] reviews these attitudes, and more particularly, shows why they can no longer be quite so easily held. But the most interesting thing, in connection with Crane's comment on *The Bridge,* is Conant's discussion of "the philosophic implications of the new physics," wherein he quotes from J. J. Thompson's *The Corpuscular Theory of Matter* (1907)[7] as follows: "From the point of view of the physicist, a theory of matter is a policy rather than a creed; its object is to connect or coordinate apparently diverse phenomena and above all to suggest, stimulate, and direct experiment."[8] *The Waste Land* was a 'creed' (how much of a creed we can now show, by means of Eliot's later work), depending on the *finality* of knowledge. But *The Bridge,* 'failure' though it was and still may seem to us, was a 'process' or 'policy,' an attempt to direct attention to a *significant* content in the American corpus, both historical and mythic, and to posit juxtapositions and methods of dealing with this material which *might* prove fruitful.

Perhaps that is all too simply opinion, mainly my own.[9] But we have damned *The Bridge* much too simply on the

[6] James B. Conant, *Modern Science and Modern Man* (New York: Anchor Books, 1953).

[7] *Ibid.,* p. 91. The reorientation which Thomson had literally accomplished in 1907 is one which many men have even yet to consider in 1953. In the art of poetry, above all, there is great need to consider the problem inherent in any such reorientation of an entire basis for the *use* of knowledge.

[8] "The poet's concern must be, as always, self-discipline toward a formal integration of experience. For poetry is an architectural art, based not on Evolution or the idea of progress, but on the articulation of the contemporary human consciousness *sub specie aeternitas,* and inclusive of all readjustments incident to science and other shifting factors related to that consciousness." Hart Crane, *Collected Poems,* Appendix B, "Modern Poetry" (New York: 1933). This was first published in 1929 — but must have been an active concept in his work long before. For comparison: "We can no longer say, The

grounds of its having failed as a poem. Certainly we are allowed to do that, and finally we must. And yet it seems to me wasteful to ignore the other implications involved. It is not even a question of giving credit where credit is due, though I should like to consider that part of it. The several questions remaining are: 1) who has answered Eliot ; 2) isn't that answer even more called for *now*, than it was then; 3) doesn't the present 'picture' of our world (again 'now') have a great, great deal to do with it.

Let me leave those as questions only. Crane's position as 'prophet,' if you will, is one which I cannot discuss very competently here. Moreover, until he is again read, as he deserves to be, any discussion must, of necessity, be meaningless. But to suggest, as Mr. Smith has done, that Crane was committed to "rebellion for its own sake . . ." is neither helpful nor true. Further, his sense of the poems as a "jumble of images thrown up by the poet's unconscious" which leave the reader to perform "the 'plastic' task proper to the poet himself . . ." does not strike me as very ade-

World is like this, or the World is like that. We can only say, Our experience up to the present is best represented by a world of this character; I do not know what model will best represent the world of tomorrow, but I do know that it will coordinate a greater range of experience than that of today." Herbert Dingle, "The Scientific Outlook in 1851 and in 1951," *British Journal for the Philosophy of Science,* II (1951), p. 86; quoted by Conant, *Modern Science and Modern Man,* p. 89. Crane's problem was not one of conception — but of means (though not at all in Mr. Smith's sense of a criticism). The essay first cited ("Modern Poetry") includes comments on a "terminology of poetic reference," etc., which indicates that, although Crane could conceive of a necessary shift in substantive qualifications, he continued to depend on nominative qualifications, when it came to the actual means. (This problem of the substantive vs. the nominative was pointed out to me by Charles Olson.)

[9]Another man holding related opinions at least is M. Elath. Cf. his article "In Another Direction" published in a double number of *Intro,* New York, Winter 1951.

quate — granted that there are reasonable alternatives to his opinion.[10]

As his critics have remarked, Crane learned a great deal from the French Symbolists, and much of his early work is dominated by what he learned. For example, Tate (speaking "logically") notes that Crane "became so dissatisfied, not only with the style of the poem ["For the Marriage of Faustus and Helen"], which is heavily influenced by Eliot and Laforgue, but with the 'literary' character of the symbolism, that he set about the greater task of writing *The Bridge* . . ." The point is that Crane had become at first a poet by way of a poetry dependent on irony, on the dissociations possible in the very surfaces of language, on a quick and nonpassive verbalism which was in direct opposition to anything then evident in English or American poetry. His 'style,' if you will, was developed in great part from this source. And this will explain much of the surface character of Crane's poetry, i.e., the rapidity of image, the disparateness, the whole sense of 'words' being used almost for their own, single character. Certainly both Eliot and Pound (as well as Stevens, Williams *et al* at home) had begun to use these same things.

But it is Crane's development away from the Symbolists, and their dependence on irony in particular, that leads to the later style, and of course to the character of language-usage which Mr. Smith dislikes. In fairness to both him and myself — not to mention Crane — it should be stated that a poem is an asserted unit of meaning, among other things. And that our appreciation of it, or disapproval of it, depends, again partially, on whether or not we can allow

[10] The "oddness" of Crane's vocabulary often produces this reaction — but is it valid? I think one had better examine the relevance of such language *in context*. Crane's worksheets (cf. Weber's biography) would defeat the sense which Mr. Smith is trying to suggest.

that the means used to effect that end provide a meaning which is apprehensible by us. Once having allowed that, we then take upon ourselves the act of judging whether or not the means used seem the most effective possible, i.e., the most proper, etc. Mr. Smith, then, is suggesting that Crane's 'jumbled images' do not properly provide for an effect of *meaning* — and that they depend on our sympathy for resolution. In any case (because a poem will be given shortly) a few lines, here, may show the nature of the difficulty, at least insofar as Mr. Smith has been thinking of it.

> Yes, tall, inseparably our days
> Pass sunward. We have walked the kindled skies
> Inexorable and girded with your praise,
>
> By the dove filled, and bees of Paradise.

Briefly the line of the sense can be given as this: that Crane and the one he speaks to share a time together which is passing, and that this time has been, to put it very simply, happy. I don't think that belies the base meaning involved, insofar as its 'action' character is concerned. So — the images, etc. The first, "our days pass[ing] sunward" with the further sense of "tall, inseparably" engenders in my mind an effect of dignity (from the "tall"), of a close love (from the whole complex of "our days pass sunward," with the echo of "sun" as life-giving, high, a source of nobility and godhead). To bypass, the next sentence comes to me as a statement of fulfillment, that they have, together, come to a sense of complete fulfillment. And that, in any case, can serve as a description, if nothing else, of how the lines begin to attain to an effect of *meaning* for me.

Now one might argue how can he talk about walking up in the sky if he has just said that his days (an apparent possession) pass sunward. How can they do that, if he is up there, etc. And — who is "inexorable" and "girded," etc. But doesn't that really come to quibbling — if an effect is achieved and sustained in rereading? And isn't this latter just what each reader must decide for himself. I suggest that Crane's use of language (i.e. such words as "inexorable," "tall," and such image complexes as in the first three lines) will invariably be attached to an *emotion* which can and will sustain them in a total pattern of *meaning*. That line of *meaning* can be determined in all of his active poems (which will serve, for a beginning, to belie Mr. Smith's "jumble of images"), and that this line will depend, precisely, on the assumedly disconnected images which some readers have balked at. Remember that an association existing between images need not be 'logical.' That term is most usually an *a priori* designation for an assumptional rationality of progression. The fact is that we do not know what we know before we know it. And a poem's line, or what to call it, of *meaning* need not be 'logical,' if it can effect its meaning by virtue of another sense of possible sequence. And, at that, Crane is really no great instance of the uses of theoretic dissociation in sequence. One might argue, in fact, that an apparent 'excess' in language was the only irony that Crane finally permitted himself.

To allow discussion to end there, however, ignores all of Crane's metrics, and all of his sense of structure in the shorter poems — particularly the latter. I have seen no comment on Crane's sense of rhythm, although it is, for me, one of the most dominant aspects of his work.[11] But the reader can judge both that, and the 'jumbled images,' for himself:

[11] All Crane's work is best read aloud. The reader can't pick up the sounds or the rhythms sufficently otherwise. A recording of a half dozen of his poems by a competent reader would do much more than any "criticism" ever will. He is one of the most *verbal* poets in the English language.

Island Quarry

Square sheets — they saw the marble into
Flat slabs there at the marble quarry
At the turning of the road around the roots of the moun-
[tain
Where the straight road would seem to ply below the
[stone, that fierce
Profile of marble spiked with yonder
Palms against the sunset's towering sea, and maybe
Against mankind. It is at times —

In dusk it is at times as though this island lifted, floated
In Indian baths. At Cuban dusk the eyes
Walking the straight road toward thunder —
This dry road silvering toward the shadow of the quarry
— It is at times as though the eyes burned hard and glad
And did not take the goat path quivering to the right,
Wide of the mountain — thence to tears and sleep —
But went on into marble that does not weep.

It is very possible to argue that this is an almost perfect
instance of form — technically. Actually, our own ears have
arrived at that conclusion upon hearing it, and our perception of the content involved make it not at all necessary to
revert to questions purely of sentiment. The poem is a good
one because of its very skillful alteration and development of
the two rhythms involved (i.e., those contained in words
like 'marble,' 'mountain,' 'maybe,' et al, and those contained
in 'sheets,' 'fierce,' 'dusk,' 'weep,' et al). The hard opening of
the poem, like a double stroke, falls then off to the softer
rhythms, then reasserts itself in the opening of the second
line — and so on to the final, broken close. This, of course,
is the usual method of 'analysis.' We may also point out
that the vowel leadings in this poem are quite equal to anything done by Yeats — although we have never heard of

them being mentioned either in this poem, or any other by Crane. Nor has there been comment on the very effective handling of line — as this poem, again, shows it, with the undulation of the lines, almost opening and closing like actual breathing, to end with the line pulling in, stumbling, unmistakable in its emphases.

All that can be said, defended — and much more can be said and defended, concerning both this one poem and at least a dozen others. My own preferences in the first book, *White Buildings,* are: "Praise for an Urn," "Lachrymae Christi," "The Wine Menagerie," "For the Marriage of Faustue and Helen," "At Melville's Tomb," and perhaps one or two others, i.e., these are only evidences of my *own* taste, and what I think I could defend as 'good poetry.' In the later book, *Key West:* the quoted poem, "The Mermen," "A Name for All," "Imperator Victus," "The Hurricane," "And Bees of Paradise," "Moment Fugue," "The Broken Tower," "The Phantom Bark," and, again, perhaps a few more, because my taste is hardly invariable.[12] But do people still read these poems, and, if they don't — how can we discuss them all so glibly, or say, so glibly, that they are this thing or that?

For an ending: the reader who saw Crane survive Weber's first book on him may have noticed this particular account, in Weber's preface to *The Letters,* concerning the death of Hart Crane's mother:

The last chapter in the Crane biography occurred in 1947. On July 30th of that year, Mrs. Grace Hart Crane, the poet's mother, died in Teaneck, New Jersey. Before her death, she told Samuel Loveman that she wished to be cremated and her ashes to be cast into the East River from the Brooklyn Bridge. The necessary arrangements were made, and the editor was one of a small party

[12] Hart Crane, *Collected Poems* (New York: 1933).

which proceeded along Brooklyn Bridge on a windy, sunlit afternoon in Fall 1947. At intervals on the Bridge, there are signs warning pedestrians not to throw anything from the structure. By the time the party reached the center of the Bridge, considerable trepidation existed about the feasibility of respecting Mrs. Crane's last wishes. It remained at last for the editor to grasp the small, undecorated tin can and shake the ashes into the air, where they swirled about for a few moments and then fell mistily into the water below. Thus Crane's mother joined him in the element which had claimed him fifteen years earlier.

But this is Mr. Smith's hero, not mine. The reader who can trust a 'character analysis' of Hart Crane coming from the same source is welcome to, but he has no reason, here, to read further.

The men who knew Hart Crane, with the authority of friendship, have said many things about him, each from the particulars of their own life. Allen Tate ends his essay, written that short time after Crane's death, by saying: "After he had lost the instinct for self-definition, and later, after the exploration of his symbol of the will had brought him back upon himself, he might have continued to breathe, but he would no longer have been alive." That whole question of will, of "the will gone all teeth" (as Charles Olson has called it in another reference), will, someday, have to be examined, and closely. Poetry, the whole art of it, had failed Crane, and that is why he could not live — even if it is not why he died.

Other men speak of him as the friend which no other man has ever quite taken the place of. Against the public that sees him as homosexual, drunkard, and all the rest, for them he was an incredible man, whom they knew. For Robert Graves, he was a 'lovely man,' however much he seemed a tragic one. For Slater Brown, the best friend he ever had.

What else is there to be said. Except that we can read the poems, and see what they are, for ourselves.

1953

[*The Free Lance,* Vol. 5, No. 1, 1960, (Wilberforce University)]

The Letters of Hart Crane,
edited by Brom Weber

IF THERE IS a ghost, or unquiet spirit, of a man ever left to us, it may well be that Hart Crane is not dead — or not in our comfortable sense of that word. I note that Brom Weber brings this up, unintentionally, in his ridiculous preface and chronology for the book in question: "Three days later, on the 27th, he [Crane] either jumped or fell into the Caribbean Sea and was drowned. His body was not recovered." (p. xvi) Perhaps we have our own fears of the sea, and also of a man not actually 'laid to rest,' not finally put under as we are accustomed to do with the dead.

But lacking the body, an age of critics can still sustain its necrophilia on the body of the work itself. Hart Crane "was admittedly not a thinker...." (p. x) Weber says, ignoring, for one thing, Williams' premise that "the poet thinks with his poem, in that lies his thought, and that is the profundity...." To prepare us, Weber speaks of Crane's "acquisitive need for sympathy, pity, understanding, affection...," (p. vi) of a man "tyrannically governed by a chronic need to love and be loved...." (p. viii) One might well say the same of *any* human being.

In any case some anger can be righteous, and some usage cannot be put up with. Lacking a present means to deal with Weber, finally — the reader is advised to bypass his comments altogether. (Or better, to judge for himself the man

writing "The last chapter of the Crane biography...."
(p. x)) He is not helpful.

Crane is, however, and we have, at last, a reasonable
addenda to the poetry itself which may serve as the gauge
we had lacked. What was Crane's conception of poetry?
"Poetry, in so far as the metaphysics of any absolute knowledge extends, is simply the concrete *evidence* of the *experience* of a recognition (*knowledge* if you like). It can give
you a *ratio* of fact and experience, and in this sense it is
both perception and thing perceived, according as it ap-
proaches a significant articulation or not. This is its reality,
its fact, *being*." (p. 237)

More than that, what was Crane's summation of his own
position — the cause back of all Weber's inanities, not to
mention his biography of Crane or Waldo Frank's fantastic
introduction to the *Collected Poems*. Was it absolutely this
fact of "Crane's tender friendships ... with boys who followed the Sea...., " and "drink ... " as "the Sea's coadju-
tor...."? So says Frank — but does it matter?

> I have a certain code of ethics. I have not as yet at-
> tempted to reduce it to any exact formula, and if I did I
> should probably embark on an endless tome with
> monthly additions and digressions every year. It seems
> obvious that a certain decent carriage and action is a
> paramount requirement in any poet, deacon or car-
> penter. And though I reserve myself the pleasant right
> to define these standards in a somewhat individual way,
> and to shout and complain when circumstances against
> me seem to warrant it, on the other hand I believe my-
> self to be speaking honestly when I say that I have
> never been able to regret — for long — whatever has
> happened to me, more especially those decisions which
> at times have been permitted a free will.... And I am
> as completely out of sympathy with the familiar whim-

pering caricature of the artist and his "divine rights" as
you seem to be. I am not a Stoic, though I think I could
lean more in that direction if I came to (as I may sometime) appreciate more highly the imaginative profits of
such a course. (pp. 299-300)

Back of this, there are the poems, forgotten for the most
part — but if this book can do anything, and one hopes
at least, it may bring us back to them somewhat sobered.
We know, we know, we know, etc., that *The Bridge* was a
'failure' — though why, and how, we are not at all quite
so sure of. Crane wrote to Allen Tate: ". . . I shall be humbly
grateful if *The Bridge* can fulfill simply the metaphorical
inference of its title. . . . You will admit our age (at least
our predicament) to be one of transition." (p. 353) It has
done that, I think.

The shorter poems, those found in *White Buildings* and
Key West, have escaped the 'failure' of *The Bridge,* but they
have also been affected, i.e., they seem to be thought less
'significant.' And there again we have the critic's help. "One
is appalled, on reading his [Crane's] explication at 'At Melville's Tomb' to realize that while he could associatively
justify the chain of metaphors comprising the poem, he was
oblivious of the difference between a random and logical
mode of association." (Which is Grover Smith, from within
his own oblivion.) But the poem?

At Melville's Tomb

Often beneath the wave, wide from this ledge
The dice of drowned men's bones he saw bequeath
An embassy. Their numbers as he watched,
Beat on the dusty shore and were obscured.

And wrecks passed without sound of bells,
The calyx of death's bounty giving back

A scattered chapter, livid hieroglyph,
The portent wound in corridors of shells.

Then in the circuit calm of one vast coil,
Its lashings charmed and malice reconciled,
Frosted eyes there were that lifted altars;
And silent answers crept across the stars.

Compass, quadrant and sextant contrive
No farther tides.... High in the azure steeps
Monody shall not wake the mariner.
This fabulous shadow only the sea keeps.

This is the GREATEST summation of Melville I have ever read. O well....

"I don't know whether you want to hear from me or not — since you have never written — but here's my love anyway...." He did all any man could.

[*Origin*, Summer 1954]

A Letter to the Editor of Goad

DEAR SCHWARTZ,

A few notes I'd wanted to get into the last letter but there wasn't time.

Anyhow, it's about the Pound article.* Certainly it's a more honest position than any I've yet met with. All the usual blatting about this and that which has attached itself to the "Pound controversy" hardly clears any of the necessary ground — or makes the least sense.

But here's what I'd like to put against the implied judgment — "How many powerful, illuminating lines are found in the published work of Pound? If you, like myself, have not found many, then you too may want to forget the whole thing."

1) Very simply, 50 years work, and at what? Criticism. Translation. Hauling over into the English of at least 3 major areas of thought, including American.

2) A principle of verse (kinetic) which has made, literally, the basic condition which now makes it possible for us to go on with it — "A Retrospect," "How to Read," "The Serious Artist — this hardly begins it.

3) A body of work, of verse, which I can mainly defend, or only, in terms of my own respect for it — it is based, surely, on a man's actuality, on his own actuality, and isn't that what, precisely, poetry is supposed to be?

*An article on Ezra Pound in *Goad*, No. 1.

There's no defense for the anti-Semitism, not even your own. There's none that I can, myself, admit. And so, perhaps, I have an even greater difficulty than yourself (if you stand back of your own statement) in adjusting to the concepts of certain of the *Cantos;* and honestly, I don't adjust — I go to that work to get what seems to me of *use*, and the rest I toss out, condemning it just by that act.

What else? If we forget the other insistences of that same book, forget the emphases on the Confucian ethic, on the literal horror of the Usury we inhabit, of all of it, one man's hardness, his ability to hold to himself, what the hell ground do we have left, to stand on, to call him: traitor? Well, tell me, because I don't know.

There remain, in any case, books that you should have there, to be going at, to answer your own problem of 'powerful, illuminating lines. . . .'

Take off on the criticism: *Polite Essays, Make It New, Pavannes and Divisions, ABC of Reading, Kulchur,* etc. I mean, go at these, and see if there isn't as hard and as direct a mind there as you've ever met with. "Damn your taste, I would like if possible to sharpen your perceptions, after which your taste can take care of itself. . . . "

Have you read his things on Dolmetsch? Did you know that he had picked up on composers like Antheil, et al, long before any public had thought of looking for them?

You should dig into these things; not be put off by a disgust with all the present palaver — it means nothing, and it will come to nothing. It's demonstrated exactly that capability already. So, to hell with it — go about your own business as you've absolute right to.

But don't lose any chance for additional clarity, which is to say, don't toss out this man's incredible sharpness. I damn well say it's there to be got — and any of the aforenoted books will give it to you straight. The *Cantos* are, first of all, an incredible condensing, as speech is, no man is going to pick up easily or quickly. They take work.

I'd say: XXX, XIII,XLVII, XLV and the section marked *libretto* on to the end of LXXXI — all will give you a straight pickup, quick, of what is here going on. Anyhow, please read them, or read them again, if you already have — tell me if I'm full of shit, and that's OK with me. Only try it. OK.

But (lord/god) let's not suggest, even by murmur, that Housman, who (did he not, damn well right he did) sold out, and cheap at that? The pretty lyrics, the cheap little sentiments, of horror, of death — that such is to be put against Pound, the implications to be: he is more?

Goddamn it, I had no sympathy there. I could not stomach that. And yet you *have to mean it* — you have no right to write what you do not mean, and do not mean exactly.

Anyhow, Housman? Christ, he is a cheap little prick; with two-bit rhymings, all the easy penance of a bankrupt man.

(Read Pound's "Housman at Little Bethel" — I mean, that's a much kinder attack than I could myself make.)

Listen:

> There died a myriad
> And of the best, among them,
> For an old bitch gone in the teeth,
> For a botched civilization.
>
> Charm, smiling at the good mouth,
> Quick eyes gone under the earth's lid,
>
> For two gross of broken statues,
> For a few thousand battered books.

Write when you can.

All best,
CREELEY

[*Goad*, Winter 1951-52]

A Note on Ezra Pound

FOR MY GENERATION the fact of Ezra Pound and his work is inescapable, no matter what the particular reaction may be. But it should equally be remembered that during the forties, that time in which we came of age, Pound's situation was, in all senses, most depressed. To the young of that period he was often simply a traitor, an anti-Semite, an obscurantist, a money crank — and such courses in universities and colleges as dealt with modern poetry frequently avoided all mention of the *Cantos*. For example, I remember in my shyness going to F. O. Mathiessen at Harvard, to ask why we had not used the *Cantos* in his own course on contemporary poetry. His answer was that he understood Pound's work too poorly, that he felt Pound's political attitudes most suspect, and that he could not finally see the value of the work in a course such as ours was.

It is hard to see, in one sense, how we were not frightened away from Pound — there was so much to persuade us of his difficulties and of those he would surely involve us with. But who else could responsibly teach us that "nothing matters but the quality of the affection," that "only emotion endures"? The work we were otherwise given was, on the one hand, Auden — wherein a socially based use of irony became the uselessly exact rigor of repetitive verse patterns — or perhaps Stevens, whose mind one respected, in the questions it realized, but again whose use of poetry had fallen to the questionable fact of a device.

Pound, on the other hand, brought us immediately to the context of how to write. It was impossible to avoid the insistence he put on *precisely* how the line *goes*, how the word *is*, in its context, what *has been* done, in the practice of verse — and what *now* seems possible to do. It was, then, a *measure* he taught — and a measure in just that sense William Carlos Williams insisted upon:

> ... The measure itself
> has been lost
>   and we suffer for it.
>   We come to our deaths
> in silence. ...

To the attacks upon Pound as bigot merely, Charles Olson — speaking in the guise of Yeats in defence of Pound, in 1946 — makes the relevant answer:

> It is the passivity of you young men before Pound's work as a whole, not scripts alone, you who have taken from him, Joyce, Eliot and myself the advances we made for you. There is a court you leave silent — history present, the issue the larger concerns of authority than a state, Heraclitus and Marx called, perhaps some consideration of descents and metamorphoses, form and the elimination of intellect.

For my own part I came first to the earlier poems, *Personae*, and to the various critical works, *Make It New*, *Pavannes and Divisions*, *ABC of Reading*, *Guide to Kulchur*, and *Polite Essays*. It was at that time the critical writing I could most clearly use, simply that my own limits made the *Cantos* a form intimidating to me. As a younger man, I wanted to know in a 'formal' sense where it was I was going, and had a hard time learning to admit that the variousness of life is as much its quality as its quantity. Or rather — akin to the anecdote Pound tells of Agassiz's student not really *looking* at the fish — I wanted the categories prior to the content which might in any sense inform them.

But it is again the sense of *measure,* and how actively it may be proposed, that I found insistently in Pound's work. Rather than tell me *about* some character of verse, he would give the literal instance side by side with that which gave it context. This method is, of course, an aspect of what he calls the *ideogrammic* — it *presents,* rather than comments upon. The emphasis I feel to be present in all his work, from the rationale of imagism, to the latest *Cantos.*

In the same sense he directed a real attention to characters of verse in the early discriminations he offered as to its nature. For example, he spoke of "three chief means" available to the man wanting to "charge language with meaning to the utmost possible degree" — in the context that "Literature is language charged with meaning":

I throwing the object (fixed or moving) on to the visual imagination.

II inducing emotional correlations by the sound and rhythm of the speech.

III inducing both of the effects by stimulating the associations (intellectual or emotional) that have remained in the receiver's consciousness in relation to the actual words or word groups employed.

(phanopoeia, melopoeia, logopoeia)

Such location of attention meant an active involvement with what was happening in the given poem — and not a continuingly vague discussion of its aesthetic 'value,' or its 'period,' or all that area of assumption which finds place in unrealized generality. Pound's discriminations were located in the poem's literal activity.

How large he was then for us, is more simply stated than described. He took the possibility of writing to involve more than descriptive aesthetics. He defined sincerity as Kung's "man standing by his word." He moved upon the active principle of intelligence, the concept of *virtu,* so that, as Charles Olson has written:

> ... his single emotion breaks all down to his equals or inferiors (so far as I can see only two, possibly, are admitted, by him, to be his betters — Confucius, & Dante. Which assumption, that there are intelligent men whom he can outtalk, is beautiful because it destroys historical time, and

> thus creates the methodology of the *Cantos,* viz, a space-field where, by inversion, though the material is all time material, he has driven through it so sharply by the beak of his ego, that, he has turned time into what we now must have, space & its live air. . . .

Beyond that sense of principle — if such 'beyonds' can exist — there is the effect of reading Pound, of that experience of an energy, of ear and mind, which makes a language man's primary act. A sound:

> And then went down to the ship,
> Set keel to breakers, forth on the godly sea. . . .

> [*Agenda,* October-November 1965]

The Release

DR. WILLIAMS* is 'unique' in no sense unfamiliar. There have been other men likewise of this intent: to hit ground somewhere, to anchor somehow to present. An autobiography can effect the impact of a recognition perhaps beyond the *art* — though I should look to nothing else but such art for major effect, or what can now be of essential use.

The present book is one of *many* by Dr. Williams, no reader can forget that. The material is, to some extent it must be, of lower intensity than that which we have witnessed before — he can not do it all over again, in any form, and the years here dealt with are those in which his other work first appeared. In 1925 *In the American Grain* recorded a like purpose, of "autobiography," and continues as informant:

> The strong sense of a beginning in Poe is in *no one* else before him. What he says, being thoroughly local in origin, has some chance of being universal in application, a thing they never dared conceive. Made to fit a *place* it will have that actual quality of *things* anti-metaphysical —

> The prose of that earlier book has, of course, been noted but not in its particulars, i.e., the first evidence of a prose *method* we have yet to acknowledge by use. "No ideas but in things."

The Autobiography of William Carlos Williams.

1

A time denies itself in thinking of *time* — the *place* is a similar escape if it be left there, and not used. It is a theme of *use*, and how one can come to fix on any *thing* some signal of his own existence. Clearly, it is not in any usual sense: "What becomes of me has never seemed important, but the fates of ideas living against the grain in a nondescript world has always held me breathless." The "world" is nondescriptive, either in our hands — to speak of it so — or in its own character. A *use* is a *relation*, and these determine no adequate symbol or metaphor beyond their very *presence* — that they exist in such permanent character.

On this the poem rests, on this presence. "The poet thinks with his poem, in that lies his thought, and that in itself is the profundity." Against the half-conceived, or the recoil — the poem also a thing — equal, if you will, to Nature or to any mass conception. In this poetry has dominance, and a *form*. It is neither explanation nor description, but *actual* in such form.

These were the years just before the great catastrophe to our letters — the appearance of T. S. Eliot's *The Waste Land*. There was heat in us, a core and a drive that was gathering headway upon the theme of a rediscovery of a primary impetus, the elementary principle of all art, in the local conditions. Our work staggered to a halt for a moment under the blast of Eliot's genius which gave the poem back to the academics. We did not know how to answer him.

A form "in the local conditions" depends on what relation is possible, and, to that end, one attacks. Particulars are relevant in their own attack on the man who wants to confront them. Released, they find form in themselves, and use any man as their declaration. It is, perhaps, that struggle is impossible against them — in this alien way. "When she died there was nothing left. In his despair he had nowhere to turn. It is the very apotheosis of the place and time."

But from that "place" or "time" there is nowhere else — either then, for Poe, or for us now. At this point we fight lacking all we might wish, or want, otherwise. In *release* from despair. The poem *begins* here. In time, if you want, and also in place. Its locus is that effect, of itself, on that corpus of the particular, the world in detail. What effect can be made is *in* the poem — not *then* alien, or strange to its locality. Our language is more uniquely ourselves than any other act, it is our marriage.

"Nothing can grow unless it taps into the soil."

2

Within my own experience I have heard Williams called "antipoetic." This is a testament, of my own — that I oppose it. "When a man makes a poem, makes it, mind you, he takes words as he finds them interrelated about him and composes them — without distortion which would mar their exact significances — into an intense expression of his own perceptions and ardors that they may constitute a revelation in the speech that he uses." All *use* is a personal act, and I have used this *sense*, of poetry, insofar as I have been capable.

Some definitions are without meaning, lacking, as they do, a ground on which to bear. Any discussion of poetry must come to the poem itself, and take there, if anywhere, its own assumption of meaning. A theory of poetry is relevant only in what it can produce, in quite literal poems. Pound notes, "I think it will be usually found that the work outruns the formulated or at any rate the published equation, or at most they proceed as two feet of one biped."

Outside

        outside myself

               there is a world,

he rumbled, subject to my incursions

— a world

        (to me) at rest

           which I approach

concretely —

("Eliot had turned his back on the possibility of reviving
my world. . . . Only now, as I predicted, have we begun
to catch hold again and restarted to make the line over.
This is not to say that Eliot has not, indirectly, contributed
much to the emergence of the next step in metrical construction, but if he had not turned away from the direct
attack here, in the western dialect, we might have gone
ahead much faster.")

No man can effect poetry without the ground of himself
— in whatever character that should be open to him. "After
it was over we rushed up — already there was a young man
telling him he was more poet than doctor (shyly) and Williams saying he was simply both & the manner of his life
affected his poetry very much he thought. . . . " Definition
would be a man's act, and so his poetry, not so much in the
character of things beyond reach, call it — but in those
things immensely to hand, in that shape they make a "world"
no matter. It is from this world a man must care *not* to
escape, having *no* other of such kind.

"He sat to read, just turning the pages & looking at the
people. Everybody I could hear near me responded in a
way that staggered me. — Dead silence, tremendous ap-
plause — and the people who have money to go to these

things don't read poetry. Common speech, and he really
got to everyone. I was maudlin, with tears in my eyes —
at the whole idea."

[*Contact* (Toronto) November-
January 1952-53]

William Carlos Williams: Selected Essays

THIS IS A DIFFICULT book to find one's way around in, because there are many apparent concerns. Most of these, however, make no more than a superficial continuity. For example, there is a surprising emphasis on poets whom one had not thought to associate with Dr. Williams' own work, since the latter has been so much beyond usual peripheries — even called at times 'antipoetic.' Of the various people whom he has chosen so to recommend, many strike one as, at best, parallel to his own practice, while some seem almost to confute it.

Pound has been one of these last for a long time, and in the early essays Williams gives us some hint* of this:

> But our prize poems are especially to be damned not because of superficial bad workmanship, but because they are rehash, repetition in another way of Verlaine, Baudelaire, Maeterlinck — conscious or unconscious — just as there were Pound's early paraphrases from Yeats and his constant cribbing from the Renaissance, Pro-

*Williams' most interesting comment on Pound (for myself) is not here included, but to note it: "Letter to an Australian Editor," published in a Williams' number of the *Briarcliff Quarterly*. There are many such omissions, and I have since learned the book represents roughly half the text originally planned by the author. Much controversial material, for example, is missing — among other things, a very succinct note on Eliot's espousal of Milton, "With Rude Fingers Forced" (printed in *Four Pages*). The resulting loss is considerable, and the reader should keep it in mind, both in reading the book itself and this review of it.

vence and the modern French: Men content with the
connotations of their masters.

(Prologue to Kora in Hell, 1918)

True or false, this is a persistent judgment, which continues in one character or another throughout Williams'
comment. But by 1934 ("A Pound Stein") he can end a
thoroughly acute perception of what both have done, saying: "It may be added that both Gertrude Stein and Ezra
Pound live in Europe." In short, Williams has had, I think,
a continual notion that men were *wrong* per se to run away
from 'local conditions'; for himself, they were all that could
generate the *forms* for which he looked. Yet there remained
the dilemma of the *success* of others, come to again and
again in both his poems and criticism:

Sometimes I envy others, fear them
a little too, if they write well. . . .

("The Cure")

Of those closer to him, in point of geography at least,
Marianne Moore is (in this selection) the most singled out:

Work such as Miss Moore's holds its bloom today not
by using slang, not by its moral abandon or puritannical
steadfastness, but by the aesthetic pleasure engendered
where pure craftsmanship joins hard surfaces skillfully.

("Marianne Moore," 1931)

Therefore Miss Moore has taken recourse to the mathematics of art. Picasso does no different: a portrait is a
stratagem singularly related to a movement among the
means of the craft. By making these operative, relationships become self-apparent — the animal lives with a
human certainty. This is strangely worshipful. Nor does
one always know against what one is defending oneself.

("Marianne Moore," 1948)

This is not a fair way of citing such things, but certain discrepancies are clear. The first note, read in its entirety, argues a completely relevant 'value,' e.g., "The 'useful result' is an accuracy to which this simplicity of design greatly adds. The effect is for the effect to remain 'true'; nothing loses its identity because of the composition, but the parts in their assembly remain quite as 'natural' as before they were gathered." The second (more a favor?) is not, however, this positive in its analyses: "... I don't think there is a better poet writing in America today or one who touches so deftly so great a range of our thought."

Such matters are, of course, minimal, a man has what friends he can have and is biased accordingly. What Williams might say of Marianne Moore's translations of La Fontaine, however interesting, would leave us still beside the point. And this *is* important to note, because it is so often the case that Williams says things in spite of his 'subject.' There are, for example, essays on the work of Robert Lowell ("It is to assert love, not to win it that the poem exists...."), on Karl Shapiro ("Shapiro speaks lovingly of his 'rime' which he defines here and there in his poem — variously, as it should [not] be defined. It is the whole body of the management of words to the formal purposes of expression. We express ourselves there [men] as we might on the whole body of the various female could we ever gain access to her [which we cannot and never shall] ..."), on Dylan Thomas ("Reading over his collected poems I have thought of what chances he had to enhance his fame by thinking again and perhaps more profoundly of what he had in mind. But what can be more profound than song? The only thing that can be asked is whether a man is content with it ....").

So it is a provocative book, for anyone who has either learned from or felt sympathy for Williams' own work. For-

getting the above for the moment (because I believe these
'occasions' to be of little importance), the last piece in the
book ("On Measure — Statement for Cid Corman") brings
to a head an issue more at root in Williams' sense of structure than even his insistence on the 'local.' It begins:

> Verse — we'd better not speak of poetry lest we become
> confused — verse has always been associated in men's
> minds with "measure," i.e., with mathematics. In scan-
> ning any piece of verse, you "count" the syllables. Let's
> not speak either of rhythm, an aimless sort of thing
> without precise meaning of any sort. But measure im-
> plies something that can be measured. Today verse has
> lost all measure.

(I would like to cite two other men here, whose practice
and/or belief may have less bearing than I think, but no
matter. I am told of an essay by an Elizabethan, Samuel Put-
man, "On Proportion," wherein he speaks of *numbers and
measure* as being *arythmus;* and of that rhythm which we
find in poems, as *rhythmus.* For him, rhythm implied ir-
regularity; he also speaks of poetic rhythm as that "regularity just out of hearing." The other man is Thomas Campion, who was both musician and poet, and who also said
he paid no attention to any 'measure.' He gave his attention
to the words and the rhythms which they carried in them,
to be related then as they occurred. This is very clear, of
course, reading any of his poems:

Kinde are her answeres

Kinde are her answeres,
But her performance keeps no day;
Breaks time, as dancers
From their own Musicke when they stray:
All her free favors and smooth words,

Wing my hopes in vaine.
O did ever voice so sweet but only fain?
  Can true love yeeld such delay,
  Converting joy to pain?

  Lost is our freedome,
  When we submit to women so:
Why doe wee neede them,
  When in their best they worke our woe?
  There is no wisedome
Can alter ends, by Fate prefixt.
O why is the good of man with evill mixt?
  Never were days yet cal'd two,
  But one night went betwixt.

To 'scan' this is hardly possible, nor, more actually, at all the point. The 'process' is literally the same as that by which Williams himself writes, or any man who can effect such things with words. In any case, here is Williams:

The World Narrowed to a Point

Liquor and love
when the mind is dull
focus the wit
on a world of form

The eye awakes
perfumes are defined
inflections
ride the quick ear

Liquor and love
rescue the cloudy sense
banish its despair
give it a home.

This is not the 'same,' granted, but see that the second verse, in particular, involves us in that same character of variation which makes Campion himself a delight.)
Williams continues:

> Most poems I see today are concerned with what they are *saying*, how profound they have been given to be. So true is this that those who write them have forgotten to make poems at all of them. Thank God we're not musicians, with our lack of structural invention we'd be ashamed to look ourselves in the face otherwise. There is nothing interesting in the construction of our poems, nothing that can jog the ear out of its boredom. I for one can't read them. There is nothing in their metrical construction to attract me, so I fall back on e. e. cummings and the disguised conventions that he presents which are at least amusing — as amusing as "Doctor Foster went to Gloucester, in a shower of rain."

The charge is reasonable enough, but for one thing — it seems to posit an either/or choice for "metrical construction" (?) versus some other means. But it is *not* metrics that are the fact in any of this, since, to compose 'metrically,' would oblige one literally to an assumption of the 'foot' and the patterns then possible well before any poem could be written. This is the confusion, I think. Also — that it seems to be 'metrical construction' as against some form of 'typographical' construction (?); "It [the poem] is all over the page at the mere whim of the man who has composed it." But Stevens, for one, answered this, when he said there were those who thought of form as if it were a derivative of plastic shape. Which it is not, etc.

> Without measure we are lost. But we have lost even the ability to count. Actually we are not as bad as that. Instinctively we have continued to count as always but it

has become not a conscious process and being unconscious has descended to a low level of invention. . . .
I have accordingly made a few experiments which will
appear in a new book shortly [*The Desert Music*]. . . .
There will be other experiments but all will be directed
toward the discovery of a new measure by which may
be ordered our poems as well as our lives.

That, in brief, is the substance of the essay in question
(here dated 1953). The first essay in the book is dated
1920. The first preoccupations are with the poem's structure — apart from content. This must be the issue of the
place where it occurs — an answer, a disattachment, to the
past. The line must be 'retaken,' reasserted, in terms of an
immediate context. Against 'old forms,' congealed casts,
which Williams names 'the sonnet.' ("To me the sonnet
form is thoroughly banal because it is a word in itself whose
meaning is definitely fascistic.") 'Measure' is first spoken of
in "Pound's Eleven New 'Cantos' " (1934):

> The line must be measured to be in measure — but this
> does not mean disfigurement to fit an imposed meter.
> It's a matter of technique or the philosophy of poetry.
> Difficult to find many who will agree about it. With
> Pound it is in itself a revolution — how difficult to com-
> prehend: unless the term revolution be well understood.

That is part and parcel with the "*relatively* stable foot"
called for in "On Measure," i.e., it is, I think, a confusion.
To take literally the first of the sentence, "The line must be
measured to be in measure. . . , " is to involve oneself in an
obviously vicious circle. No poem was ever written "in this
direction."

So, then, what does it all come to. That the words in a
poem must cohere in terms of their rhythms and sound
weights — this is reasonable enough. We have lost con-

siderable ground — if one wishes to speak of it all as ground covered — by thinking too literally of 'quantitative verse,' and then, in a form of reflex, of that which we have been given by poets in our own immediate tradition. But 'measure,' bitterly enough, has most usually been that means by which lesser men made patterns from the work of better — so to perpetuate their own failure. There is even a hint of this in a review published in the *London Times Literary Supplement*, of Williams' *Collected Later Poems:*

> But his forms are so irregular in outline that there is no way of measuring them. Any metrical ideas which the reader retains while reading him will be an interruption.

So much for 'measure' (which has nothing to do with *rhythm*, which, as Olson reminds us, the "pedants of Alexandria made it"). But Williams no longer trusts rhythm — "an aimless sort of thing without precise meaning of any sort."

It all goes around and around. That I suppose would hold as true of the world as anything else would. Let's measure that?

[*Black Mountain Review*, Winter 1954]

A Character for Love

WE CAN HOPE that the woman be merciful, a kind of repose (and our rejection in part) for that for which she attacks. And yet there is no woman either to be kind or to live with a kind man, and rightly. The man who would come to her comes with his own weapons, and if he is not a fool, he uses them.

That much might well be dogma — an apology only to those who have gone down before its alternative, the 'undrestanding.' It was this that Lawrence fought all his life, perhaps more closely (more desperately) than any man before or since. Because we can have no way to declare love, except by the act of it.

Here* it is that Dr. Williams not so much rests as still persists — in that persistence, which, because it knows itself (and will not understand), is love too.

        THERE ARE MEN
                who as they live
                        fling caution to the
        wind and women praise them
                        and love them for it.
                                Cruel as the claws of
        a cat . .

You do not describe this thing, neither you nor I. Married, the world becomes that act, or nothing.

*William Carlos Williams: *The Desert Music*.

112

THE FEMALE PRINCIPLE of the world
      is my appeal
         in the extremity
to which I have come.

I think that much of this content (by no means to beg
it) came from him from the first, and, to that extent, American poetry had something even Poe (whom Williams alone
saw this in) could not in his own dilemma give it. It is interesting, certainly that, to read the last part of the Poe
essay in *In the American Grain* — where Poe's attempt to
register himself is so characterized as this persistence, this
hammering at the final edge of contact.

And this is the same force of Williams' stories, the best
of them I think, even that possible vagueness in the one
about the returning doctor, at the friend's house (also a
doctor), and of the friend's wife who comes in and sits
there, in the dark, by the edge of the bed, lies down on it,
because *he* cannot sleep.

           You are a woman and
  it was
      a woman's gesture.
           I declare it boldly
  with my heart
      in my teeth
          and my knees knocking
together. Yet I declare
    it, and by God's word
      it is no lie.

The *Autobiography*, more than any of his other books,
now, is the place where the materials of his work are given
— not done, but there to be found and related, if that is the
purpose, to their forms in his art. What the poem is — beyond his sense of this service as "capsule for punishable

secrets" or including it — comes again and again to the fact of women. In the preface to the book he speaks of that 'form' which men have given to his life, but it is women who have made for the 'energy.' And energy begins it.

Of asphodel, that greeny flower,
            like a buttercup
                        upon its branching stem . . .
save that it's green and wooden . . .
            I come, my sweet,
                        to sing to you.
For what reason, to sing, even to be a 'poet'?
                        I *am* a poet! I
am. I am. I am a poet, I reaffirmed, ashamed

Now the music volleys through as in
a lonely moment I hear it   Now it is all
about me. The dance! The verb detaches itself
seeking to become articulate

There shall be no other judge — *not* judge, but she who will take it. And for that reason, that it begins where all things *(mind you)* begin, the dance is the plain fact of contact, god help us.

You seem quite normal. Can you tell me? Why
does one want to write a poem?

    Because it's there to be written.

Oh. A matter of inspiration then?
                        Of necessity.

Oh. But what sets it off?

            I am that he whose brains
            are scattered
                aimlessly

At this point one turns, to laugh (ha), because it is what you wanted? Well, put it that here we are thrown out, not by Williams but by that which he knows, perfectly. We shall get no thanks for what we do, 'poets' or not. Nor can we lie down, asking it.

There is, in short,
a counter stress,
             born of the sexual shock,
                          which survives it
consonant with the moon,
             to keep its own mind.

We have had so much hope, both in love and in poetry, that I wonder what is or can be left. Yet put them together and you will have nothing at all. You cannot sit in a woman's lap, however comfortable. And, despite the humiliation, the door must be shut of necesssity — until you can bang it down or open it.

You understand
             I had to meet you
                          after the event
and have still to meet you,
             Love
                          to which you too shall bow
along with me —
             a flower
                          a weakest flower
shall be our trust
             and not because
                          we are too feeble
to do otherwise
             but because
                          at the height of my power

I risked what I had to do,
   therefore to prove
      that we love each other
while my very bones sweated
   that I could not cry out to you
      in the act.

Let men do what they will, generally — there will be no statement beyond this. It is fantastic, to me, that Williams at such a time as now confronts him should be so incredibly clear. Yet, what else to be —

   Hear me out
      for I too am concerned
and every man
   who wants to die at peace in his bed
      besides.

     [*Black Mountain Review*, Summer 1954]

The Fact

THERE IS NO simple way to speak of this book.* It is so singularly the work of a man, one man, that it moves thereby to involve all men, no matter what they assume to be their own preoccupations.

What shall I say, because talk I must
    That I have found a cure
       for the sick?
I have found no cure
    for the sick
       but this crooked flower
Which only to look upon
    all men
       are cured . . .

                ("The Yellow Flower")

The insistence in our lives has become a plethora of plans, of solutions, of, finally, a web of abstract commitments — which leave us only with confusions. Against these Dr. Williams has put the fact of his own life, and all that finds substance in it. He had earlier insisted, "No ideas but in things," meaning that all which moves to an *elsewhere* of abstractions, of specious 'reliefs,' must be seen as false. We live as and where we are. It is, for example, literally *here*:

*William Carlos Williams: *Pictures from Breughel and Other Poems.*

117

The World Contracted to a Recognizeable Image
at the small end of an illness
there was a picture
probably Japanese
which filled my eye

an idiotic picture
except it was all I recognized
the wall lived for me in that picture
I clung to it as a fly

What device, means, rhythm, or form the poem can gain
for its coherence are a precise issue of its occasion. The
mind and ear are, in this sense, stripped to hear and
organize what is given to them, and the *dance* or *music*
Williams has used as a metaphor for this recognition and
its use is that which sustains us, poets or men.

But only the dance is sure!
make it your own.
Who can tell
what is to come of it?

in the woods of your
own nature whatever
twig interposes, and bare twigs
have an actuality of their own

this flurry of the storm
that holds us,
plays with us and discards us
dancing, dancing as may be credible.

("The Dance")

It is equally that music which informs our lives with a
coherence beyond their intention or apparent significance.
In "The Desert Music" (the title poem of an earlier collection [1954] included in this present book, as is also *Journey*

to Love [1955]) this music is "a music of survival, subdued,
distant, half heard. . . ." And against the external music of
the juke-box, band, or whatever, the "nauseating prattle,"
Williams puts "the form of an old whore in / a cheap Mexican joint in Juárez, her bare / can waggling crazily. . . . ":

> What the hell
> are you grinning
> to yourself about? Not
> at *her?*
>   The music!
> I like her. She fits
> the music   .

And again, finding the form of no shape, no identity, "prop-
ped motionless — on the bridge / between Juárez and El
Paso — unrecognizeable / in the semi-dark. . . . ":

> But what's THAT?
>
>   the music! the
>
> *music!* as when Casals struck
> and held a deep cello tone
> and I am speechless   .

The *dance,* the acts of a life, move to that *music,* the life
itself, and it is these which it is the poet's peculiar responsibility to acknowledge and recover by his art:

> Now the music volleys through as in
> a lonely moment I hear it.   Now it is all
> about me.   The dance!   The verb detaches itself
> seeking to become articulate   .
>
>   And I could not help thinking
>   of the wonders of the brain that
>   hears that music and of our
>   skill sometimes to record it.

Coming then to the later poems, what can be said now is that there is all such truth, such life, in them. I cannot make that judgment which would argue among the poems that this or that one shows the greater mastery. I think there must come a time, granted that one has worked as Williams to define the nature of this art, when it all coheres, and each poem, or instance, takes its place in that life which it works to value, to measure, to be the fact of. As here:

To Be Recited to Flossie on Her Birthday

Let him who may
among the continuing lines
seek out

that tortured constancy
affirms
where I persist

let me say
across cross purposes
that the flower bloomed

struggling to assert itself
simply under
the conflicting lights

you will believe me
a rose
to the end of time

[First draft of a review published
in *The Nation*, October 13, 1962]

Louis Zukofsky: "A" 1-12 & Barely and Widely

Louis Zukofsky's poetry is compounded of great love, equal care, and a singular perception of the nature of words in all their manifold senses. There is no one who writes with greater intelligence of what our common world is, nor of the tradition of the family in it, nor of the mind itself asked to see reason in the flux of war and economic confinement. His long poem, "A" (here collected to the 12th book, with another twelve now planned), is itself a singular history of a man's will to relate, in all senses, the circumstances in which he lives. There is also purpose which cannot be so simply described:

> River, that must turn full after I stop dying
> Song, my song, raise grief to music
> Light as my loves' thought, the few sick
> So sick of wrangling: thus weeping,
> Sounds of light, stay in her keeping
> And my son's face — this much for honor....

The poem turns upon many senses of value, "values / The measure of use who conceive love...," sees:

> We are things, say, like a quantum of action
> Defined product of energy and time, now
> In these words which rhyme now how song's exaction
> Forces abstraction to turn from equated
> Values to labor we have approximated....

So we are led to know that:

When men count
They do not err
In their minds.
No one desires
To be blest —
To act well
Or live well —
Who will
Not desire
To exist.
This is virtue
The more so
All have it . . . .

The terms of a world depend on that intelligence which
can relate them, making of senseless sound, a music, as
Bach's — or here:

Take and owe nothing.
Everybody take. Here,
And owe nothing. . . .

But such quotation tends to make too small the area involved, which is no less complex than the world's:

People   people   people
There is no whisper but vibrates
Your body
No voice but that you
Speak it. . . .

Louis Zukofsky's use for poets now is very great. The
note on poetry at the end of this book — and the book itself
— are primary evidence. He teaches the articulation of consciousness, the modes of apprehension which words can
make clear. So it is "The thought in the melody moves . . . ,"
making order, moved by love.

Barely and Widely, in holograph facsimile, is also a lovely book in all senses. It is a collection of shorter poems written 1956 to 1958 (the first sections of "A" are dated 1928 and the last section 1951) and includes "4 Other Countries" — again evidence of his great, compassionate power. Having spoken of the Roman's love of domesticity and family, for example, the poem continues:

. . . unlike
  the Christians
in the catacombs
  who burying theirs

In their walls
  must have turned
in distraction
  to give joy

To one another
  in carving
good shepherds
  and their flocks

Or painting fish
  or ravens
when their hymns
  and prayers

Brought no daily
  bread—and for fear no
other speech than
  out of their wild eyes. . . .

[*The Sparrow,* November 1962]

"paradise / our / speech ..." *

LOUIS ZUKOFSKY has defined his poetics as a function, having as lower limit, speech, and upper limit, song. It is characteristic of him to say that a poet's "... major aim is not to show himself but that order that of itself can speak to all men...." It is his belief that a poet writes one poem all his life, a continuing *song*, so that no division of its own existence can be thought of as being more or less than its sum. This is to say, it *all* is.

Williams wrote of him, "The musician and the poet should be taken as a critical unit in our effort to understand the poet Zukofsky's meaning." It was his own thought that "It was never a simple song as it was, for instance, in my own case...." But that complexity which Williams noted can be deceptive if it proposes that something intently difficult is involved with whatever sense of purpose. In many instances, the *song* of both men is similar, and it is necessary to isolate the character of *music* either might mean. For example, here is a poem of Zukofsky's in which the "tune" is defined deliberately as a consequence of rhythms and sounds:

> The lines of this new song are nothing
> But a tune making the nothing full
> Stonelike become more hard than silent
> The tune's image holding in the line.

(20, *Anew*)

All: The Collected Short Poems, 1923-1958.

124

Again as Williams has said, "He uses words in more or less
sentence formation if not strictly in formal sentence patterns, in a wider relationship to the composition as musical
entity. . . ." I had first understood this possibility by means
of a poem of Williams', "The End of the Parade":

> The sentence undulates
> raising no song —
> It is too old, the
> words of it are falling
> apart. . . .

That is, I *heard* the fact of the poem's statement as well as
understood its meaning. Such hearing is immediately necessary in reading Zukofsky's work insofar as meaning is an
intimate relation of such sound and sense. It can be as close
as —

> Crickets'
> thickets
>
> light,
> delight . . .
>   (16, "29 Songs")

— or move with an apparent statement, seeming to "say"
enough to satisfy that measure; but again it will be that one
hears what is so said, not merely deciphers a "meaning":

> And so till we have died
> And grass with grass
> Lie faceless as the grass
>
> Grow sheathed with the grass
> Between our spines a hollow
> The stillest sense will pass
> Or weighted cloud will follow.
>   (19, *Anew*)

❖   ❖   ❖

                    Strange
To reach that age,
                    remember
      a tide
And full
      for a time
                    be young.
                  (36, *Anew*)

The consequence of such a way leads to a recognition of
what is being heard at each moment of the writing, or reading, and the effect is evident in either:

. . . Having seen the thing happen,
There would be no intention 'to write it up,'

But *all* that was happening,
The mantis itself only an incident, *compelling any writing*
The transitions were perforce omitted.

Thoughts' — two or three or five or
Six thoughts' reflection (pulse's witness) of what was
                                      [happening
All immediate, not moved by any transition.

Feeling this, what should be the form
Which the ungainliness already suggested
Should take? . . .

                  ("Mantis," An Interpretation)

It leads to other distrusts of any kind of *plan* which distorts
the actuality of feeling:

            . . . Understanding:
            I wasn't going to say
          for fear
            You didn't want to hear.

That's the worst
of understanding,
a handshake
would be better. . . .

("4 Other Countries")

The way of such feeling is clear in the words, as "for fear /
You didn't want to hear" or "understanding, / a handshake,"
and trusts to that sense, *"The vowels / abide / in consonants /
like / / Souls / in / bodies—"* for the life of what it says.

This life—*All: The Collected Short Poems, 1923-1958*—
is evidence of Zukofsky's own, but not as some biographical
record, although much detail of that kind can be taken from
it. It is, rather, that by virtue of the occasion so shared each
has come to live in all the diversity of either. In this respect,
I can think of no man more useful to learn from than Zukofsky, in that he will not 'say' anything but that which the
particulars of such a possibility require, and follows the *fact*
of that occasion with unequalled sensitivity. But to *hear* it,
is necessary —

. . . That song
is the kiss
it keeps
is it
The
unsaid worry
for what
should last. . . .

("4 Other Countries")

[*Poetry,* October 1965]

Louis Zukofsky:
All: The Collected Short Poems, 1923-1958

IN HIS PREFACE to *A Test of Poetry* (1948) Louis Zukofsky notes at the outset, "The test of poetry is the range of pleasure it affords as sight, sound, and intellection. This is its purpose as art..." In his long poem *"A"* he qualifies its occasion as *"Out of deep need...."* Then, continuing:

Who had better sing and tell stories
Before all will be abstracted.
So goes: first, *shape*
The creation —
A mist from the earth,
The whole face of the ground:
Then *rhythm* —
And breathed breath of life;
Then *style* —
That from the eye its function takes —
"Taste" we say — a living soul.
First, glyph; then syllabary,
Then letters. Ratio after
Eyes, tale in sound. First, dance. Then
Voice. First, body — to be seen and to pulse
Happening together.

("A" 12)

It is a sense that proposes poetry to be evidence as to its own activity, apart from any other sense of description or of a convenience to some elsewise considered reality of things. More, it is a belief, deeply committed, that what is said says 'what-is-said' — a complexity of no simple order. For example, the first poem in *All* notes by the fact of its activity that any *said* thing exists in its saying and cannot be less than said — each time it is. It is interesting that this poem is called "Poem beginning 'The'" — which article is itself a determined emphasis upon what is defined in speech. In this case, a method as well takes form in this poem, as William Carlos Williams points out in his essay "Zukofsky," included in "*A*."* It is based, I feel, upon the premise that all that is, as whatever has spoken it, may occur as it is, each time it is spoken. In other words, there is nothing which anything so existent is 'about,' that will go away in time, so as to embarrass the actuality of such existence. Zukofsky makes a lovely note of *time* in the 28th of 29 Songs, which is pertinent to all such facts of *factness*: ". . . And for years it was four o'clock, — not time which would have broken the hour and placed a statue of David in history, but an ornamental herb of that name, — with flowers that grow in Peru of a great variety of color. So that for years it was four o'clock and the same as bloom from 4 P.M. till the next morning."

There is one poem which I would feel very useful for many senses of Zukofsky's poems, both in that character with which I have been concerned and also, very much, in the full complexity of their involvement with the man who is writing them. The poem is "Mantis" and there is a note as to its date of writing, November 4, 1934. At a time when so much concern has come to center on assumptions of form, and remembering also that Empson's *Seven Types of Ambiguity*, for one such instance, was published in the early thirties — this poem makes clear a context of possibility and response itself a manifest of the poem's writing. The osten-

*Origin Press edition (1959).

sible form of the poem is a sestina, and in " 'Mantis,' An Interpretation" — a close response to the poem's writing and concerns which follows in the next — Zukofsky says:

> The sestina, then, the repeated end words
> Of the lines' winding around themselves,
> Since continuous in the Head, whatever has been read,
>   whatever is heard,
>   whatever is seen
> Perhaps goes back cropping up again with
> Inevitable recurrence again in the blood
> Where the spaces of verse are not visual
> But a movement,
> With vision in the lines merely a movement . . .
>
> One feels in fact inevitably
> About the coincidence of the mantis lost in the subway,
> About the growing oppression of the poor —
> Which is the situation most pertinent to us —
> With the fact of the sestina:
> Which together fatally now crop up again
> To twist themselves anew
> To record not a sestina, post Dante,
> Nor even a mantis.

What I am most intent to point out here is that Zukofsky feels form as an intimate presence, whether or not that form be the use or issue of other feelings in other times, or the immediate apprehension of a *way* felt in the moment of its occurrence. The distinction is, then, against what appropriates the outline sans an experience of its intimate qualities — as Zukofsky notes in this same section:

> What is most significant
> Perhaps is that C— and S— and X— of the 19th century
> Used the "form" — not the form but a Victorian
> Stuffing like upholstery

> For parlor polish,
> And our time takes count against them
> For their blindness and their (unintended?) cruel smug-
>   [ness.
>
> Again: as an experiment, the sestina would be wicker-
>   [work —
> As a force, one would lie to one's feelings not to use it.

There is no reason I would credit to prevent a man's walking down a road another has made use of — unless the road,
by such use, has become a 'road,' an habituated and unfelt
occasion. But as "force" its possibility is timeless.

Given the briefness of these notes, I am embarrassed to
deal with all that in this poem excites and informs me. It
is a peculiar virtue of Zukofsky's work that it offers an extraordinary handbook for the writing of poems. His particular sensitivity to the qualities of poetry as "sight, sound,
and intellection" mark the significance of his relation to
Ezra Pound, who dedicated *Guide to Kulchur* "To Louis
Zukofsky and Basil Bunting, strugglers in the desert." It is
Bunting who says that his own first experience of poetry as
an unequivocal possibility for himself came with the recognition that the order and movement of *sound* in a poem
might itself create a coherence of the emotions underlying.
In this respect, the following note by Zukofsky merits much
thought:

> How much what is sounded by words has to do with
> what is seen by them, and how much what is at once
> sounded and seen by them crosscuts an interplay among
> themselves — will naturally sustain the scientific defini-
> tion of poetry we are looking for. To endure it would be
> compelled to integrate these functions: time, and what
> is seen in time (as held by a song), and an action whose
> words are actors or, if you will, mimes composing steps

as of a dance that at proper instants calls in the vocal
cords to transform it into plain speech.

("Poetry," in "A" [Origin Press edition])

The brilliance, then, of these poems is their grace in such
a recognition, that they can move so articulately in all the
variables of a life. I can make no selection because, as their
author has said, one writes one poem all one's life, and there
can be no significant division. But as one moment, this may
stand as token of all:

> Strange
> To reach that age,
> remember
> a tide
> And full
> for a time
> be young.

(36, *Anew*)

[*Agenda,* Summer 1966]

A Note*

THERE IS A POSSIBILITY in reading and writing, which knows
words as in the world in much the same way that men are,
and that each may know that possibility which Herrick defines:

> And when all bodies meet,
>   In Lethe to be drowned,
> Then only numbers sweet
>   With endless life are crowned.

There is no presumption in the fact that Louis Zukofsky
puts two poems of Herrick's together with his own song,
"Little wrists," as an instance of *grace* in his comparative
anthology, *A Test of Poetry*. One hears in the possibility
another has articulated what may thus bring clear one's
own, and though there are three hundred years intervening,
the measure of grace is not variable.

Zukofsky says, one writes one poem all one's life. All that
he has written may be felt as indivisible, and all *one* — which
word occurs frequently in the text in this sense.

Another word found often is *leaf*, echoing, specifically at
times as in the latter part of "*A*" 12, Whitman's *Leaves of
Grass*. Despite what seem dissimilarities, they are like men
in that both would favor — with Shakespeare as Zukofsky
has proposed — the "clear physical eye" as against "the

*Introduction to Louis Zukofsky: "*A*" *1-12* (New York: Doubleday,
1967).

133

erring brain." The experience of one's life as one is given
to have it, and as relationships of its nature are found, un-
fold, then, as *leaves*, finding home in time far past or in the
instant now:

The music is in the flower,
Leaf around leaf ranged around the center;
Profuse but clear outer leaf breaking on space,
There is space to step to the central heart:
The music is in the flower,
It is not the sea but hyaline cushions the flower —
Liveforever, everlasting.
The leaves never topple from each other,
Each leaf a buttress flung for the other.

This is taken from "*A*" 2, written in 1928. In "*A*" 11,
twenty-two years later:

Honor

His voice in me, the river's turn that finds the
Grace in you, four notes first too full for talk, leaf
Lighting stem, stems bound to the branch that binds the
Tree, and then as from the same root we talk, leaf
Over leaf of his thought, sounding
His happiness: song sounding
The grace that comes from knowing
Things, her love our own showing
Her love in all her honor.

"... His voice in me. ..." That men do so move, one to
one, here grandfather, to father, to son — but that also, as
Zukofsky thinks possible, it may be that Shakespeare had
read Catullus, and that men who may so read the same text
may so *in time* relate. Certainly, as the outset of the work
makes clear, Zukofsky *hears* Bach, and after hearing:

I walked on Easter Sunday,
   This is my face
   This is my form.
Faces and forms, I would write
                  you down
   In a style of leaves growing.

One may well quote Pound, as Zukofsky has, to give measure for such occasion:

Hast 'ou fashioned so airy a mood
   To draw up the leaf from the root?

                 •   •   •

and the rest as time has cleft it

The title "*A*" itself is what one might call initial, and initiating, evidence of the kind of intelligence Zukofsky has — seeing and hearing words in the world as the specific possibilities they contain. He has said, in fact, that "a case can be made out for the poet giving some of his life to the use of the words *the* and *a:* both of which are weighted with as much epos and historical destiny as one man can perhaps resolve." How much "world" can lie between *the* and *a* is hardly for either *a* or *the* grammarian to decide.

We may speak of *the* as some thing previously noted or recognized, and of *a* as that which has not been thus experienced — but think too that, "from A to Z" may mean something, and that if one looks at an A, it may very possibly become a sawhorse:

Horses: who will do it? out of manes? Words
Will do it, out of manes, out of airs, but
They have no manes, so there are no airs, birds
Of words, from me to them no singing gut.
For they have no eyes, for their legs are wood,
For their stomachs are logs with print on them;

Blood red, red lamps hang from necks or where could
Be necks, two legs stand A, four together M.

Horses and *leaves:*

You keep up to date
On all fours
That canter sometimes
Before boughs that grace trees.
Sparks from hoofs:
There is horse....

So year to year —
Nor do the arts
Ever end.
How can man say
"I am certain"
For certain and uncertain
Do not make certain.
Only forever is previous
And not a horse's forever.
If someone stole off with its body
Be sure that its spirits
Canter forever.
Blacksmith, creator, shapes his shoe
Into substance.

Born in New York's lower east side, Zukofsky's life cannot
have been simple, and the kinds of complexity one realizes
do confront him here are deeply to be considered. In the
opening movements there are bitter terms of death, poverty,
war —

"I beg your pardon
I've a— "h" begins the rhyme here,
Shall we now?"

"You misconstrue—uh
Men's rue—eh,
Anyhow!"

The sailors in the carousel
   looking for a place to
      bury—Ricky;
Seaweed, fellow voters, and
   spewn civic sidewalks.

Thus one modernizes
His lute,
Not in one variation after another;
Words form a new city,
Ours is no Mozart's
Magic Flute—
Tho his melody made up for a century
And, we know, from him, a melody resolves
                           to no dullness—
But when we push up the daisies,
The melody! the rest is accessory:

My one voice. My other: is
An objective—rays of the object brought to a focus,
An objective—nature as creator—desire
   for what is objectively perfect
Inextricably the direction of historic and
                        contemporary particulars.

He was first published in *The Exile* by Ezra Pound in the
twenties. The poem was "The," which is relevant, and it led
subsequently to his publication in *The Dial* and other magazines of the period. In 1931 he edited an issue of *Poetry* in
which he presented a number of writers, among them Carl
Rakosi, Kenneth Rexroth (for whom it was his first publication), William Carlos Williams (whose poem "The Alphabet of the Trees" gained him one of his first awards),

and others of like significance. Asked for some tag, whereby to identify the group, Zukofsky used the term "objectivist"— which he once spoke of in conversation as follows:

> I picked the word simply because I had something very simple in mind. You live with the things as they exist and as you sense them and think them. That's the first thing, and that I call *sincerity* in an essay that was printed at the back of that *Poetry* number. Otherwise how sincere your intentions doesn't matter. The rest is, once you do that, you do put them into a shape that, apart from your having lived it, is now on its own, and that's what goes into the world and becomes part of it.

He has been long and quietly about his work, and, in the passage of time, he has written other books which complement it significantly—*All*, the collected short poems in two volumes (1923-1958; 1956-1964) and *Bottom: on Shakespeare* (published in 1963) among them. What he has said of the latter makes a useful focus here. First, despite that it is written in prose, he calls it "a long poem on a theme for the variety of its recurrences." The theme is, "that Shakespeare's text thruout favors the clear physical eye against the erring brain" and "that this theme has historical implications." Second, a "valid skepticism, that, as 'philosophy of history' taking in the (arts and sciences) my book takes exception to all philosophies from Shakespeare's point of view, that is, the physical eye against the erring brain." Third, "a continuation of my work on prosody in my other writings. In this sense my wife's music [her setting of Shakespeare's *Pericles* is the second volume of this work] saves me a lot of words, and she did a note to every syllable of *Pericles*." Finally, it is "a poet's autobiography as involvement of twenty years in a work shows him up, or, as in the case of Shakespeare, his words show him, are his life. . . ."

About *All*, Mr. Zukofsky says: "In a sense *All* is an autobiography: the words are my life ... Or to put it in other
words, the poet's form is never an imposition of history, but
the desirability of making order out of history as it is felt
and conceived."

In the title story of *It was*, a collection published in 1961,
the story itself having been written twenty years earlier, one
finds: "This story was a story of our time. And a writer's attempts not to fathom his time amount but to sounding his
mind in it. I did not want to break up my form by pointing
to well-known place names and dates in the forty years that
I had lived — events familiar to most of us, to some more
than myself. I wanted our time to be the story, but like the
thought of a place passed by once and recalled altogether:
seen again as through a stereoscope blending views a little
way apart into a solid — defying touch. I was saying something that had had a sequence, like the knowledge of taking
a breath, and hiding it, because one breathes without pointing to it before and after. . . . " "Thanks to the Dictionary,"
the final piece of this same book, written in 1932, begins:

"A." Quoting the dictionary. Remembering my saw-
horses, my little a.'s abbreviated for afternoon, perhaps
for years, this afternoon.

Quoting Satie, "born very young in a world already old,"
he has said of "A," "The idea is much as the brain does err,
it will willynilly get down, and sometimes the eye sees — the
form in that sense organic, or all of one's life, and this is the
life, and for the rest nobody else's business. It's written in
one's time and place, and it refers to other times and places
as one grows, whatever way one grows. It takes in books
that survive — say, well, like Bach's music it can go down,
it can go up, that's the interest of it and all to come through

the form of the thing. To hold it together, I don't know — a
song?" From "A" 12:

> You remember
> The houses where we were born
> The first horse pulsed
> Until the evening and the morning
> Were the first day?
> I'll tell you
> About my *poetics* —
> $\int$ music
>   speech
> An integral
> Lower limit speech
> Upper limit music . . .

❈   ❈   ❈

> *Time qualifies the fire and spark of it.*
> I can't improve *that.*
> That closed and open sounds saw
>   Things,
> See somehow everlastingly
> Out of the eye of sky.
>
> Poetics. With constancy . . .

❈   ❈   ❈

> As I love:
> My poetics. . . .

❈   ❈   ❈

> Better a fiddle than geiger?
> With either there is so much in 1
> And in one:
> $\quad\quad\quad 1 \quad\quad \int \; \text{sound}$
> $\quad\quad -1 \quad\quad\quad \text{story} - \text{eyes: thing thought}$

❈   ❈   ❈

Courses tide, and a tide
       brings back folk
       after twenty years,
A cycle a light matter or more,
So my song with an old voice is whole:
Another way of saying
You cannot take out of the circle—what was in it. . . .

Thus to *hear*, as he would hear Catullus, in the translation
he has made with his wife— "fact that delights as living hint
and its cues" being *"facit delicias libidinesque"*—"which is
much more simple in the Latin. It has to do with pleasures
and desires . . . " So "A" 9 is an extraordinary reading of
Guido Calvacanti's *Donna mi prega,* the *experience* of val-
uation, and of love, with Marx as he stems from Aristotle
included — the form a canzone, which demands that fifty-
four of the one hundred and fifty-four syllables occurring in
a strophe be rhymed, extending to seventy-five lines in all.
As Zukofsky notes, "it's all wound in," which impulse the
sonnet form reverses. Here he has composed two distinct
canzones — the first, of value, the second, of love — not a
literal translation of Calvacanti but rather an intensive
experience of the intimate situation of his writing, as fact of
sounds in the rhythms then relating. The second canzone
repeats, almost verbatim, the rhymes of the first:

    (1)

An impulse to actions sings of a semblance
Of things related as equated values,
The measure all use is time congealed labor
In which abstraction things keep no resemblance
To goods created; integrated all hues
Hide their natural use. . . .

(2)

An eye to action sees love bear the semblance
Of things, related is equated — values
The measure all use who conceive love, labor
Men see, abstraction they feel, the resemblance
(Part, self-created, integrated) all hues
Show to natural use....

To know what men say, one must hear them, and to hear
them means moving with the intimate means of their occasion —

Out of deep need
Four trombones and the organ in the nave
A torch surged—
Timed the theme Bach's name
Dark, larch and ridge, night:
From my body to other bodies
Angels and bastards interchangeably
Who had better sing and tell stories
Before all will be abstracted.

Buffalo, N.Y., April 2, 1967

A Personal Note

I HAVE NEVER understood very clearly why a man of Basil Bunting's accomplishment should have so little use in his own country. We have had like situations here – in the case of Louis Zukofsky, only recently 'discovered' after many years indeed of exceptional writing, and I can remember as well how resistant the elders of my own generation were to the work of Williams and Pound. H. D. remains for the most part an obscure figure, despite the fact that she is so uniquely a major one.

But if no one shouts, or keeps the insistence active, then these things do happen. Some years ago, when *Origin* was first being published, I wrote to Bunting to ask his help with finding active people in England and especially to see if he might have poems himself to send. He answered most kindly that his life had never been 'literary,' and since much of it had been spent in Persia, he was not aware of what might be of use then (roughly 1952) in England. He said he saw few English writers, and that when Alec Waugh, for example, had visited him, they talked of the water table and of the migration of game.

I had known of his work for some time, associating it with that of Pound, in whose *Active Anthology* I had first had chance to read Bunting's poems. *Kulchur* is also dedicated to Bunting and Zukofsky, "strugglers in the desert" of all too real a fact. Then in 1950 the Cleaners' Press published his

Poems, and we had our first chance to see the range and
subtlety of what he had done. Shortly after, *Poetry* published his long poem, *The Spoils* (1951).

But then the silence settled in again. When I visited last
October in England, of the many literary men I saw, only
two had occasion to speak of Bunting. One, George Fraser,
loaned me his copy of *Poems* to take back with me to London, in hopes someone there might be interested. The other,
Charles Tomlinson, was curious to know what Bunting's
present circumstances might be.

So I knew as little as ever. Then, coming down from Scot-
land, I stopped to read in Newcastle, at the invitation of Tom
Pickard, and there to my great pleasure and surprise was
Bunting himself.

I value that occasion very much, simply that there are men
who are measures of all possibility, in what they do literally
and in how they do it. I can't report all of the conversation
we had, but, again, it continues to serve me as measure both
of my own circumstances and of what poetry itself can be
as an active art. With respect to Eliot, he questioned the
rhythms, finding them "gross" I think his word was, yet
pointed out that the diction — the literal vocabulary of his
work — was very clear indeed. He made a useful distinction
between organizations of sound as one meets them in a
lyric — where the briefness of the poem's length gives them
a necessarily emphatic situation — and in a long poem, where
their texture may accumulate relationships without the
reader being aware of their singular condition. He talked
of Pound, more parallel he felt to Spenser than to Chaucer,
in that each man gives an encyclopaedia of possibilities to
those who then come after.

Of his own condition he said little. We walked above the
Tyne, back of the village of Wylam where he lives. When he
was a boy, there were several fisheries along that river, but

now industrial wastes and like circumstances made it un-
likely that even a casual fisherman would find much to
catch. He told me the Northumberland clans were the last
to give in to the organizations of county, more implacable
even than the Scots. He spoke of the reforestation program
in Northumberland, and in all he said there was evidence of
a deep sense of place and of his own commitment to it.

There is such a clarity to him, and in what he has written.
I wonder it is not seen more simply, but happily that situation now changes. There is no one else who can help as
much, both in the fact of his work — it offers, I feel, the most
real occasion for the work of younger men now — and himself, of all men unique in the quiet determination of what
he has valued.

> Have you seen a falcon stoop
> accurate, unforseen
> and absolute, between
> wind-ripples over harvest? Dread
> of what's to be, is and has been —
> were we not better dead?
> His wings churn air
> to flight.
> Feathers alight
> with sun, he rises where
> dazzle rebuts our stare,
> wonder our fright.

(from *The Spoils*)
[*Granta*, 6 November 1965]

A Note on Basil Bunting

THE PUBLICATION OF Basil Bunting's poems in England regains a possibility that has been equivocal for some time, if not literally absent. I am not the one to write of it simply that I am not English, nor of that particular root which Bunting has such use of. R. S. Woolf, reviewing *Loquitur* and *Briggflatts* in *Stand* (8, No. 2), puts emphasis on the almost flat pessimism, the insistence of death, throughout Bunting's work. It is there without question as it is equally in Samuel Beckett's, or in Dunbar's *Lament for the Makers*. Also relevant is the tone and manner of Michael Alexander's translations, *The Earliest English Poems*, from which comes the following:

> A man who on these walls wisely looked
> who sounded deeply this dark life
> would think back to the blood spilt here,
> weigh it in his wit . . .
> Alas, proud prince! How that time has passed,
> dark under night's helm, as though it never had been!
>
> ("The Wanderer")

Beckett, translating *An Anthology of Mexican Poetry*. comes to a very like tone (which is more than the transposition of a content evident in the Spanish):

> This coloured counterfeit . . .

146

is a foolish sorry labour lost,
is conquest doomed to perish and, well taken,
is corpse and dust, shadow and nothingness.

> (Juana de Asbaje, "This coloured
> counterfeit that thou beholdest...")

In short, I am curious to know if an implicit quality of language occurs when words are used in a situation peculiar to their own history. *History,* however, may be an awkward term, since it might well imply only a respectful attention on the part of the writer rather than the implicit rapport between words and man when both are equivalent effects of time and place. In this sense there is a lovely dense sensuousness to Bunting's poetry and it is as much the nature of the words as the nature of the man who makes use of them. Again it is a circumstance shared.

I am caught by the sense of himself Bunting defines:

I hear Aneurin number the dead and rejoice,
being adult male of a merciless species.
Today's posts are piles to drive into the quaggy past
on which impermanent palaces balance.

> *(Briggflatts)*

It is the hierarchal situation of *poet* going deeper in time than one could borrow or assume, and hence the issue of some privileged kinship with the nature of poetry itself in one's own language. Pound's "heave," with the trochee, proved him sensitive to it and makes clear one aspect of the relation between Bunting and himself. Bunting, from the earliest poems in *Loquitur* to the greatness of *Briggflatts* itself, is closely within the peculiar nature of his given language, an English such as one rarely now hears. In the earlier poems he makes use of a Latin, call it, appropriately enough:

Narciss, my numerous cancellations prefer
slow limpness in the damp dustbins amongst the peel
tobacco-ash and ends spittoon lickings litter
of labels dry corks breakages and a great deal

of miscellaneous garbage picked over by
covetous dustmen and Salvation Army sneaks
to one review-rid month's printed ignominy,
the public detection of your decay, that reeks.
> ("To a Poet who advised me to
> preserve my fragments and false starts")

But the insistent intimate nature of his work moves in the
closeness of monosyllables, with a music made of their
singleness:

Mist sets lace of frost
on rock for the tide to mangle.
Day is wreathed in what summer lost.

> *(Briggflatts)*

Presumptuously or not, it seems to me a long time since
English verse had such an English ear — as sturdy as its
words, and from the same occasion.

> [*Agenda*, Autumn 1966]

Three

Charles Olson: Y & X

ANY MOVEMENT POETRY can now make beyond the achievement of Pound, Williams, et al, must make use of the fact of their work and, further, of what each has stressed as the main work now to be done. We can't discard either of these men by calling them 'experimentalists' or by thinking that however right their method may be for their own apprehension of *form,* we can now ignore its example in our own dilemmas. Unless we also can find for ourselves a *method* equal to our content, show some comprehension of the difficulties involved, we stay where we are.

A recent comment of Dr. Williams notes one of the headaches. "To me the battle lodges for us as poets in the poetic line, something has to be done with that line — it's got to be opened up.... " I cite this here, since a good many feel that it's just the opposite that should be done, that the line must be tightened, pulled in, fixed. We should by now have a clear idea as to what this kind of *tightness* implies. To begin with, it's an external *tightness,* having more to do with the poem's pattern than with the movement of its sense. And it's this same *tightness* which Stevens has damned by implication: "There is, however, a usage with respect to form as if form were a derivative of plastic shape."

The five poems in this present collection of Olson's work demonstrate a technique set squarely against this *tightness.* They mark the alternatives. For Olson the line becomes a way to a movement beyond the single impact of the words

which go to make it up, and brings to their logic a force of
its own. Instead of the simple wagon which carries the load,
he makes it that which drives too, to the common logic,
the sense of the poem.

The first poem, "La Préface," is an illustration. Here the
line is used to make the ground logic beyond the single
'senses' of the words. The poem can't be understood, lacking
a comprehension of the work the line is doing here. What
it does do then, is give the base pattern which pulls the
poem's juxtaposition of *action* and *thing* to a common center
where the reader can get to bedrock. Meaning.

> Put war away with time, come into space.
> It was May, precise date, 1940. I had air my lungs
>   [could breathe.
> He talked, via stones   a stick   sea rock   a hand of earth.
> It is now, precise, repeat. I talk of Bigmans organs
> he, look, the lines! are polytopes.
> And among the DPs — deathhead
>   at the apex
>   of the pyramid.

The line is the means to focus, is that which says 'how' we
are to weight the various *things* we are told. And as it is
there, to do this work, so the words break through to their
sense.

Perhaps enough to find this use of line in these poems, but
Olson is a good deal more than a competent technician,
There is a reach in these five poems, a range of subject and
a depth of perception, that mark him exceptional. His
language is exact, hangs tight to the move of his thought.

> Shallows and miseries shadows from the cross,
> ecco men and dull copernican sun.
> Our attention is simpler

The salts and minerals of the earth return
The night has a love for throwing its shadows around
                                        [a man
a bridge,   a horse,   the gun,   a grave.

                                ("The K")

Again, if poetry is to get further, develop, it will depend
on those who, like Olson, make use of its present gains, push
these beyond. Olson's work is the first significant advance.

                        [*Montevallo Review*, Summer 1951]

Charles Olson: In Cold Hell, in Thicket

ERNST ROBERT CURTIUS has described Charles Olson's talent as returning us to that same presence, of force, which is evident in a Mayan glyph. The point is that Mr. Olson's work represents a sole and major content in contemporary American poetry.

This content is most clearly demonstrated in one of the several long poems here included, "The Kingfishers." Its first line gives us the basic preoccupation: "What does not change / is the will to change. . . . "

Not one death but many,
not accumulation but change, the feed-back proves,
                                            [the feed-back is

the law
                    Into the same river no man steps twice
                    When fire dies air dies
                    No one remains, nor is, one

It is this change, and the force which demands it, which hold the only 'continuity' possible. If a culture is to maintain itself, it can do so only by a *use* of this force, and the problem is as Mr. Olson puts it:

                    I am no Greek, hath not th'advantage.
                    And of course, no Roman:
                    he can take no risk that matters,
                    the risk of beauty least of all.

But I have my kin . . .

Despite the discrepancy (an ocean courage age)
this is also true: if I have any taste
it is only because I have interested myself
in what was slain in the sun

   I pose you your question:

shall you uncover honey / where maggots are?

   I hunt among stones

Such problems of change, and origin, are common to the
American temper, but their occurrence in American poetry
has become less and less frequent. Or, perhaps better, they
have been absorbed in other attitudes or left as "European,"
i.e., relating to a past shared in effect with poets either in
England or on the continent. But this is a simplification of a
useless sort. The American, for example, has this reference
to contend with:

(of the two who first came, each a conquistador, one
                                    [healed, the other
tore the eastern idols down, toppled
the temple walls, which, says the excuser
were black from human gore)

hear
hear, where the dry blood talks
   where the old appetite walks

He can only quiet it, by confronting it. Similarly, the
whole area of how we now live, or can live, is part of Mr.
Olson's attack. The title poem is a form of 'lyricism' brought
from the instant, or the single and abrupt emotion, to bear
on all there is for any man, or woman — "Or, if it is me, what
/ he has to say. . . . " So it is that:

... hell now
is not exterior, is not to be got out of, is
the coat of your own self, the beasts
emblazoned on you   And who
can turn this total thing, invert
and let the ragged sleeves be seen
by any bitch or common character? Who
can endure it where it is, where the beasts are met,
where yourself is, your beloved is, where she
who is separate from you, is not separate, is not
goddess, is, as your core is,
the making of one hell . . . .

The value of any poem is not at all the fact of any technique, however much it is necessary to be the master of just
such things. For the reader, beyond the way a poem is written or made, is the ultimate impact of its *meaning*, what it
either can or does mean — to us. Mr. Olson's poetry provides
for much more than delight.

[*New Mexico Quarterly*, Autumn 1953]

Charles Olson: The Maximus Poems, 1-10

IN POETRY THE attentions can come to govern, as a man might be governed by what he loves or despises, or what number of things his hands can hold. Seeing the thing, even so it remains outside him until he can give it substance in the multiple involvement — which means only that he and the thing, and the possibility which has no limit, can coexist in a form which it is his own responsibility to effect. "The thing" is an ugly word for it. But it is ugly only because we have so degraded what confronts us, that we ride in on our own isolation thinking not to see anything, and hating that which we have to.

The Maximus Poems are, or seem first to me, the modulation of a man's attentions, by which I mean the whole wonder of perception. They are truth because their form is that issue of what is out there, and what part of it can come into a man's own body. That much is not sentimental, nor can anything be sentimental if we make it that engagement. The local is not a place but a place in a given man — what part of it he has been compelled or else brought by love to give witness to in his own mind. And that is *the* form, that is, the whole thing, as whole as it can get.

I think we will be fools to be embarrassed by it. We know the other neatness possible, the way of the neat pattern, and the dodging which it must call for. Grace has no part in that. At some point reached by us, sooner or later, there is no longer much else but ourselves, in the place given us. To make that present, and actual for other men, is not an embarrassment, but love.

1953

Preface to Mayan Letters *by Charles Olson*

SOMETIME TOWARD THE end of 1950, it was in December I think, but the letter isn't dated, I heard that Charles Olson was off to Yucatan. A sudden "fluke" — the availability of some retirement money owed him from past work as a mail carrier — gave him enough for the trip, "not much but a couple of hundred, sufficient, to GO, be, THERE...." By February I had got another letter, "have just this minute opened this machine in this house lerma...." From that time on I heard from him regularly, and so was witness to one of the most incisive experiences ever recorded. Obviously it is very simple to call it that, that is, what then happened, and what Olson made of his surroundings and himself. Otherwise, it is necessary to remember that Olson had already been moving in this direction, back to a point of origin which would be capable of extending "history" in a new and more usuable sense. In his book on Melville, *Call Me Ishmael*, he had made the statement, "we are the last first people ... "; and in his poetry, most clearly in "The King-fishers," there was constant emphasis on the need to break with the too simple westernisms of a 'greek culture.'

Yucatan made the occasion present in a way that it had not been before. The alternative to a generalising humanism was locked, quite literally, in the people immediately around him, and the conception, that there had been and *could* be a civilization anterior to that which he had come from, was no longer conjecture, it was fact. He wrote me, then,

"I have no doubt, say, that the American will more and more repossess himself of the Indian past. . . . If you and I see the old deal as dead (including Confucius, say), at the same time that we admit the new is of the making of our own lives & references, yet, there is bound to be a tremendous pick-up from history other than that which has been usable as reference, the moment either that history is restored (Sumer, or, more done, Chichen or Uaxactun) or rising people (these Indians, as camposinos ripe for Communist play — as ripe as were the Chinese, date 1921, June 30). . . . " The problem was, to give form, again, to what the Maya had been — to restore the "history" which they were. For in the Maya was the looked-for content: a *reality* which is "wholly formal without loss of intimate spaces, with the ball still snarled, yet, with a light (and not stars) and a heat (not androgyne) which declares, the persistence of both organism *and* will (human). . . ."

In editing the present selection, I have tried to maintain a continuity in spite of the limits of space and the loss of some letters which it has meant. I have indicated excisions with dots (. . .), whenever such were necessary.

February 12, 1953

Olson & Others: Some Orts for the Sports

WHERE WRITING WILL GO TO, what comes next, or the answers to any of those profoundly speculative questions bred of Saturday afternoons in comfortable surroundings — god alone knows. Where it's all come from is another question, and a few sentences may serve as well to answer it as any more documented or descriptive account. For example, in 1950 Cid Corman, the subsequent editor of *Origin*, had a radio program in Boston called *This Is Poetry*, which by a fluke of air waves I heard one night in Littleton, N.H. The guest was Richard Wilbur, who read with such graceful accents I was filled with envious ambiton to read also, although I had none of his qualifications; and some weeks later, after correspondence with Cid which that night began, I convinced him I was good enough, or he was tolerant enough, and so I read one Saturday night while I was in Boston showing chickens at the Boston Poultry Show. Literary history is like that, and this event would be altogether unnotable, were it not that a magazine which I then tried to start (with much the same motives), but could not get printed, was absorbed in the first two issues of Cid's *Origin* — and that among the contacts so contributed were Charles Olson, Paul Blackburn and Denise Levertov.

Charles Olson is central to any description of literary 'climate' dated 1960. I don't think any of those involved knew, at the time, he had written *Call Me Ishmael;* and I remember my own dumbfounded reception of that book —

from a man I had assumed to be sharing my own position of unpublished hopefulness. The Olson I knew, and wrote to daily if possible, was the one whose Y & X had been published by Caresse Crosby's Black Sun Press, who had among other poems in manuscript a long one called "The King-fishers," and whose own letters were of such energy and calculation that they constituted a practical 'college' of stimulus and information. Some of this last can be seen in an article he published at that time, partly derived from letters as it happens, which he called "Projective Verse" (*Poetry New York*, No. 3, 1950; reprinted with addenda, N.Y.: Totem Press, 1959). He outlines there the premise of "composition by field" (the value of which William Carlos Williams was to emphasize by reprinting it in part in his own *Autobiography*); and defines a basis for structure in the poem in terms of its '*kinetics*' ("the poem itself must, at all points, be a high energy-construct and, at all points, an energy discharge"), the '*principle*' of its writing ("form is never more than an extension of content"), and the '*process*' ("ONE PERCEPTION MUST IMMEDIATELY AND DIRECTLY LEAD TO A FURTHER PERCEPTION"). Olson equally distinguishes between breathing and hearing, as these relate to the line: "And the line comes (I swear it) from the breath, from the breathing of the man who writes, at that moment that he writes...."

Some distinctions are now possible. Verse practice today splits in point of several emphases, and this is reasonable enough. Most familiar are those poets who have looked at a re-informing of traditional structures, at times with great ability. It is not at all a question of falling back into the same old sofa, etc., but to manage a use of that which the man back of you has given in such fashion that you will both honor him and those differences which the nature of time seems to insist upon. There are also those men, most definitive in the thirties, who extend to their writing of verse concerns which haunt them, again reasonably enough, in the other areas of their living.[1] They are in this way poets of 'content,' and their poems argue images of living to which the contents of their poems point. They argue the poem as a means to recognition, a signboard as it were, not in itself a structure of 'recognition' or — better — cognition itself. Some, then, would not only not hear what Olson was saying, but would even deny, I think, the relevance of his concerns. The great preoccupation with symbology and levels of image in poetry insisted upon by contemporary criticism has also meant a further bias for this not-hearing, since Olson's emphasis is put upon prosody, not interpretation.

Those who were sympathetic, who felt as Dr. Williams did ("it is as if the whole area lifted . . ."), were those equally concerned with prosody. "Prosody," said Pound, "is the articulation of the total sound of a poem." This is an obviously difficult and painstaking requirement; and, again, a division of method appears between those who make use of traditional forms, either for discipline or solution, and those who, as Olson, go "by ear," by, in effect, the complexly determined response to work literally in hand. Robert Duncan's discussion precludes mine; I refer you to that ("Notes on Poetics Regarding Olson's *Maximus*," *Black Mountain Review*, No. 6, 1956). But, to suggest its relevance here, Duncan writes, using the image of "The coming into life of the child . . .":

[1]Kenneth Fearing would be one man I'd think of in this connection, though that may be simply my own circumstances. Names are deceptive in any case, since they tend to develop a false chronology, granted men change. The point is that the *sociology* which the thirties develops is present in poetry also, both as methodology and sense of purpose. The methods and concern are felt later in Ciardi, Shapiro, et al. It's also in Weldon Kees. The contrast is the early work of Rexroth, Carl Rakosi, George Oppen, and very certainly Zukofsky.

> ... that the breath-blood circulation be gaind, an *inter-jection!* the levels of the passions and inspiration in *phrases;* second, that focus be gaind, a *substantive,* the level of vision; and third, the complex of muscular gains that are included in taking hold and balancing, *verbs,* but more, the *movement of language,* the *level* of the ear, the hand, the foot. All these incorporated in mea-sure. [2]

At this point it becomes necessary to read, which is, after all, what we are here for. The following books are, at best, a partial list of materials — yet serve to indicate others, so that much is served:

(1) Charles Olson, *The Maximum Poems 1-10, 11-22* (1953, 1957). Olson's handling of the poems as an 'open field,' using a variable measure as concerns of content, and the emotional or informational character thereof, indicate, show what *range* can be managed.

(2) Louis Zukofsky, *Some Time* (1956), *Barely and Widely* (1953), and "A" (1960). Zukofsky teaches *prosody* — and these are only three of the books which might be cited. One should also see his *A Test of Poetry:* "The test of poetry is the range of pleasure it affords as sight, sound, and intellection...." By a complex of juxtaposed examples (following Pound's *ideogrammic* method), "a means for judging the values of poetic writing is established by the examples themselves...."

(3) Robert Duncan, *Letters* (1958), and *Selected Poems* (1959). The second book includes *The Venice Poem* — again a study in *formal* solutions, for those who will read it with attention. Duncan's other books are

---

[2]Italics mine. Duncan has given, *in fine,* the steps of a poetic *grammar.*

also valuable — *Fragments of a Disorderd Devotion* (1952) and *Caesar's Gate* (1955). His notes and articles should be searched out as well.

Etc. Because the list continues, happily: to books like Denise Levertov's *Overland to the Islands* and *Here and Now;* to Paul Blackburn's *Proensa* and *The Dissolving Fabric;* to Allen Ginsberg's *Howl*[3]; to first books like Joel Oppenheimer's *The Dutiful Son,* and the as yet uncollected poems of Edward Dorn. All of these relate to the same areas of technical concern, surely. Otherwise, 'content' in every man is singular; which fact is a happy one.

Meeting Christopher Logue in Paris in 1956 — an English poet who looked so Englishly like that illustration of the Mad Hatter in *Alice in Wonderland* — his first question, hoarsely yelled at me because the cafe whereto I had been brought by his friend Alex Trocchi, was so noisy, etc., was: "Tell me about Olson." Later we went to Logue's room where he showed me his Pound books (which are as much a currency in some areas as dollar bills in others) and gave me, as I left, a carbon he had made of Pound's Cavalcanti translations. He will be amused to know that I am still trying to 'explain.' Logue knew as much about American writing as I did, or, better, he knew the problems shared in common — because such things are only secondarily national these days.

You must read, then, to know what is happening. All poets seem to suffer certain things in common, as certainly all men do: difficulties of self-support, or, if a family is involved, some means of sufficiencies in common, and the dignity any

---

[3]Ginsberg's *Howl* has been read too simply as 'social document' and its technical concerns ignored. See his discussion in "Notes Written on Finally Recording Howl" (*Evergreen Review,* No. 10), e.g., "So these poems are a series of experiments with the formal organization of the long line . . . No attempt's been made to use it (Whitman's line) in the light of early XX Century organization of new speech-rhythm prosody to *build up* large organic structures."

man has right to claim, granted it has never been his purpose
to ask for it. We all of us live in an increasingly pinched
world, pinched emotionally, pinched referentially — despite
the fact that the moon comes closer. "How shall I love you?
Let me count the ways" is too often a proposed calculus of
possibilities; and that, alone, is no good. In despite, relationships, here as elsewhere, continue, serving a common need
for survival and growth. The issue is the poem, a single event
— to which, as to the Battle of Gettysburg, or the Pan American Highway, many men may well contribute — *"aperiens
tibi animum. . . ."* Like, you dig the 85th Canto? Like —
that's all.

[*Big Table*, No. 4, 1960]

Some Notes on Olson's Maximus

EYES HAVE A MAJOR PLACE in this work as anyone familiar with it will know. And despite the easiness of the pun, an 'eye' here is 'i,' not the singular psychologic misfit of contemporary society — but the major term of relation to external world, in just the sense that as one *sees* a thing, he may then deal with it or be dealt with by it, in a manner to which he is a party. In that way Olson makes clear, early in the poems, that:

polis is

eyes . . .

And also:

There are no hierarchies, no infinite, no such many as
[mass, there are only
eyes in all heads,
to be looked out of . . .

Polis, at first a *town,* grows in no sense otherwise—it is never more than the aggregate of people who have so joined themselves together, and its members define it. Their perception constitutes their city.

There is another point to be made in this respect. John Burnet in his *Early Greek Philosophy* characterizes the Pythagorean concept of society in this way:

In this life there are three kinds of men, just as there are three sorts of people who come to the Olympic Games.

167

The lowest class is made up of those who come to buy and sell, and next above them are those who come to compete. Best of all, however, are those who come to look on . . .

Burnet then claims these last as proving the significant relation to science — but it is most to the point to see that *seeing* here is not a passive act akin to spectacles — it is a looking in order to see in the place *(in situ)*, and to understand in that way.

2

Olson's kinship with Pythagorean thought, and with the pre-Socratic sense of world more generally, is very marked. It occurs as a reference directly in, for example, an early poem, "The Praises," wherein are found these proposals:

What has been lost
is the secret of secrecy, is
the value, viz., that the work get done, and quickly,
without the loss of due and profound respect for
the materials . . .

The danger he sees here is that "dispersion which follows from/ too many having too little/ knowledge . . . " "What is necessary is/ containment,/ that that which has been found out by work may, by work,/ be passed on/ (without due loss of force) for use . . . "

Or again:

What belongs to art and reason is
                                   the knowledge of
                                      consequences . . .

It is a sense of *use*, which believes knowledge to be necessarily an *active* form of relation to term, with the corollary, that *all* exists in such relation, itself natural to the conditions.

It is not, then, knowledge as a junk-heap, or purposeless accumulation of mere detail — which seems to derive too frequently from the manner of classification which follows upon the pre-Socratic world-view. It is knowledge used as a means to relate, not separate — which senses must, *per se,* prove very different. That is why the term, *use,* is to be met with so frequently in Olson's writing.

3

The pre-Socratics had also the question of *nominalization* to deal with. Parmenides of Elea gives a good sense of it:

> The thing that can be thought and that for the sake of which the thought exists is the same; for you cannot find thought without something that is, as to which it is uttered . . .

All of "Tyrian Businesses" seems to me much involved by this question, as this quotation will illustrate:

> There may be no more names than there are objects
> There can be no more verbs than there are actions . . .

And, too, the use in this section of *Maximus* of a *particularizing* vocabulary (e.g. "futtocks, we call 'em" or "the honey in the lion, the honey/ in woman . . . ") forces thought to specific terms — much against a progress of easy, generalized understanding. Words, here, are forced to be seen specifically.

This character of language — and the use of language — is much to be found throughout *Maximus,* and as well in the writing before it. One such instance in earlier work is the first part of "ABC's," like this:

> b l a c k   eat a peck of storage batteries 'fore
>   I die . . .

All meaning is local to an instance, wherefrom it derives, but also, whereto it returns. If a writer promotes a sense of language that floats in a middle way, neither here nor there, he is reasonably to be suspected. It becomes clear that this emphasis is one Olson shares with Williams ("No ideas but in things . . .") and with Pound who has given much emphasis to the problem of terminology, an aspect of nominalization. (It is Pound who tells of Santayana, that he had said, it doesn't so much matter what books they read in college, say, so long as they read the *same* books — and thereby have means for a *common* reference for terms. That we greatly lack at present, and our society tends to give prizes to men who can think up new 'terms' for old ones, not really changing anything at all but further confusing the so-called issue, a bothersome kind of euphemism.)

"Letter 5" in Olson's *Mayan Letters* is another reference for this question — and a very useful one for those who have means to check it. There Olson says the problem is "to bring any time so abreast of us that we are in this present air, going straight out, of our selves, into it . . ." In fact, that might well serve as a sense of the purpose in *The Maximus Poems* themselves, and it is no fluke that such a thing had been on his mind. He felt then (March 8, 1951) that a too simple "nomination" and/or name-reference as part of a traditional use of 'history' would fail to realize that, as he saw it, the shift had become "substantive" (i.e., broke free of 'great men' to consider the question of maize, as in Carl Sauer's work) — a parallel to what men in the allied fields of anthropology, archaeology, geography, physics, etc., had already begun to document toward the end of the 19th century. I.e., the world had been *prior* to its reference in historical texts, where too often its use was simply "the passage of time & time's dreary accumulations by repetition . . ." A man writing had now to find his 'names' in terms that would free them for use *now* — not simply leave them caught in the trap of the 'past.'

The reference, in that way, could no longer be a question of memory.

I find myself hammering at this for several reasons, as 1) the use of historical materials in *Maximus* will not be realized until one understands that they are being brought into a context of the *present* — no one is 'going back' to them, nor is there any question of the 'good old days'; and 2) that just as Mencius can say, how is it far if you think it, so Olson: how is it past, if you think it. All that can inhabit the present, is present. That is why, I think, such documents as John Smith's "The Sea Marke" or the list of what the fourteen men left at Stage Head had for provisions are given literally — to see as of *now*, else we see nothing sufficiently of that literal ground we occupy, a place accomplished by men. In that there may well be much of *time*, perhaps, yet those men are *there* too, and by no simple trick of language — we do not finally have to remove ourselves to a future, in which we will all be dead, to understand that fact. All is, as it is, where it is, when it is — and the dead in that respect do bury the dead, altogether.

4

A parallel statement is Gertrude Stein's comment: "... the making of a portrait of anyone is as they are existing and as they are existing has nothing to do with remembering any one or anything ... " In *Maximus* the "portrait" is a place, Gloucester, with all that may thereto be related — first of all, men, since "polis is/ eyes ... ", and then the 'measure' of those men and that place, as:

I measure my song,
measure the sources of my song,
measure me, measure
my forces ...

or the literal 'mapping' of "Letter, May 2, 1959," and as well, the sense that "metric then is mapping, and so, to speak modern cant, congruent means of making a statement . . . "

5

Again, in an earlier poem, "Concerning Exaggeration, or How, Properly, To Heap Up," Olson has this question, "how / can you be otherwise than / a metaphor . . . " The sense of the sign that men make as, and of, themselves continues into *Maximus,* and is also an explanation of *Maximus* himself — the metaphor for a man not simply 'large' but more, the Pythagorean 'looker-on,' the measurer of terms and relation-ships. In that sense he stands at the apex of human activity in this same order.

(I do not propose a catalogue of all such 'metaphors' in the poems, but this way of thinking of it may help to explain the Ferrini section — where Ferrini proves token, or sign, for one kind of activity and its apparent value and the Burke section, another. Men are to this extent consistently the face they wear, and the things which they do, in the place given them. Anecdotes have a like function I think, as here:

was such a man
he was embarrassed
to ask for the rent . . .

They make a vocabulary of activities, which in turn are freed from category by virtue of their being *local.*)

6

Were the poems simply social criticism, they would not be very interesting. What they do offer, and work to provide, is just such a 'vocabulary' as I have mentioned. Williams has said with persistent desperation:

> The measure itself
> has been lost
> and we suffer for it.
> We come to our deaths
> in silence . . .

What does this mean. It means that we have lost control of the very terms by which we propose to live — that we can, say, argue 'limited war,' or defensive armament, for peace, which seem the most bloated instances one can quickly think of. It means that we are committed to suffering and desperation for specious reasons — since there is *no* reason except the duplicity of our reference. We fear commitment and risk of quite another kind. It is the contrary of all this I believe Olson to know:

> He left him naked
> the man said, and
> nakedness
> is what one means
>
> that all start up
> to the eye and soul
> as though it had never
> happened before

[*Yugen*, No. 8, 1962]

Introduction to Charles Olson:
Selected Writings I*

THERE IS A RELEVANT MEASURE of Olson's situation to be
found in William Carlos Williams' notes upon a parallel
figure — a man equally embarrassed by conveniences — Sam
Houston. Of him Williams writes:

> He wants to have the feet of his understanding on the
> ground, his ground, *the* ground, the only ground that he
> knows, that which *is* under his feet . . .

It is simple enough to generalize the American situation
itself by reference to its pragmatism, its lack of traditional
objectives, so to speak. But to turn it to use, the form of this
world requires from the first an adamant recognition of
place, of a literal geography such as John Smith could manage, so that, as Olson says, "The sort of knowledge Smith
gave Hudson . . . Hudson went straight to the river." Smith
is not, in Olson's context, the enlarged issue of a *hero*, but
rather a primary instance of conduct, the *how* a man might
demonstrate given the fact of himself in an environment that
will only admit him as he *can* be there.

But I slur here too quickly into a sense of will, which is
not to the point. However much a man may want something,
the possibility is still not his to determine, although it is certainly his to recognize. One had much better see that no
relief comes of any enlargement, or recourse to some sense

*Original version.

174

of the world as *idea* merely. That "euphoria" which Olson
defines in "Tyrian Businesses" is the result of a kind of containment, which is not one at all — but, instead, a spilling
over of the "personality," a false measure of human presence, onto all that confronts it.

There can be, then, no relief of such an order. I am most
impressed that, in Olson's writing, these several measures
of human term are adamant: 1) that the instant is human
time and/or all that can be so felt must be so present, or else
cannot exist; 2) that human content and possibility are the
issue of acts, and are only absolute in that finiteness; and
3) that the *geography,* the complex of place — not at all the
simplicity of a humanistic 'nature' — is the complement of
all human condition.

So it is that the first essay of this collection insists that,
for a man, "It is his body that is his answer, his body intact
and fought for, the absolute of his organism in its simplest
terms, this structure evolved by nature, repeated in each
act of birth, the animal man; the house he is, this house
that moves, breathes, acts, this house where his life is. . . . "
Elsewhere he writes:

> I have this sense
> that I am one
> with my skin
>
> Plus this — plus this:
> that forever the geography
> leans in
> on me. . . .

When reality is so confronted, much occurs that is otherwise lost in the roar of good intentions. Olson's criticism of
those systems of logic and classification, and of those senses
of symbology inherited by our humanists from the Greeks,
has as its basis his assertion "that a thing, any thing, im-

pinges on us by a more important fact, its self-existence, without reference to any other thing, in short, the very character of it which calls our attention to it, which wants us to know more about it, its particularity...." "Human Universe" is a brilliant qualification of this circumstance, and the same thinking underlies his premise in "Projective Verse":

> The objects which occur at every given moment of composition (of recognition, we can call it) are, can be, must be treated exactly as they do occur therein and not by any ideas or preconceptions from outside the poem, must be handled as a series of objects in field in such a way that a series of tensions (which they also are) are made to *hold,* and to hold exactly inside the content and the context of the poem which has forced itself, through the poem and them, into being.

The point is that no form can exist as a possibility apart from that which informs it, the content of which it is the issue. The idealism of a sense of absolute form is answered as follows:

> Here again, as throughout experience, the law remains, form is not isolated from content. The error of all other metaphysic is descriptive, is the profound error that Heisenberg had the intelligence to admit in his principle that a thing can be measured in its mass only by arbitrarily assuming a stopping of its motion, or in its motion only by neglecting, for the moment of the measuring, its mass. And either way, you are failing to get what you are after — so far as a human goes, his life.

This leads him to a kind of writing that is never more, nor less, than 'what it has to say.' It is primarily what he calls "language as the act of the instant" since — as he also makes clear — "the habits of thought are the habits of action," however difficult such action may prove. But at no moment may one step aside — to think *about* the world, rather than *in* it or *of* it or *as* it. Again, there can be no relief in such a generalization.

The poems themselves are, then, the issue of an engagement, of an impingement, a location that is constantly occurring. They are not a decision of forms more than such forms may be apprehended, literally gained, as possible in the actual writing. "But a field/is not a choice...," however much within it may occur that sense of "choice" he takes care to qualify as *recognition*.

It is in this sense that Olson has been *given* Gloucester, which I may note briefly is a city in Massachusetts, a seaport up the coast from Boston. But that is merely what it is *for me*, which is not the point — nor is it even interesting to think of what it is *for Olson*. It is how Olson is involved with this place, that is interesting, how it is that he is "caught in Gloucester," in "The Librarian," or in another context, quite otherwise:

It rained,
the day we arrived.
And I have rowed the harbor since,
out the window of Johnny's Candy Kitchen,
through that glass and rain through which I looked
the first time I saw
the sea.

These are statements, themselves their own occasion. It is relevant that Olson's discussion of Shakespeare's late plays and the character of the verse they develop provides the most useful measure of his own verse that I can offer. For example, he says "logicality persists in the syntax and image but the thinking and weighing in of the quantity stop twist and intensify the speech, thus increasing the instancy." The insisted upon 'forms' of the language and its 'subjects' are still evident, then, in the patterns of syntax and image, in these plays, but the words in their own literal occurrence, and in what they so think of, gain an *immediate* context, one momently present. "Some Good News" demonstrates a like gain, but also moves in its syntax and image free of an external limit, as here:

> . . . shoals, worse
> than rock because
> they do blow shift lie,
> are changing as you sound —
> on this crooked sand
> Portuguese (when?)
>
> had a fishing station.
> It wasn't new,
> what happened,
> at Cape Ann. It's where
> and when it
>
> did . . .

But it seems wisest, now, to stop such illustration, and to enter directly upon the writing. Its selection has been as arbitrary as I, or any one, must be, and much is left out — as the whole of *Call Me Ishmael*, his study of Melville, which will not admit to what were here the necessities of choice. One will, in any case, want to read more, and there is much more of Olson to read. This is a beginning, echoing what was my own, upon a way of being in the world which made clear to me and I hope now to you —

> There are no hierarchies, no such many as mass, there
> [are only
>
> eyes in all heads,
> to be looked out of

February 12, 1965

Introduction to Charles Olson: Selected Writings II*

IT IS SIMPLE enough to note the main details of Charles Olson's background. Born December 27, 1910, he lived for some years in Worcester, Massachusetts, and his family spent summers while he was still quite young in Gloucester, on the coast of the same state. I once saw a picture of him, aged about eleven, taken together with the whole summer camp community at that time, some forty people who vacationed in this part of Gloucester, separated from the main town by the Cut or channel that runs in to the inner harbor. He is sitting on the edge of a roof and his legs hang down very evidently, giving a sense of the size he will later have as a man. He was to be tall indeed, roughly six foot eight or nine.

Subsequently he went first to Wesleyan, then to Yale, and Harvard, where he worked toward the Ph. D. in American studies. His jobs were various. He was a mailman for a while in Gloucester, he worked on a fishing boat, he taught at Clark and Harvard for relatively brief periods, he was chairman to foreign language groups for the Democratic Party during Roosevelt's campaign for a fourth term. Then, in the late forties, he took a job vacated by Edward Dahlberg, at that point a close and significant friend, to teach at Black Mountain College in North Carolina on the in-

*New York: 1966.

vitation of Theodore Dreier and Josef Albers, then rector
of the college. Albers soon after went to Yale, and in the
early fifties Olson became rector. Although it was a difficult
time financially for all involved, and the college had relatively few students, nonetheless Black Mountain proved a
focal point for much significant activity in the arts. John
Cage, Robert Duncan, Merce Cunningham, Franz Kline —
all of whom were present at one time or another during
this period — show briefly the range and intensity of what
was then happening. The students — John Wieners, Robert
Rauschenberg, Edward Dorn, John Chamberlain, Michael
Rumaker, Cy Twombly, Joel Oppenheimer, Dan Rice,
Fielding Dawson, to name several — were equally notable.

Olson had come to Black Mountain following publication
of a most singular critical work on Melville, *Call Me Ishmael*
(1947), which he had written with the help of a Guggen-
heim Fellowship.[1] In that book he makes clear his relation
to a responsiveness and decision in such writing to be found
only in such comparable works as D. H. Lawrence's *Studies
in Classic American Literature*, W. C. Williams' *In The
American Grain*, and Edward Dahlberg's *Can These Bones
Live*. In this respect, criticism is not only a system of notation and categorization — it is an active and definitive engagement with what a text proposes. It is not merely a
descriptive process. *Call Me Ishmael* begins:

> I take SPACE to be the central fact to man born in
> America, from Folsom cave to now. I spell it large be-
> cause it comes large here. Large, and without mercy.
> It is geography at bottom, a hell of wide land from
> the beginning. That made the first American story
> (Parkman's): exploration ...

[1]Shortly after, Olson received a second fellowship, for a book on the
morphology of American culture.

Olson had also been in touch with Ezra Pound, who had recently been returned to the States to face trial on the charge of treason. There is a very moving defense of Pound written by Olson for the *Partisan Review*,[2] for whom he acted as a "reporter" in order to gain admittance to Pound's first arraignment in Washington. It is called "This Is Yeats Speaking" — the title itself a clear measure of those circumstances Pound's accusers were preparing to ignore. As Yeats, he says:

> We were the forerunners — Pound only the more extreme — but our time was out of phase and made us enders. Lawrence among us alone had the true mask, he lacked the critical intelligence, and was prospective. You are the antithetical men, and your time is forward, the conflict is more declared, it is for you to hold the mirror up to authority, behind our respect for which lay a disrespect for democracy as we were acquainted with it. A slogan will not sufffice . . .

2

Olson's approach was thus twice removed from the terms of any other critical intelligence of that period. He spoke of "geography" and that was clearly antiliterary. He proposed a sense of the literal nature of this country quite distinct from those critics influenced by European traditions. If he was involved with particular European evidences (as witness his translation of Rimbaud's last recorded poem, "Ô saisons, ô châteaux . . . ," in "Variations Done for Gerald van de Weile"), he so involved them that they became the American context equally:

[2]Vol. XIII, No. 1, Winter 1946.

I offer, in explanation, a quote:
si j'ai du goût, ce n'est guères
que pour la terre et les pierres...

("The Kingfishers")

If I have any taste, it is only for earth and stones... Or to
continue with Rimbaud's text from which this is also taken:

Je déjeûne toujours d'air
De roc, de charbons, de fer. [3]

Daily I dine on air,
rock, coal, iron...

It is relevant, then, that Olson's particular nature should
lead him in Yucatan [4] to just such exploration as he values
in Parkman, or equally in Herodotus ("I would be an historian as Herodotus was, looking/for oneself for the evidence of/what is said...," "Letter 23," *The Maximus
Poems*). In *Mayan Letters* we have unequivocal evidence
of a *kind* of intelligence which cannot propose the assumption of content prior to its experience of that content, which
looks, out of its *own* eyes. This does not mean that conjecture is to be absent, insofar as *jacio* means "throw" and *con,*
"together" — however simply this point may note the actual
process. It is a consistent fact with Olson that he does use
his legs, and does depend on what his own instincts and intelligence can discover for him. In this way he *throws
together* all he has come to possess.

But humanism, as a system of thought or ordering of
persons in their relations to other things in the world, is
distinctly absent. Even the most sympathetic ordering of

[3] "Faim," *Délires* II.

[4] Olson lived in Lerma from February to July 1951. *Mayan Letters* is
a selection made from letters written to me at that time. In 1952 he
was awarded a Wenner-Gren Foundation grant for further study of
Mayan hieroglyphs.

human effects and intelligence leads to unavoidable assumptions and the test — which is the reality of one's quite
literal being — denies any investment of reality prior to its
fact.

> There are no hierarchies, no infinite, no such
> [many as mass, there are only
> eyes in all heads,
> to be looked out of

("Letter 6")

This commitment is further proposed and defined in "Human Universe," written, significantly, during that same
period in Yucatan. We are not here involved with existen-
tialism, despite the apparent closeness of sympathies at
times. That is, Camus may speak of a world *without appeal*,
but the system of discourse he makes use of is still demonstrably a closed one. What he seems most despairing about
is that language cannot make sense of the world, that logic
and classification do not lead to conclusions and value —
but open only to the dilemma of experience itself. But
L'Étranger is again a closed demonstration, a "fiction" proposed as example, and this, of course, is to stay within that
universe of discourse which Olson distrusts.

> ... such as analysis only accomplishes a *description*,
> does not come to grips with what really matters: that a
> thing, any thing, impinges on us by a more important
> fact, its self-existence, without reference to any other
> thing, in short, the very character of it which calls our
> attention to it, which wants us to know more about it,
> its particularity. This is what we are confronted by, not
> the thing's "class," any hierarchy, of quality or quantity,
> but the thing itself, and its *relevance* to ourselves who
> are the experience of it (whatever it may mean to some-
> one else, or whatever other relations it may have).

("Human Universe")

Camus despairs of his inability to fit experience to possible orders of language, whereas Olson would insist that language be returned to its place *in* experience, neither more nor less than any other act.

3

William Carlos Williams had said, "No ideas but in things," thereby insisting that reality was a real matter. Pound equally insisted, "Any tendency to abstract general statement is a greased slide." Both men have clearly to do with possibilities in writing of which Olson is further evidence, but his own qualifications of either man are also relevant. For example, Pound he felt limited to an "ego-system":

> Ez's epic solves problems by his ego: his single emotion breaks all down to his equals or inferiors....Which assumption, that there are intelligent men whom he can outtalk, is beautiful because it destroys historical time, and thus creates the methodology of the *Cantos*, viz, a space-field where, by inversion, though the material is all time material, he has driven through it so sharply by the beak of his ego, that, he has turned time into what we must now have, space & its live air . . .
>
> *(Mayan Letters)*

The gain is that any instance of intelligence is relevant insofar as it proves so, that what was said in 500 B.C. can be actively heard in 1965—and in that sense "time" is denied as a limit of such a possibility. But the dilemma it leads to is that the ego or mind is made the sole measure of such experience.

In contrast, Olson feels that Williams offers an *emotional* system, which does not limit the context of writing to an assumption of *understanding*—or, better, it attains a way of writing that *feels* as it goes as well as *sees*. This allows the experience of writing to be more sensitive than the ego alone can admit.

In the second part of "Projective Verse,"[5] Olson makes this useful summary:

> Objectism is the getting rid of the lyrical interference of the individual as ego, of the "subject" and his soul, that peculiar presumption by which western man has interposed himself between what he is as a creature of nature (with certain instructions to carry out) and those other creations of nature which we may, with no derogation, call objects. For a man is himself an object, whatever he may take to be his advantages, the more likely to recognize himself as such the greater his advantages, particularly at that moment that he achieves an humilitas sufficient to make him of use.

4

When Williams first read "Projective Verse," his response was immediate:

> I share your excitement, it is as if the whole area lifted. It's the sort of thing we are after and must have . . . Everything in it leans on action, on the verb; one thing *leads* to another which is thereby activated . . .[6]

It was an excitement which many of us shared, because what confronted us in 1950 was a closed system indeed, poems patterned upon exterior and traditionally accepted models. The New Criticism of that period was dominant and would not admit the possibility of verse considered as an "open field."

But, thinking now of what else was clearly happening, that attitude was already losing ground. If one reads Jackson

[5] "Projective Verse" was first published in *Poetry New York*, No. 3, 1950. The date is significant.

[6] I take this from a letter Williams wrote me at the time. His interest is further demonstrated by the fact that he includes a substantial section of Olson's "Projective Verse" in his *Autobiography*.

Pollock's comments on his painting at that time, he can note for himself the obvious parallel:

> When I am in my painting, I'm not aware of what I'm doing. It is only after a sort of "get acquainted" period that I see what I have been about. I have no fears about making changes, destroying the image, etc., because the painting has a life of its own. I try to let it come through. It is only when I lose contact with the painting that the result is a mess. Otherwise there is pure harmony, an easy give and take, and the painting comes out well.[7]

A like situation was clear in the work of John Cage, which involved the introduction of "chance" factors and reconsidered the whole context of a "melodic" modality in music. And similar circumstances were very clear in the sciences as well. "Formal" order, taken as a *sine qua non*, could no longer be assumed as a necessary virtue.

How, then, manage its alternatives—in such a way that the result be not random but rather the most precise discrimination and attention of which the man writing is capable? Olson's premise is this:

> A poem is energy transferred from where the poet got it (he will have some several causations), by way of the poem itself to, all the way over to, the reader . . .
>
> ("Projective Verse")

This means, very literally, that a poem is some *thing*, a structure possessed of its own organization in turn derived from the circumstances of its making. Thus far, it could, of course, be a sonnet—and under given circumstances well might be, supposing that the man writing discovered that

[7] "Problems of Contemporary Art," *Possibilities* I, 1947-48.

possibility as he did, in fact, write. But what one is saying has intimate relation to how one is saying it—and/or the content, in this sense, is that which qualifies the possibilities of form. Valéry, in *The Art of Poetry*, qualifies as *lyric* that mode of poetry in which the content and the form are realized simultaneously. Neither one can precede the other as a possibility. It is this sense, then, which Olson extends to all occasions of writing in verse. It is hardly a careless procedure, in that no order more than that so recognized can be gained. Apropos the syllable, "the king and pin of versification," Olson writes:

> It is by their syllables that words juxtapose in beauty, by these particles of sound as clearly as by the sense of words which they compose. In any given instance, because there is a choice of words, the choice, if a man is in there, will be, spontaneously, the obedience of his ear to the syllables . . .
>
> ("Projective Verse")

The capabilities of that ear will have no other evidence to support them but that which they define. "Prosody," Pound said, "is the articulation of the total sound of a poem." In the note to which this serves as motto, so to speak, Olson says:

> It's as though you were hearing for the first time—who knows what a poem ought to sound like? until it's thar? And how do you get it thar except as you do—*you*, and nobody else (who's a poet
>
>   What's
> a poem?
>   It ain't dreamt until it walks   It talks   It spreads its green barrazza

Listen closely, folks, this poem comes to you by
benefit of its own Irish green bazoo. You take it, from
here.

                    ("A Foot Is to Kick With,"
                        Human Universe and Other Essays)

5

The range of materials here collected is not evidence of
"subjects" or of some preoccupation with any such term of
argument. "Letter 15" notes that clearly enough: "He sd,
'you go all around the subject.' And I sd, 'I didn't know it
was a subject . . .'" It is worth some thought.

Where one lives is a complex occasion, both inside and
out. What we have as *place* is defined in "The Resistance,"
and, again, it is not only "existential." When a man walks
down a street, he walks it only *now*—whether the date be
1860, 1960, or so-called centuries ago. History is a literal
story, the activity of evidence.

In short, the world is not separable, and we *are* in it. The
fact of "Apollonius of Tyana" is not *then*, so to speak—at
some remove in time because its person is, as we might say,
historical. Each moment is evidence of its own content, and
all that is met with in it, is as present as anything else.
Apollonius *is* a present instance.

The most insistent concern I find in Olson's writing is the
intent to gain the particular experience of any possibility in
life, so that no abstraction intervenes. "In Cold Hell, in
Thicket" makes clear the difficulties, and "To Gerhardt,
There, Among Europe's Things," the situation of the
specifically American:

                    . . . Or come here
                    where we will welcome you
                    with nothing but what is . . .

A dream *is*—as clearly as whatever else. The circumstance of "The Librarian" or "As the Dead Prey upon Us" will not be confusing to any who admit what they *know* to be a total content, rather than one divided by assumptions of understanding. "In dreams begin responsibilites . . ." I was moved on hearing Williams use that quotation from Yeats at the outset of his acceptance speech for the National Book Award in the early fifties. But it is not only "responsibilities," but also "This very thing you are . . ."

Meaning is not importantly *referential*. Reference may well prove *relevant*—but I can make myself clearer by quoting a sense of *meaning* which Olson used at the Berkeley Poetry Conference this past summer (1965): *That which exists through itself is what is called meaning.* He also noted, as a usable context for that "mapping" or measure of how one is where one is, these four terms:

> earth
> Imago Mundi
> history
> Anima Mundi

By "earth" is meant all that literal ground we walk on and its specific character, including water and sky; by "Imago Mundi," that way of seeing or view of existence evident in any particular circumstance of life; by "history," all the condition and accumulation of human acts and effects, as these exist; by "Anima Mundi," that which informs and quickens life in its own condition, the spirit—or what we speak of in saying, "the *quick* and the dead." I offer these simply as measure, for the relevance of what follows.

Placitas, New Mexico
October 3, 1965

"A Foot Is to Kick with" *

THE WORK OF CHARLES OLSON is a complex and densely articulate sequence of poems and critical notes. Those familiar with his earlier study of Melville, *Call Me Ishmael* (1947), are aware of the compactness of his statement, the extraordinary manner in which the juxtaposition of terms effects a shorthand of reference, a quickness of mind not often met with in such studies. For example, here is a charaterization of Melville's situation taken from the opening section of that book:

> Beginner—and interested in beginnings. Melville had a way of reaching back through time until he got history pushed back so far he turned time into space. He was like a mignant backtrailing to Asia, some Inca trying to find a lost home.
>
> We are the last "first" people. We forget that. We act big, misuse our land, ourselves. We lose our own primary.
>
> Melville went back, to discover us, to come forward. He got as far as *Moby-Dick*.
>
> Ortega y Gasset puts it that the man of aniquity, before he did anything, took a step like the bullfighter who leaps back in order to deliver the mortal thrust.
>
> (*Call Me Ishmael*, p. 14)

*Charles Olson: *Human Universe and Other Essays; Proprioception;* & *A Bibliography on America for Ed Dorn.*

190

Human Universe and Other Essays is a collection written primarily since the publication of *Call Me Ishmael,* the only exception being, I think, "This Is Yeats Speaking," which Olson wrote for the *Partisan Review* on the occasion of Pound's trial. Again the quality of the intelligence is remarkable, in its speed, in its complexity of reference, in the juxtaposition of terms it can accomplish. The title piece, "Human Universe," makes evident the basic nature of Olson's qualification in all senses, which I may make clear here by a brief sequence of quotes:

We have lived long in a generalizing time, at least since 450 B.C.

❈   ❈   ❈

The distinction . . . is between language as the act of the instant and language as the act of thought about the instant.

❈   ❈   ❈

It is not sufficiently observed that logos [what Olson calls "discourse" and the promoter of abstraction and of the sense of a "UNIVERSE of discourse"—"the refuge of all metaphysicians . . ."], and the reason necessary to it, are only a stage which a man must master and not what they are taken to be, final discipline. Beyond them is direct perception, and the contraries which dispose of argument. The harmony of the universe, and I include man, is not logical, or better, is post-logical, as is the order of any created thing.

❈   ❈   ❈

Here again, as throughout experience, the law remains, form is not isolated from content.

❈   ❈   ❈

Art does not seek to describe but to enact.

❈   ❈   ❈

In other words, the proposition here is that man at his peril breaks the full circuit of object, image, action at any point. The meeting edge of man and the world is also his cutting edge. If man is active, it is exactly here where experience comes in that it is delivered back, and if he stays fresh at the coming in he will be fresh at his going out. If he does not, all that he does inside his house is stale, more and more stale as he is less and less acute at the door. And his door is where he is responsible to more than himself.

❋ ❋ ❋

It is unbearable what knowledge of the past has been allowed to become, what function of human memory has been dribbled out to in the hands of these learned monsters whom people are led to think "know." They know nothing in not knowing how to reify what they do know. What is worse, they do not know how to pass over to us the energy implicit in any high work of the past because they purposely destroy that energy as dangerous to the states for which they work—which it is, for any concrete thing is a danger to rhetoricians and politicians, as dangerous as a hard coin is to a banker.

("Human Universe")

The fact of such loss, of a literal energy, of men's disposition toward their own confronting of the particular world given them, is an insistence throughout this collection. "The Gate and the Center" calls to attention primacies both of conduct and of possibility—the point that "energy is larger than man, but therefore, if he taps it as it is in himself, his uses of himself are EXTENSIBLE in human directions & degree not recently granted." "Apollonius of Tyana" enacts literally as dance and speech the classical possibility of a man so determined by himself: "Apollonius' assumption is that any image around which any people concentrate and commit themselves is a usable one just because it is theirs, that truth is never more than its own action, and that all that ever needs attention is the quality of the action." "The Resistance" equally states that it is a man's "body that is his answer, his body intact and fought for, the absolute of his organism in its simplest terms, this structure evolved by nature, repeated in each act of birth, the animal man; the house he is, this house that moves, breathes, acts, this house where his life is, where he dwells against the enemy, against the beast."

The complement and extension of the materials in this first section of *Human Universe* are found in *Proprioception* wherein Olson, by means of quick notation and relevant chronology and bibliography, makes evident the content of any man as literal experience in and of his *body* — not a "psychology" (which he feels as "the surface" merely) but "the data a depth sensibility/the 'body' of us as object which spontaneously or of its own order produces experience of, 'depth.' . . ." This placement, so to speak, yields a brilliant view in the discussion of grammar. The subject's agency in the middle voice (as distinguished from the active voice, and also what becomes the "copulative" passive in present habit, although it was not so then) is qualified as follows:

1. on himself	make oneself go, proceed, persuade oneself, trust, obey	[*will!* [*belief!*
2. for himself	buy for oneself,	
	send for a person to come to oneself, summon,	[*grace!* — or command
	send for	courtesy!
	to take to the field, march	[*obey!*

3. on some- thing be- longing to oneself	loose one's own, ransom bring one's own	[each takes care of themselves!

Such a system of discourse gained a literal function for the experience of men's recognition of themselves.

Again, it is such recognition that all three of these books insist upon. In *Human Universe* I would call particular attention to "Against Wisdom as Such," "Quantity in Verse, and Shakespeare's Late Plays," "Letter to Elaine Feinstein," "Equal, That Is, to the Real Itself," and to much of the material in the fourth section, especially that concerned with John Smith, Billy the Kid, to the review of Cyrus Gordon's *Homer and Bible,* and to the active distinctions found in the discussion of Ernst Robert Curtius. These are, to my own mind, major matters indeed.

The last essay is called "The Contours of American History" and is the review of a work by William Appleton Williams having the same title. But for the involvement it proposes I think one is better advised to go to *A Bibliography on America for Ed Dorn,* just that Olson gives here his own procedure for the recognition of such history as men in complement with place and time do make actual. He says at one point, "Best thing to do *is to dig one thing or place or man* until you yourself know more abt that than is possible to any other man. It doesn't matter whether it's Barbed Wire or Pemmican or Paterson or Iowa. But *exhaust* it . . ." In the note on Williams' book there is the lovely point about "synthesis having always that advantage, that it gives intellectual experience . . ." It's always up to each man what he makes of anything.

[*Poetry,* October 1966]

"A light, a glory, a fair luminous cloud"

A MAN IS MADE BY what he makes, the poet (*makar*) also. Robert Duncan* makes clear, "It is not expression nor creation that I seek; but my inventions are addressed to an adventure. The medium of words." This *medium* is both path and declaration, for it is the way by which the poet moves and the way, also, by which all moves to him. It is:

a word giving up its ghost
memorized as the flavor
  from the vowels (the bowels)
  of meaning
       (BE STILL THY BRATHE AND HEAR THEM SPEAK . . .)
               ("For a Muse Meant")

The image of what I am talking about begins to come: it is a fair land, a life, a language. And we, poets, are made up by it — it is a maker — and we in turn making ourselves up are of it.

                   ("With Bells Shaking")

The *Letters* then make a character for the initial communication, serve as communicants here, as everywhere and always. We know that what we see finds "images more powerful than our own power of sight." This is the truth of "the full splendour of poetry in which we blindly see."

It were a good thing to begin a book with Blake's beginning: HEAR THE VOICE OF THE BARD! for it is the

* *Letters.*

imagination who listens then — but the Bard is the voice
of the listener, who hears, sees, the ancient trees, the
Holy Word walking there, crying.

("Figures of Speech")

In finding this, as we read, we find ourselves discovered,
by the writer, as ourselves discover him.

An imaginary woman reads by her lamplight, inclining
her head slightly, listening to the words as I write them:
we are there, as the poem comes into existence — she
and I — losing ourselves in the otherness of what is
written. I too then am imaginary.

("At the End of a Period")

Relationships derive from this ground, read or unread.
The forms which sustain us are those devices of conjecture,
force, or need, making ourselves the device of their forms.
They wear us as their sign.

But — "Cezanne restored the destroyed mountain . . ." So
Coleridge may write, "O Lady! we receive but what we
give,/And in our life alone does Nature live . . ."

> Is there another altar than the fact we make,
> the form, fate, future dared
>   desired in the act?

("Upon Taking Hold")

Loss may well live here:

> the reaching out, risk of the touch,
> rhymes that mimic much of loss, ghost goings,
>   words lost in passing, echoed
> where they fall, againnesses of sound only.

("Words Open Out upon Grief")

Yet how else should we live, despite that "Never to this
fullness I came, that fills me"? Such risk defines the poet,
makes him as the poem.

Then with that triumph of assertion, that dear courage in which the creature addresses the creator — for we have in faith to take our stand with God, and say IT IS GOOD — I sign my name, I, Robert Duncan, made this, as best I know.

("Preface: L'Oeuvre de Vivant L'Oeuvre de fantôme")

... now I, who did not see, see.
Friend, you have given your hand to me.

[*Poetry,* April 1960]

"To disclose that vision particular to dreams"

Roots and Branches is characteristic in its title, as in all other respects, of a continuing work which no brief note can report with much accuracy. For one thing, Robert Duncan is of that most rare order of poets for whom the work is not an occasional exercise, nor a demonstration of metrical abilities, nor any other term of partial commitment, however interesting. This book is the eleventh of a sequence, of a life, in fact, which can only be admitted or experienced in that totality.

But I can note, albeit briefly, some of the major insistences of his work as one meets with them in this book as well as in every other which he has written. Most primary is the assertion that what one *can* say, in any circumstance of poetry, is informed by a "voice" not ours to intend or to decide. So Eve (who is first Erda, "the earth daughter," then Eve, "Imagination's child . . . Womb-man of Adam's life") in answer to Adam's "Now in your eyes I see the tree is fair / in which I lose myself thru you" —

> There's a way of speaking that's most like this
> where thought and feeling is not our own
> but belongs to a voice that would transmute
> into a music joy and grief, into one living tree
> in which beyond our selves we find release.

> "Rime" the demon calld it and made a wry face
> as if it were wrong
> where words are obedient to song's measure
>   beyond our will.
> But the daimon calld it "Melody"
> and spoke, again, of our Author's delight
>   in various Truth.
>
> (*Adam's Way*)

Equally, Eve as "Womb-man" and "earth daughter" figures
in part a sense of earth met with in "Apprehensions" an
extraordinary poem indeed which I would place with those
others equally notable in his earlier books, *The Venice
Poem* and "A Poem Beginning with a Line by Pindar."
Here the earth is sensed as complexly the occasion of
births, "pitted with young," "a chain of caves," in a dream
which is instruction. Then the last poem in the book, "The
Continent," plays variations on the recurring theme:

> A diary poem
> to Day, Gaia, Earth
> — murther, murmurer, demurrer.

And this "murther" elsewhere echoes as "But, of that other
Great Mother/or metre, of the matter . . ." in "Two Presentations" which confront the circumstances of his own
birth and relation to his mother with a deeply moving
intimacy.

I am also most interested in Duncan's sense of Adam, who
is wakened to Eve by the angel Michael:

> The Night is done. From your base elements
> you are removed, and Day's your bride . . .
>
> (*Adam's Way*)

I read a curious parallel then in the opening line of
"Apprehensions": "To open Night's eye that sleeps in what

we know by Day . . ." Here the need is to disclose that
vision particular to dreams so that its orders may take part
in that waking life otherwise given to us.

Again, might one manage it in such short space, it would
be of great use, and interest, to make explicit the changes
rung on these divers themes — and I have by no means
noted all those which seem to me relevant. But apropos that
sense of "Night's eye," for example, here is the opening
verse of "A New Poem (for Jack Spicer)":

> You are right. What we call Poetry is the boat.
> The first boat, the body — but it was a bed.
> The bed, but it was a car.
> And the driver or sandman, the boatman,
>   the familiar stranger, first lover,
> is not with me.

Or to follow the circumstance of false instructions, as
contest of those to be honored, that he makes the issue of in
"What Happened: Prelude":

> Betrayd,
> the structures of the poem or play of mind
>   (angelic instructions)
>   broken,
> the genii come to life,
>   touch fire to ice in the living bone
>   and waken
> fearful consequence. They take
> offense who'd promised happiness.

Or to find the various person, Isis, Helen, Eve, Erda, in all
her presence here. But there can be no end to it here.

> Feeling and motion, impression and expression,
>   contend. Drama

is the shape of us. We are
       ourselves tears and gestures of Isis
as she searches for what we are ourselves,

Osiris-Kadmon into many men shatterd,
       torn by passion. She-That-Is,
our Mother, revives ever   His legend.
       She remembers. She puts it all together.
So that, in rapture, there is no longer
       the sensory-motor-homunculus
subduing the forces of Nature, Horus contending
                                    [with Set,

              but the sistrum

              sounds through us.

       The Will wherein the gods ride

          goes forward.
                         ("Osiris and Set")

              [*Humanist*, January-February 1966]

"An intensely singular art"

POETRY FOR THE American has been an intensely singular art. Poe fights early for a separation from European attachments; and Whitman provides the example, basing himself on an ultimate personalism. We have, equally, Emily Dickinson, whose minutiae of personality and perception in effect pick out a world from the four walls of one small room. It is the *me* and *you* which have concerned us — the interstices of human relationships brought home, so to speak. It is there that we have most constantly begun.

This character of placement continues in contemporary verse. Sometimes the sound is belligerently self-assertive, revelatory and painful. The *I* is worn as a merit in itself; all forms break to it, and what hope of relationship to others there may once have been, is lost. This is, of course, the isolation which the American so often carries like a sore, marking him as lonely, lost, and a little pathetic.

The counter to this is the attempt to move into form, again, with others, with one's wife, husband, children — the sudden instances of relationship, the worn ones, all of it. How hard that seems. We cannot speak, now, of any very large aggregate of things to hold us together; and our sociality has become a business maneuver, or else (most hopefully) that the garageman does remember us, the postman smiles! We want so much to be liked.

All three of these books* relate to this one center: how to
live. It is not, how to stay alive, because that is something
else again, almost now beyond our determination. But — in
the time we have, what shall we do? Do you love me? Where
are we? These are interesting questions.

The youngest of these poets, Joel Oppenheimer, came of
age at the end of the second World War: a shocked time,
with "love" a kind of down payment, it seemed, on a house,
or perhaps a refrigerator. One didn't know. One tries,
however:

The Couples

if i dont bring you
flowers. if i dont have any
flowers. delicate grubby violets.
chrysanthemums for your coat.
only children. what has that got
to do with it.

any child is isaac.
brushwood and sticks.
the burning bush in the hill's side.
jesus strung from a dogwood.

if it is not fair
where is fairness. if she is not
fair where is fairness. if flowers.
apples. peaches and pears
for the summer. an edible potato.

the stain of the dogwood
is in you. what now.
mushrooms. or underground
truffles. a pig with a ring

*Denise Levertov: *Here and Now;* Joel Oppenheimer: *The Dutiful
Son;* Louis Zukofsky: *Some Time.*

in his snout. he is hungry.
the stain of the dogwood.

who cries for another's
pain hasnt enough of his own.
where are my children they
leave me here knocking wood.

what is there i havent invented
contrived cut out of the
whole cloth. some day to
make it easier, with more
pleasure. that is a pleasure.

how else to be fecund if not
to put up with a man.

It is a sturdy defense, I think, written in like manner. But
the women know too, what there is to know. God knows they
feel it — no kindnesses, or expectancies, or money. It is
different. Denise Levertov is English, but that doesn't
matter. One says (grandly!) she knows:

> *The Bird*
> That crazy bird
> always laughing —
> he sits on the wall they are building,
> the wall
> which will hide the horizon,
> and laughs like mad every time
> we open our mouths to say
> I love you I hate you etc.
> He came only since
> the green rain came and
> softened everything, making
> mud of the cracked
> selfrespecting earth and rotting

> the red flowers from their stems. Yes,
> the rain, the trucks full
> of pink bricks, that crazy
> eavesdropping bird, came
> together and finished
> the days of burning,
> and silence, and distance.

Thank God for the relief of it all. Personalism is of course only interesting insofar as it does contain "That crazy bird . . ." One begins with oneself perhaps, and to that entity one joins one other; and from that it may well be that a third is conceived. And so on — because this is what the world is all about. And the birds laugh. It is a good thing. Men and women grow whole in this image.

There is also wear, certainly, and the time that passes. But the determination, to live with others, holds true, once chosen. And a poet, like any man, thoughtfully enough arrives at the choice common to all. Louis Zukofsky is older than either Denise Levertov or Joel Oppenheimer, and has been alive consistently. He has a family much in evidence in his poems, a wife and son. His book is, in fact, a complexly woven evidence of this basic relationship, so that I cannot, by quoting, make it all clear. But the substance of it can be made so, and the craftsmanship whereby it is given form — and, again, the world in which it obtains.

Sequence 1944-6 (4)

> Having outlived self-offense
> And that of my friends
> I became brother to loneliness
> And love the fact more than the word.
>
> All that is human is
> Alien and not alien.
> All carefully chosen words
> Are here — fairly shadows.

You have music to accord.
A child
At a remove from love
Holds leaves in my hand.

Where the world is headed
We do not say
As stars
Sun and surf

Flash in the sky. Were it said
Among twigs
"And then the world went
And then — "

Only our thoughts
Might seek it
In further woods.

It was never easy — but there was what there was to do. It may well be a simplification to posit ways at all, this or that. I don't know. Who is to say who is known? Each of these three poets knows the isolation of being alive, and of that counter will, to move to someone, to move with some-one. They celebrate *family* — America's archaic institution, but America will not decide it this time. Let it be simple as Zukofsky:

> *Lights* (8)
> See:
> My nose feels better in the air.

[*New Mexico Quarterly*, Spring — Summer 1957]

The New World

WE DESCRIBE OUR TIME as one in which relationships, rather than the hierarchies to which these might refer, are dominant. What is meant by politics, marriage, education, religion, or love itself, become modalities, terms between, people, the *you* and *me* of the subjective universe. If it is not *my* hat, then possibly it is *yours*; or if not yours, *his*, or *hers* — or *theirs*, a collective enterprise, yet one (as religion or philosophy, at present) given meaning by a *possessional* insistence. The hat itself is an occasion.

It is clear that poetry will reflect this sense of emphasis, and, if the given instance be sensitive, it will succeed in forcing a passage between individual sensibility and shared commitments (to live, to endure, and the like). Poems themselves are peculiarly suited to the present environment, because they are basically relational. In this way Charles Olson defines "A poem [as] energy transferred from where the poet got it (he will have some several causations), by way of the poem itself to, all the way over to, the reader . . ." The poem is not a signboard, pointing to a content ultimately to be regarded; but is, on the contrary, a form inhabited by intelligence and feeling. It is the way a poem speaks, not the matter, that proves its effect, and although this is an old insistence, it is one hard at times to remember when a great variety of desperations want a solution, a content capable of relief.

Gary Snyder's first book, *Riprap,* calls for a ground-sense
of place, a world of substantial place, even primeval. Its
manner is quiet, low-keyed like they say, with much solidity
and peace — and that is a pleasure, offered as it is by a
working intelligence and care:

No paradise, no fall,
Only the weathering land,
The wheeling sky,
Man, with his Satan
Scouring the chaos of the mind.
Oh Hell!

So that if we cannot escape, at least we can know, as
Stendhal:

The pleasure brought by the cessation of pain consists:
1. In conquering all the successive obstacles that one
   erects for one's self.
2. In visualizing all the advantages of which one was
   about to be deprived.

From specific images of work-lines, farmhouses, intensities
of physical life, the poem may come to:

Thinking about a poem I'll never write.
With gut on wood and hide, a plucking thumb,
Grope and stutter for the words, invent a tune,
In any tongue, this moment one time true
Be wine or blood or rhythm drives it through —
A leap of words to things and there it stops.

But if it does *not* stop — if there the relation shatters, or,
rather, shivers, oscillates, flips back and forth in an ecstasy
of qualification. Ah well. It is again only an old enough
irresolution — "no ideas but in things" — *things?* What are
things but ideas, until we bump our heads finally, and that's
an end to it:

Allowing such distinctions to the mind:
A formal garden made by fire and time.

Arrived at such peace, then, all the landscape changes, and
men walk quietly, enhanced by their relationships, defined
by them, as women also. It is a beautiful and painstaking
world which Snyder wants to live in, has by his poems made
to live in — a successful relation of hope.

❋   ❋   ❋

But the fires burn elsewhere, in other characters, and
"No man can purify another."

Evil is done by the self alone, by the self alone
is evil left undone, by self alone is one purified.
Purity and impurity depend on one's own self.

(*Dhammapada*)

Perhaps the present attraction of the *Dhammapada*, or
other Buddhist texts, is just this emphasis — that the self is a
self-isolated event, yet one which must find relationships.
When contact is broken, becomes the touch of the mind,
then hell becomes particular, and not at all a place where
bad people go, etc. When the imagination projects for itself
a world more real than that which it literally experiences,
this is hell, a forfeit, as Dante said, of the goods of the
intellect. Because such 'goods' are relational, *joiners*, describe a method of being-with, otherwise impossible.

The self grown huge is a common aspect of the Romantic,
but it might be remembered that its size is one of *sensation*,
of what is felt, and is not otherwise of magnitude. The
danger inherent is what Lawrence called *sensationalism*, i.e.,
the repetition of a known sensation is sensationalism. This is
what happens when all qualification exists as a method of
feeling rather than as a posited consequence of actions.

Michael McClure* describes the hair-edge of feeling *qua* sensation and feeling *qua* effect:

> The poem
>
> is confusion. Love, Sex, Death, are within
> us and we give them many names. Naming only
>
> ---
>
> the heads, when the bodies are wound, woven
>   together. Making
>
> ---
>
> the parts of us abstractions, Knees unreal
> their qualities are vagaries

It is McClure's virtue as a poet, that he gives to his language a space, a flux in language, held by a structure of *words* — not a program of predetermined measures, either metrical or ideological. It is, in this way, as much his risk, in writing, as it is ours, in reading — to undertake a composition.

McClure, reading aloud, speaks flatly, without color, so that the words fall into relationships which they themselves, almost alone, seem to determine. In the poems capitalization is used for divers lines as a point of enlargement, a center and/or focus for the movement. Like this:

> Sleepwalkers . . . Ghosts! Voices
> like bodies coming through the mists of sleep,
>   we float about each other —
>
>   bare feet not touching the floor.
>   Talking in our lover's voice
> NAMING THE OBJECTS OF LOVE . . .

The movement of the poems makes clear an insistent disattachment, or better, a recognition of distance qualified as separation, perhaps forever. There is a vacuum all but un-

---

*Hymns to St. Geryon and Other Poems.

entered by purpose, form, consequence — wherein events relay between a shifting possibility of relation, to come to:

I am sure of my movements I am a bulk
  in the air.

✻   ✻   ✻

This center of *self* (rather than 'we' or 'they') has become a mark of the new poetry, to my own mind not unreasonably since it depends on real crises in real homes. It is very hard to make one's self understood, most of all by another — sadly, truly, etc. If culture now derives from mass orientation — and it seems that it does — kitchens and bedrooms and ultimately bathrooms house, god knows, the shaken egos of our time. Poetry, beginning with the protest of the thirties (a self-centered evaluation), moving through the chaos of the forties, loss of meaning and the huge arrival of apparently nonhuman activity (the atom, then hydrogen and cobalt, bombs, and too, such devices as the blowing up of an air liner to kill a mother-in-law, i.e., the new potential seen as property of the individual, also) comes through the fifties finding a language in a common hysteria, a nervously singular presence of mind, in which feelings are dominant as they are felt, are registered as static blurring the voice of ordinary explanation, which says that everything is all right (when it is patently not all right). At times it will, as parody, take on, in grotesque approximations, the 'walk, don't run' character of current political and social jargon. Death, love, hope, and other qualities of attitude, will appear then as crudely erected statues in vacant lots, i.e., vacant states of mind aroused by a scarecrow of desire. From all this, this vacant density, appear to come many crowded voices — as if each 'I' wanted to believe it was to be, in some miraculous way, taken away from all this, and was to wake up to a warm familiar bed, in which its place was assured.

In this situation the intelligence becomes primary, is itself
the contact with the real. But being so used, it is almost
necessarily suspect, and so must be itself examined — as a
possible last ditch of the deception suspected. *Self-Portrait,
from Another Direction* is an instance of "Philip Whalen,"
a series of mentally approximate images of this man's
activity. One day it may be, as Norbert Wiener suggests,
"that one might conceivably travel by telegraph, in addition
to traveling by train or airplane." States of mind seem to
show relay points in the complex which, admittedly with
an overweight of emphasis, we call *self*. Whalen is not
engaged in vindicating, nor in revealing, himself, but in
thinking himself: "I think what is thinking . . ." He presents,
then, all the dilemma, and all the gain, of a man wandering
around in a battle area with the constant question, *what's
happening:*

> Now it is here.
> Now it is falling.
> Now it is there.
>   which we agree upon . . .
> What comes next?

❋   ❋   ❋

> Any word you see here defies all fear doubt destruction
>   [ignorance & hatefulness
> All the impossibilities unfavorable chance or luck . . .

Whalen's formal invention develops as the range of his
intelligence increases, not wisdom-wise but methodologi-
cally, to contain those relationships overtly, which mentality
in itself seems to involve. It is hard to suggest, much more to
say, where such an emphasis may lead. Yet the areas of
consciousness which are related (as in Whalen's poem) by
such attention are argument enough. Conditions of thought

are now too volatile, too open to a variety of persuasion, not to be examined; and Whalen makes a good lighthouse.

❋   ❋   ❋

In *The Human Use of Human Beings* (quoted previously) Norbert Wiener says also: "the individuality of the body is that of a flame rather than of a stone, of a form rather than of a bit of substance." The human entity, person or self, depends on its environment as a context for its reality. Such proves the modulation of its own reality, felt more than known or determined. What is so new about this — except that time has entered space, and place itself is insubstantial. So both poems and men rely upon an act of thought.

It is hard to live, yet by use of the resources given, and responsible consciousness, one may find a sudden reassurance — as Loewinsohn's: *

> The thing made real by
> a sudden twist of the mind:
> relate the darkness to a face
> rather than
> impose a face on the darkness
> which has no face, in reality.

Ron Loewinsohn knows the common institutions of marriage, working, and friends, and in that way his poems are common too. The intelligence is, however, very specific, again an instance of *self* determination and need.

> The stillness of the poem
> a moment full of silence &
> portent, like
> the sudden halt of great machines.
> Silence that becomes a fabric
> to clothe the consciousness . . .

*Watermelons.

What do we want from it? I don't know, but think that
the poem is a form, derives its nature from the language of
which it is made, is "charged" by the emotion(s) of its
writer. But into that then comes the great modality of the
occasion, the where and when — on some time-screen with
blurred and shadowy presences. A man cannot live without
the use of his intelligence. There may be, now, no common
union except in the attempt to survive that intelligence, the
risk of all writing or thought. Synder, McClure, Whalen,
and Loewinsohn each make their own form *qua* poem, and
the world whereto these relate comes after, or at the same
time:

> . . . A small room
> without windows & only one door;
> its accoustics make even laughter dissonant.
> Every ocean, orchard, city, speech,
> sin, book & body I've ever known
> lie scattered all over the place.
>   (Loewinsohn)

[*Yugen.* No. 7, 1961]

Edward Dorn in the News

THE PUBLICATION OF Edward Dorn's *The Newly Fallen*
makes at last possible a *place* to read him simply, and in
that way, ought not to be missed. The 'news' is the *line,* as
in the very first poem, like this:

I know that peace is soon coming, and love of common
[object,
and of woman and all the natural things I groom,
[in my mind, of
faint rememberable patterns, the great geography of my
[lunacy.

If "lunacy," it is gracefully apropos — and moves with the
neat lightfoot way of quick sense and specific commitment.
He takes hold of things, common as the "red Geranium"
Indian woman of this first poem, and makes no mistake —
nor invites you to any, who are so often smothered with
confidences that prove bullshit. Partly the book is a 'making
peace,' a necessary and valuable operation, with the old
places, as "oh, mother/I remember your year-long stare/
across plowed flat prairielands . . ."

Place is even more absolute in "Sousa," and in the variations of "A Country Song" — as the last lines:

Then in front of the fire
We talk of Spring

An obscure slight offering . . .

the beauty of the thought, and *line*, throwing back upon the melody as it fades and ends here. So "If it should ever come . . ."

> And we are all there together
> time will wave as willows do
> and adios will be truly, yes . . .

Shy in love, he is accurate and final in his condemnations, hardly to be denied:

> Will Fidel feed his people before his own stomach
> is filled? Can Jack
> hold up his grimy hands and shade us
> from that vileness falling in particles . . .

The *line* is, after all, the *measure* of the man writing, his term, peculiarly, as he writes, weighing, in the silence to follow, the particular word sense, necessary to his own apprehension of the melody, the tune — that he *hears*, to write. So, of secondhand clothing sold by charity:

> Of wearing secretly a burden,
> clothes fitting as casually as though
> they were stolen,
> from the wealth
> of the nation.

It is an anger that *must* make its terms understood, and so makes them a music no man can deign (wow!) to avoid.

[*The Floating Bear*, No. 6, 1961]

Edward Dorn's Geography

THIS BOOK returns to the orders of feeling and response a kind of intelligence that has been long absent from poetry written in America and England. There have certainly been 'political' poems in abundance, but these (with specific exception of the work of Allen Ginsberg, Robert Duncan, and Charles Olson — from each of whom Edward Dorn remains singularly distinct) have largely argued a *use* of existing evils in a way that seemed too simply satisfied with the fact of such circumstance, just that it provoked the poems in question. In short, such writing tended to promulgate the very attitudes and situations it seemed most to condemn, in a convenience of 'description' — in a luxury of hate and dissatisfaction that was otherwise not to be enjoyed.

But here — much as an anger is evident — there is a ranging knowledge of literal terms, a *geography* of actual location and of the space it has been forced to accept as a kind of time measured in miles and days and persons and things of an endless debris and confusion. Movement becomes 'A modern group in cars . . .'

> In the bitterness of the great desert
> they tried to get comfortable in car seats.
> Utterly left behind was
> a mixed past, of friends and a comfortable house.
> They felt sorry for themselves perhaps
> for no real reason, there had never

been in their baggage more than a few stars
and a couple of moons, you've seen their surfaces
in pictures.

("West of Moab")

Edward Dorn speaks literally, so that the experience of
these poems, both for himself and the readers of them, is
neither a symbolism nor an imaginative transfer of reality
into some relieving change. It is, rather, the dry, tough,
drawn, harsh, *unrelieved* experience of the world as the
mind and senses are permitted to disclose it, if they *will* stay
unremittingly attentive to the specific qualities *and* quan-
tities it manifests. There is the undistracted fact, then, of
Mr. Dorn's belief that 'the poem is an instrument of in-
tellection/thus a condition/of the simultaneous . . .' Thus it
is issue of what perception can afford in the instant of time
when things are, as they are, met by nothing more than their
recognition.

One might well note the relevance of this condition to
much that has preceded it in America — for example, the
dryness of Poe's intelligence and yet the sensuality of his
experience; or what another poem of Mr. Dorn's from an
earlier collection, *Hands Up!*, makes so evident:

Insofar as life can be lived
and can be *stated*, H D T
did well to write about it.
Became more than living, that hapless verb.
Became a survey of more than a hubbub
of the days in which axes & bread,
ponds, window with bars out of which
to look and be disobedient, mere tools
of distraction. Altho I don't
say much for the crabby writing.
I like the clarity. Nor have much use

for the temper, but he was alive.
Knowing we can't be forever waiting for the appraisor.
In america every art has to reach toward some
clarity. That is our hope from the start.

("The Land Below")

That Thoreau gained *particularity* in writing is much to the
point here — and that Edward Dorn shares with him in that
particularity the fact that —

My desire is to be
a classical poet
my gods have been men . . .
and women.

("Idaho Out")

Or also:

Thus a window
is that seemingly clear opening our tested knowledges
pass through and the world shakes not at all
before the weight of our disappointments, you will
and would be part of the new hemisphere
until it dies of the same old loosely wrought manifestoes.
All those sounds from the broken washing machine
are trying to tell you something sweetheart don't laugh
one day it will speak and not stop
all things have an insistence of their own.

("Six Views from the Same Window
of the Northside Grocery")

There is so much that instructs in this book — not as an
aggression or cheap privacy, but as the intensity of such
careful thought and weighed insight at times it is heart-
breaking to realize how much the possibilities of speech
mean to this man. He is possessed of a *lovely* ear:

If the world
or a life
or all of this
love,
all the pleasures
we do not sow
and those we do
love,
sometime end . . .

                ("Song")

These are poems of a deeply articulate beauty, and, at
moments, of such a catch of fragmented relief —

    Daffodil Song
The horns of yellow
      on this plain resound
      and the twist on the air
of their brilliance
      Say where
say where I will find
a love
      or an arabesque
of such rash fortune.

                    [*Stand*, VIII, 2, 1966]

Rainer Gerhardt: A Note

I FELT VERY CLOSE to this man — selfishly, because he gave me knowledge of a world I had otherwise no means of knowing. We were of the same age, but the life he had been given was far from that I knew. When he spoke of growing up in the Hitler *Jugend*, of the final chaos of his feelings and senses of possibility after he had been drafted into the army — of his desertion, then, to Tito's forces in Yugoslavia — finally, of all the world of chaos after the war, of his marriage and his two young sons who had to go daily through streets of collapsed buildings often with bushes pushing through the rubble — of the hope of a magazine, then small books, of what Ernst Robert Curtius characterized as *the most hopeful sign to come out of postwar Germany*, the first issue of *Fragmente* — when one witnessed the complexity of his life and all that it had been forced to acknowledge, there was no easy way to resolve all that he did, in his own person, force one to see.

I most clearly remember him, not tall, somewhat stocky, dark haired, his skin a little heavy with all the starches that made up the common diet — or more clearly, the curious concentration, persistent, often enthusiastic, but never a whim only or a momentary excitement. He took such care with things — of myself, when I came to see him with a friend, Ashley Bryan. We found them living in Freiberg in one room, Rainer, his wife, and the two children. They gave us their beds and slept on the floor. I had a pair of old,

scuffed combat boots I was wearing, and found them the
next morning polished to a high shine, by Rainer's wife.
Then Rainer came back with myself and Ashley, by way of
Paris, to Aix-en-Provence, close to which we lived in a small
town called Fontrousse. He stayed with us there a week,
and it was his hope that he and his family might immigrate
to France. They never managed it. I remember the day before he was to leave, I had come down, it was morning, and
he was standing looking out through a window in the door,
at the long side of Mt. Sainte Victoire, that faced our house
across the fields. He was crying without sound, one could
see the tears on his face.

He spoke to me of what he felt to be the community, the
complex of people any city or town describes. He felt that
a writer was not distinct from such a unity, but rather
helped very literally in its definition. In contrast, he felt an
isolation in Americans which bewildered him.

What he hoped to do was so much, and is most simply
illustrated by a partial list of the contents of the first two
issues of *Fragmente* — all that he was able to publish before
his death: Pound, Bunting, Michaux, Césaire, Olson, W. C.
Williams, Montanari, Perse, Artaud, Alberti, Lu Chi. He
wanted to bring back into the German context all that writing he felt the war had blocked, and at the same time he
could not accept such makeshift 'official' translations as
would leave out eleven lines of *The Waste Land* on the
grounds 'they were too difficult.' He wanted it right with
such an unremitting intensity.

The last year of his life I had too little sense of, involved
as we then were with our immediate living. I realized that
money continued a large problem, and his ability to get
some income from radio scripts and like work had been
affected by his increasing depression. They had lost the
room they had been living in, and for a time depended on

a tent. Another passing friend told me of having been in Germany, and of meeting Renate, Rainer's wife, standing out on the road hitchhiking in a heavy rain to the city where she hoped to sell some of Rainer's scripts. She told him that Rainer now went for long periods all but incapable of speaking, and that he would sit by himself in the park, where she would then go to sit by him, for what moments he could speak, or work, trying to continue with all that he had undertaken.

To speak of his poems is for me most difficult, because I could not read them simply in German, and, beyond that, had only a partial sense (very much so then) of what specific difficulties and possibilities German poetry had as context. He said once, *the idyll is our weakness.* Trakl was close to his own terms of imagination. Benn's technical facility he respected, and he found, also, accuracy in the deep irony with which Benn characterized the world. But I was certainly aware that in his last book, *Umkreisung* (1952), all the care he had given to his translations of men as Pound, and Olson, and Williams, was beginning to find root in his own work. He seems to have read the necessity very deeply.

I felt such a bitter waste, at the news of his death. I feel it still, simply that he was so much the cost of his own time and place — and so incredibly brave in his confrontation of that fact in himself. There was no way to move in any easy sense beyond the past, and there never will be.

January 20, 1964
[*Work*, Winter 1965-66]

Four

A Note on Canadian Poetry

THE FIRST Canadian poet was probably the Frenchman who came over with Champlain, and had intelligence a good deal beyond the ordinary in that he saw the new world even as Champlain did. Before leaving, and almost on the dock, he had written his "Farewell to France," and by that act intended a new life, one might say; at least it was his own decision. There is an account in Parkman of how Champlain came back to Port Royal (I think it was) after a miserable voyage down the Atlantic coast. Putting in for water, he had been attacked by Indians, and off Mount Desert he had almost lost his ship in the heavy seas. In any case he came back bitter and tired out, and was utterly dumbfounded to find himself met by men in strange costumes chanting alexandrines – a true poetic homage to himself.

As Parkman has it, the Frenchman was not lazy, and if the old world could not be translated quite so literally to the new, it was an honest sense that had made the attempt. The masque was the old form, but the context was altogether a new one.

Canadian poetry might always be this attempt, not so much to fit, say, into an environment but to act in the given place. If there is no 'major' poet in Canada, if there never was one, etc., I think it is a part of this same problem. A theoretic embarrassment of 'culture,' all the tenuosities of trying to be local and international at the same time, etc., take an energy otherwise of use in the making of an idiom peculiar to the given circumstances. In this way Canadian poetry, in its earlier forms, has much in common with the American poetry of Lowell, Longfellow, et al. The model is English, and it is precisely the English which is of no use whatsoever. "Like some grey warder who, with mien sedate, etc." comes too late, and too borrowed, to be helpful. It is incredible to think of the man writing it, even then, being where he must have been. The impact of the place is dulled in the overlay of the English rhythms, and the politenesses which couldn't have been actual.

The Frenchman with Champlain was, finally, a poet in a much, much deeper sense, and it was he who catalogued a good many of the plants around their camp, and also made a garden which kept them all in vegetables. There is that sense of it, of where, particularly, one is. I think that is more 'poetic vision,' call it, than any other sense could be. The Frenchman has size in his intention, and more than that, what he intends he does, i.e., the garden, and the masque in the dead of winter, completely improvised and successful.

I don't see any other way to do it. The problems of form and content, and all the other contentions of poets, are utterly intimate with each man writing, and where he is writing, and what he tries with what's around him. Canadian poetry becomes, in each instance, which man or woman it is, and what their work can effect.

[*Contact* (Toronto), No. 8, 1953]

Canadian Poetry 1954

A ROUNDUP OF Canadian poetry, A.D. 1954, would probably bring in little else but these.* The American reader is, or may well be, familiar enough with the work of A. M. Klein, P. K. Page, and perhaps one or two others — but I think that Irving Layton, for one example, may well have escaped him, despite the fact that he is a better poet than either of the two noted. Why this is so, like they say, is of course simple enough to guess. Local conditions, and a prevailing provincialism, have kept the Canadians wedged between England on the one hand, and the US on the other, and it takes a somewhat trusting soul to stick his nose out.

Contact Press, however, has broken out of this usual dilemma by way of both books and a magazine, and if a reader wants to see where actual conditions for a healthy literature can be found, he might well look here. For example, *Contact* (the magazine) is nothing very much to look at, nor does it have many of those great names well-calculated to keep the reader buying. But it is, in spite of itself, *international* — insofar as its tone is open, its critical sense almost sufficient, and because it prints in each issue four or five good poems, demonstrably good poems, by men

*Contact (An International Magazine of Poetry) No.'s. 4-8, edited by Raymond Souster; *Cerberus* by Louis Dudek, Irving Layton, Raymond Souster; *Twenty-four Poems* by Louis Dudek; *The Black Huntsmen* by Irving Layton; *Love the Conqueror Worm* by Irving Layton; *Canadian Poems 1850-1952* (Toronto: Contact Press, 1953).

writing all the way from Freiburg to Mexico City. Not to
mention Montreal.

That, in itself, is something — and with the canons of good
taste, and good business, so well-set in the States, one can
do worse than subscribe to such a magazine — if only for
the fine sense of air, and openness, it does have.

To maintain such a thing is not of course simple, either
for the men writing, or the editors thereof. It is a considerable scramble to get together enough material and enough
money for a decent issue of any magazine, of any length,
coming out four times a year. And the Canadians, in spite
of ingenuousness and an almost sticky goodwill toward
Literature, are by no means apt to run out and buy something by people who are not quite acceptable. Raymond
Souster, in *Cerberus*, is eloquent enough.

> Turning the crank of a mimeograph
> In a basement cellar to produce the typical
> "Little magazine" perhaps fifty will read,
> Twenty remember (and with luck) five will learn from.

The delights of the literary salon etc., are by no means what
these men know:

> Engaged through the week at Usura,
> Loaning the rich the poor man's money,
> And kidding yourself it does not leave
> The marks of its uselessness upon you.

So that to say something, *anything*, in protest, has been of
necessity their payment.

Back of that is the problem of how to say it, if one is
writing poetry, and this is much the same headache, for
Canadians, that it is for anyone else. And they have no all-
pervading tone, to sneak by with, no Great Men for a shield.
Dudek, in both *Cerberus* and *Twenty-four Poems*, founders,
I think, on this lack of patent authority. Or else he has not

yet got to his own idiom — and too much resembles, at
present, a very desperate man in a very crowded store, trying on thousands of hats, coats and gloves, in hopes to find
something to fit, before the clock strikes five-thirty. On the
other hand, more relaxed, he can be very graceful:

An Air by Sammartini

It was something you did not know
     had existed — by a dead Italian.
Neither words nor a shape of flesh
    but of air;
       whose love it celebrated
        and "cold passion"
Amoroso Canto, a crystal
     that fell from musical fingers —
As a cloud comes into the eye's arena,
    a certain new tree
      where the road turns,
   or love, or a child, is born,
      or death comes:
Whatever is found or is done
    that cannot be lost or changed.

Which, in defiance, really, of the 'love,' 'death,' etc., ends
with as hard and simple a statement as any man might ask
for. Because 'general statement' is Dudek's *bête noire,* on
other occasions, and no matter all the goodwill in the world,
his preface in *Cerberus* (with its "The way to freedom and
order in the future will lie through art and poetry . . .") is
incredibly naive.

Layton seems to have sprung from somewhat more hard-
ened stock. One can imagine him biting nickels, etc., at a
much earlier date. His poetry is tougher, and at the same
time more gentle. His idiom, to call it that, is much of the

old and even 'traditional' way of it, except that he has a
very sharp ear, and a hard, clear head for rythms:

Mrs. Fornheim, Refugee

Very merciful was the cancer
Which first blinding you altogether
Afterwards stopped up your hearing;
At the end when Death was nearing,
Black-gloved, to gather you in
You did not demur, or fear
One you could not see or hear.

I taught you Shakespeare's tongue, not knowing
The time and manner of your going;
Certainly if with ghosts to dwell,
German would have served as well;
Voyaging lady, I wish for you
An Englishwoman to talk to,
An unruffled listener,
And green words to say to her

Layton may well be, for the historian of literature at any
rate, the first Great Canadian Poet — he has his bid in at
least, not that it is not, in some of these poems, too brief
and too random. But Canadian, English, American, or whatever, his poetry can be very good.

And *how* good can well be judged, thanks again to
Layton, together with Dudek this time, by means of an
anthology of Canadian verse which they have edited — as
Pound would say, "an anthology based on terrible knowledge," if one remembers how many poems both must have
read in order to produce what they come up with here. It
may well be that any anthology is terrifying, not just this
one. I should hate to see the same job done on American
verse, all put together like this, 1850-1952. And yet one can
see the use — if only to settle, once and for all, that there was

and is a Canadian poetry, however dark some of its 'periods' may now seem.

Some of it is by no means as bad as all that; we have written much worse. Robert W. Service is much the same pleasure:

> I dreamed I saw three demi-gods who in a cafe sat,
> And one was small and crapulous, and one was large
> > [and fat;
> And one was eaten up with vice and verminous at that.

The editors do not rate him strictly as a poet, i.e., "a rough-house rhymester whom everybody welcomes but no one rates strictly as a poet." I would, I think. At least he is much more of a poet than, say, F. R. Scott?

> This is our gardening
> And this our hardening,
> There is no pardoning:
> We cannot be forgiven
> For what we have not striven.

Some of it may come from an idea of 'poetry' (not the act, but the noun) which is, after all, a matter almost apart from what Dr. Williams, for one, calls, the poem. Canadians, if any of these people are evidence, or if Souster has not been beating his head on stone, are writing more and more poems.

[*Black Mountain Review*, Spring 1954]

Kenneth Patchen: Fables & Other Little Tales

Another prose book by Kenneth Patchen brings up all kinds of memories — dull as that occupation often is. But Patchen was always unclassifiable, his earlier books were an excitement altogether separate from what, say, Henry Miller amounted to. There was a wild kind of *purity* to them, and a conception few men would have dared to attempt.

All this is too simple to say. The old gimmick of breathing heavily about a man's past performance is too often an excuse for ignoring him all the same. In Patchen's case this has been so much the fact, that it is tantamount to insult, finally, to invoke these older things at the expense of what he is now doing.

The new work is not a simple matter. For once, I think, it is legitimate to speak of Patchen himself, i.e., the man writing this book, and the particular problems with which he has been damned through no fault, certainly, of his own. Various appeals for medical help for him have of course appeared from time to time in almost all the magazines — though the response to them has been hardly enough. For a long time Patchen was thought to be suffering from a form of arthritis, until finally it was found that the cause of all the hell he had gone through with his back came from an 'exploded' disc, in the spinal column. An operation partially helped this — but he is far from done with it. And the same need for money, for medical expenses, continues.

What that has to do with this present book may be vague — though I doubt it. We ask a man to tell us what he knows, and what Patchen knows must be pain, constant pain, pain moving, sitting up or trying to, pain walking. Every single day of his life. It's not a question of 'excusing' the flaws, call them, of this book — or even of feeling that, after all, the man we had known, with his incredible tenderness, and gentleness, is at last a victim even of that world he believed in. He still is there, very much there. And if it is, or seems, by inversion — a care turned inside out — I hardly think this can be called the end of it.

The tone in the book is neither very 'funny' nor anything else. It seems to me almost ugly, and almost necessarily so. What else? The punning, the discontinuous sequence, etc. — he is not the first man to call attention to horror, to the horror now on us, by the use of its own methods. It is that things *don't* 'follow,' not now — that you begin saying this, you end saying that. And who knows why, in time? Perhaps that is very far from either Patchen's intention, or, better, the book's actual point, but it is a sense that comes very strongly from it.

"Never mind that," interjected the impatient Kraken. "Those pleasant little minnows there — " indicating the orphans, who were now contentedly belting one another with planks their steaks had come on, "I know damn well that their shoes will fit me. Only thing is, I wouldn't want to hurt their feelings . . . so I guess I'll have to eat them first."

In defiance of the jacket blurb, the book is anything but "sad, beautiful gaiety." But it may well be the beginning of, and the reasons for, an attack. Toward the end of the book he writes "Every stick points two ways, and people like you and me have either got to get an easy, knowing grip on the dirty end or else let go altogether . . ."

[*Black Mountain Review*, Spring 1954]

Kenneth Rexroth: In Defense of the Earth

In Defense of the Earth is the first more or less substantial collection of Kenneth Rexroth's poems since the publication of *The Dragon and the Unicorn*. The latter was a long philosophical travel-poem, so that the book I am reviewing more literally goes back to *The Signature of All Things* (1949), and is (as that book was) an accumulation of poems and translations of varying length and determination.

> Many of these deal with similar locations and events, seeking over and over again for the changing forms of an unchanging significance in stars, insects, mountains and daughters. They do not of course try to answer, "Why am I here?" "Why is it out there?" — but to snare the fact that is the only answer, the only meaning of present or presence... [Foreword by Kenneth Rexroth to *In Defense of the Earth.*]

Reading a book, or reviewing it — one comes to ask, what does the book have, for its ideas; and, how clearly are those ideas made evident? Rexroth's title demonstrates the area of his concern, large though it surely is, and open as well to the pitfalls of an overzealous generality. But one can, as he does, begin there.

The opening poems are for his wife, Marthe, and his daughter Mary. Those for his wife have, among them, some of the book's best writing.

> ... What do I know now,
> Of myself, of the others?
> Blood flows out to the fleeing
> Nebulae, and flows back, red
> With all the worn space of space,
> Old with all the time of time.
> It is my blood. I cannot
> Taste in it as it leaves me
> More of myself than on its
> Return ...

This is the first idea. It is as well a broadening, in effect a deepening of something, such as:

> ... Just born to die
> Nobody will ever know anything about it
> And I have nothing more at all to say.

Which is taken from *The Art of Worldly Wisdom* (1949), a book which marked the last large instance of Rexroth's experimentation in poems akin (as he notes) to those of Stein, Lowenfels, Arensberg, and Louis Zukofsky. After that time he made clear his intention to write in more "common" forms, and to give up at least the intensity of his concern to that point with syntactical formation, personally based. Perhaps my own statement here is unclear, but what was meant seems simply this: he became concerned with a poetry which people, in a half-hoped for generality, might be able to read, as put against that which apparently they could not — or at least this was not to be the concern of the writer.

This is the second idea, clear in this book — that people, who are being loved, attacked, or subjected to the varying attitudes of the writer, be obliged to hear that concern. The poem "Thou Shalt Not Kill" (for the memory of Dylan Thomas, who was himself proposed as a common voice) speaks like this:

I want to run into the street
Shouting, "Remember Vanzetti!"
I want to pour gasoline down your chimneys.
I want to blow up your galleries.
I want to burn down your editorial offices
I want to slit the bellies of your frigid women.
I want to sink your sailboats and launches.
I want to strangle your children at their finger paintings.
I want to poison your Afghans and poodles.
He is dead, the drunken little cherub.
He is dead,
The effulgent tub thumper.
He is Dead . . .

But — one knows what one 'speaks,' or else not. Put too
blandly, such address is perhaps only equalled by the equal
exhortations, to buy this bread, that butter, and to eat it all.
More reasonably — the addition of 'launches' to 'sailboats'
belies the echoing tiredness of the man writing, it may be,
with the whole 'idea.'

More quietly (less 'common') :

What can you say in a poem?
Past forty, you've said it all.
The dwarf black oak grows out of
The cliff below my feet. It
May be two hundred years old,
Yet its trunk is no bigger
Than my wrist, its crown does not
Come to my shoulder . . .

I read the book making notes, so that I should not be
overly embarrassed, coming to write of it. Which was my
dilemma, but these poems are marked as follows: "Seven
Poems for Marthe, My Wife" ('Positions of love — physical — loneliness. Images of possible loss — flat line. Praise.')

"The Mirror in the Woods" ('Good — fairy story quality. Mirror.'); "For Eli Jacobsen" ('Good — old-timers, liberals, workers — the good old days — won't come again. Courage — makes taste & feelings better. Ok.'); "Time Is the Mercy of Eternity" ('Philosophical — "on poetry." Up in the mts. Images of *moments:* description. Clear. *Alone.* All strips *away to "knowledge"'*), etc., etc.

Perception, inside or out, is 'earth,' equally to be defended. In the 'Japanese Translations' at the book's end, there is this one (by Ishikawa Takuboku):

> I do not know why
> But it is as though
> There were a cliff
> Inside my head
> From which, every day,
> Clods of earth fall.

[*New Mexico Quarterly,* Winter 1956-57]

"To Build Castles in Spain"*

To ANTHOLOGIZE ten centuries of any country's poetry would seem a very ambitious job — and the more so, when the country is one so vague in our minds as is Spain. I don't know that either Miss Turnbull's selection, or that of Cohen, succeeds altogether in giving the necessary orientation. But such success would be in any case extremely relative. Briefly, I would prefer Cohen's book for these reasons: 1) his system of identifying authors in the table of contents is uncomplicated and allows quick reference; 2) his prose translations, running beneath the Spanish text on each page in the character of unpretentious footnotes, make a very usable "trot"; and 3) his material, although paralleling Miss Turnbull's in great part, seems to me a more solid continuity. To these things, I should add the fact that his anthology costs $1.50 less than Miss Turnbull's; and consider the matter settled.

There is, however, a tendency evident in Miss Turnbull's book that might be mentioned — because it seems without justification. The translations which she has provided are often very curious. They include, for example, Henry Wadsworth Longfellow's translation of the formalist, Jorge Manrique's "Coplas por la Muerte de su Padre" — and also Lord Byron's translation of "La Perdida de Alhama," which he calls "A Very Mournful Ballad on the Siege and Con-

*Eleanor L. Turnbull, ed.: *Ten Centuries of Spanish Verse;* J. M. Cohen, ed.: *The Penguin Book of Spanish Verse.*

quest of Alhama" reasonably enough. And there are a number of other translators present, who have that strangely insistent tone of great enthusiasm and limited perception. Again, that is why I favor the workmanlike continuity of Cohen's prose notes. But an instance may make the point more clearly:

> ... *Como al partir del sol la sombra crece,*
> *y en cayendo su rayo levanta*
> *la negra escuridad que el mundo cubre,*
> *de do viene el temor que nos espanta* ...
> (Garcilaso de la Vega, from *"Egloga Primera"*)

> ... As when the sun departs the shadows grow and, as its rays sink, the black darkness rises to cover the world, whence comes the fear that strikes us...
> (Cohen)

> ... As at the set of sun the shades extend,
> And when its circle sinks, that dark obscure
> Rises to shroud the world, on which attend
> The images that set our hair on end...
> (Turnbull: Jeremiah H. Wiffen, translator)

Miss Turnbull would, I think, have been better advised to follow her own abilities; *Contemporary Spanish Poetry* (another of her anthologies, wherein she used translations of her own) seems to me a much happier example of her care and intelligence.

That done, there remains Spanish literature to be spoken of; and I feel as tentative here, as the usual American must. Both books are, in effect, a substantial offering of that literature, but I wonder how simply a reader will find their materials available, lacking much acquaintance with either literature or the peculiar characteristics of the national temper of which it is the form. It is true enough, as Cohen notes, that "For the majority, Spain is the country of a single prose masterpiece, *Don Quixote* . . ." For the American, we may add background instances of Spanish temper, such as Cortes, Coronado, et al., and of course Columbus (by Robert Graves' conjecture quite probably Spanish also, i.e., a Mallorquin from Soller, etc.). But then our orientation moves north. And although one may see bullfights in Nimes, Arles, and other French cities close to the Spanish border, there is no such acquaintance with Spanish form allowed in Texas.

So then the background for this literature is also a problem, and we are left here with what references we can manage, wherewith to take hold of this work. Granted writing comes from a *place*, and the complex of attitudes there to be found effectual, I would recommend as a primer William H. Prescott's *History of the Reign of Phillip the Second* (1855), simply because it conveys with all the singularities of 19th-century American intelligence, a world unequivocally *Spanish*, in a variety of relationships, both European (because this period was one in which Spain, contrary to usual position, was much involved in European politics) and Moorish (the opening chapters of Book V will place that relationship clearly in the reader's mind). What we have, in short, to manage is even the most minimal sense of what that "world" was — for ten centuries. Prescott will usefully let one look both backwards and forwards, and that is more to the point here than would be a work perhaps more modern or more accurate.

Continuing this sense of background, I would also cite a few *ideas*, more than actual references, which may have bearing. I don't know that we see, or can see, such areas "all of a sudden"; yet an idea, a perception of some aspect of that reality, can do much to help, no matter what questions of bias or opinion. For example, Stendhal comments on the Spanish character in his *A Life of Napoleon* as follows:

Ferocious yet generous at one and the same time; hospitable yet unrelenting; lazy yet tireless when on the move, burned by his sun and his superstitious beliefs, the Spaniard offers all the freakish characteristics of an irascible temperament carried to extreme.

Continuing:

The specific character of the priests is perhaps the main characteristic which divides Spain from the rest of Europe. The clergy in Spain is *resident*.

In her *Autobiography* Gertrude Stein writes:

She always says that americans can understand spaniards. That they are the only two western nations that can realise abstraction. That in americans it expresses itself by disembodiedness, in literature and machinery, in Spain by ritual so abstract that it does not connect itself with anything but ritual. . . . They have no close contact with the earth such as most europeans have. Their materialism is not the materialism of existence, of possession, it is the materialism of action and abstraction.

Ramón Sender calls the Spanish poet ("if he survives") the most civilized man in the world today. I note that Elie Faure in an introduction to a collection of Goya's etchings speaks of "a kind of equivocal atmosphere wavering between Catholic cruelty and life on the one hand, and Protestant hypocrisy and morals on the other . . ." It will be, then, by such apparently disrelated comment, often incisively personal, that our own reaction may be stimulated, to supply that contact on which these, or any poems, will be dependent.

There are many poets in the two collections, otherwise, who will enlarge anyone's concept of Spanish or, equally, of

world literature. Juan Ruiz, Jorge Manrique, Garcilaso de la
Vega, Fray Luis de León, Baltasar del Alcazar — to note only
those to the time of Shakespeare — are such men. Yet to say
it that way quickly falls into speciousness. It is better to
think of one poem. "Antonio Machado (1875-1939), a poet
of great and individual simplicity, sober and reflective, and
a great interpreter of the Castilian landscape. He defended
the Republic, and died on the French side of the Pyrenees
when its armies were defeated" (Cohen). This is one of his
poems:

Siesta

En memoria de Abel Martín

Mientras traza su curva el pez de fuego,
junto al ciprés, bajo el supremo añil,
y vuela en blanca piedra el niño ciego,
y en el olmo la copla de marfil
de la verde cigarra late y suena,
honremos al Señor
— la negra estampa de su mano buena —
que ha dictado el silencio en el clamor.

Al Dios de la distancia y de la ausencia,
del áncora en la mar, la plena mar . . .
Él nos libra del mundo — omnipresencia —,
nos abre senda para caminar.

Con la copa de sombra bien colmada,
con este nunca lleno corazón,
honremos al Señor que hizo la Nada
*y ha esculpido en la fe nuestra razón.**

---

*Whilst the fiery fish traces his arc beside the cypress, beneath the
tallest indigo-plant, and the blind boy disappears into white stone,

and in the elm the ivory verse of the green cicada beats and booms,
let us honour the Lord — the black trace of his kindly hand — who
has compelled silence among the clamour.

To the God of distances and absence, of the anchor in the sea, the
sea at high tide ... He frees us from the world, — he is omnipresent —
and opens us up a path to travel.

With cups overflowing with shadow and with this never filled heart,
let us honour the Lord who made Non-existence and sculpted our reason out of faith. (Cohen.)

[*Poetry,* December 1958]

Ways of Looking*

THERE ARE MANY THINGS to tell us the nature of the world in which we live. A pragmatic response to such nature, for example, would place the house where water is to be found, and would avoid, equally, the desert or whatever other situation might be supposed impossible. Our reference is this nature, and in our use of it we cite the nature of ourselves, the needs and suppositions which describe us as actual. Perhaps at last it is all a dream — as they say — some ultimate mistaking of purpose. That aside, in poems as elsewhere, a description is, like it or not, made use of, to speak of worlds and to live in them. Adaptations of form and of purpose follow as an outline, an acknowledgment of exterior presence.

Barriss Mills works between a part-time wish and (also hopeful) a rejection of an easy taking, of anything, so that his poems are, often, wryly wanting something he feels may not be had. An image of his father becomes:

> ... Remembering
> now my father and the begonias
> he could love and they, thirsty, silent
> accept unknowing his silent care.
>
> ("Remembering My Father and the Begonias")

*Barriss Mills: *Parvenus & Ancestors;* Carol Ely Harper, ed.: *Experiment Theatre Anthology No. 1;* Kenneth Koch: *Kô, or A Season on Earth;* Jack Kerouac: *Mexico City Blues;* Irving Layton: *A Red Carpet for the Sun;* Judson Crews: *The Heart in Naked Hunger* and *The Feel of Sun & Air upon Her Body.*

Is that given as the despair, or the triumph, of care; or is it habit, maintained to secure a continuity? The problem, as ever, is meaning — and relationship, as Iago elsewhere says:

> . . . I'll prick them
> till they've lived (and felt
> the world rush in upon them)
> a moment, before they die.
> ("Interlude: Iago Addresses the Audience")

Mills feels, I think, the nature of women as both a relief and a curious threat, or problem, of adaptation, in the ease of relationship suggested, not with men but with all that men fumble in, the world of things and intention:

> No man can feel it —
> the aplomb women are born to.
>
> ("Helen")

The poems in his book are often a happy balance of good humor and a wistful attention to discrepancies. They are small in the range of their attention, and seem even meant to be so, e.g., notes on the "classical" moon, Venus, *Everybody Cried at Our Wedding*, Pygmalion's "icy art," and money: "The money? nobody knew/by now where it had gone." In that sense they are occasional — or better, purpose described as provoked attention not so much lacking as falling beside a more deliberate sense of purpose.

Purpose itself, of course, may well be ridiculous, implying relationships where none may exist — so that no tunnels to China succeed. The *Experiment Theatre Anthology* fails partly in this sense. It is not so much that one rejects, just like that, "the *petit drame* or One-Minute Play" which the preface to this book describes, nor even the "arena theatre in every living-room." But to say that "We can develop a Shakespeare so in a hundred years . . ." strikes me as pretentiously overhopeful.

The plays themselves, insofar as they depend on poetry
for a means, seem garbled and cribbed, echoes of a high-
school "Shakespeare," who is all too present as it is. Bad
writing stays bad writing no matter what the occasion, and
it is a poor trick to attempt to blur that fact by removing it
all to a play:

> LEAH: Jacob, hear me now,
> For I am yours, as night has been our vow:
> You cannot love, I see, but give me room
> To lay my heart, and God will bless my womb.
>
> (Jacob Hofstädter")

Which is unfair, out of context, and there are many other
"tones" at work in the collection. For myself, however, there
is little of interest and/or it is a world so cutely begged
that it becomes offensive, the Living Room *qua* Ultimate
Refuge for pains quite real enough but never, I believe, to
be exorcised in this manner. Our world seems desperate
enough to make us want to turn all possible occasions to use.
But to say with the complacency of Carol Ely Harper, "We
have taught young poets, unfamiliar with playwriting, to
make the One-Minute Play from one's own poem, preferably
an unsuccessful one . . ." makes cosy what is not cosy, and
turns such art as her Shakespeare's into a harmless pastime.

It is this sort of easy reference (which the *Experiment
Theatre Anthology* implies) that Kenneth Koch lampoons
with a very gracious viciousness. It is a character of the
urbane to play upon discrepancies, and to leave the unify-
ing and observing intelligence — with final limits of sky
and ground and people thereon — as the only real term.
Koch's "epic," mocking and clever, marches upon all sorts
of things, the cliché of Great Baseball Teams (the Dodgers)
and of Great Events (the Coronation) among them. The
hero, or one of the heroes at least, is, rightly enough,

Japanese, and the progress of the story, so to speak, leaps about like a kid's flipping stations on a television set. The villain of it all is Dog Boss, whose farcical origins are much attached to a German shepherd, who had bitten his mother's seducer, etc., while all were living on a houseboat, etc.:

Dog Boss was there, a child of five; tears welling
In both his eyes, he ran to shore to farms
And cried for help, but none could understand him.
'Twas summer, blazing. Then a cool breeze fanned him,
And he saw at his side a German shepherd
With wagging tail, who understood! They hurried
To where the lust-crowned living-boat was tethered
And found the pair. The shepherd roared and buried
His teeth in Blickly's thigh, whose muscles severed.
From that day onward, sailing down the Surrey'd
Be nothing to the boy, without a dog;
Sheep could not substitute, nor could a hog.

Finally the whole thing comes to a fading end, because the problem with such work must be that it can, patently, go on forever. As can likewise the world which it reports, with such inventive humor. But laughter, like love, among the ruins seems a reasonable act. It doesn't change things, so to speak. It simply makes them entertaining.

If Koch's world depends upon a satiric response to a chaos of value, then Jack Kerouac's becomes a simplification of that chaos, familiar to us now in Zen teaching. For example:

> You start with the Teaching
>   Inscrutable of the Diamond
> And end with it, your goal
>   is your startingplace,
> No race was run, no walk
>   of prophetic toenails

Across Arabies of hot
meaning — you just
numbly don't get there.

(113th Chorus)

Kerouac's book is a series of improvisations, notes, a shorthand of perceptions and memories, having in large part the
same kind of word-play and rhythmic invention to be found
in his prose. It seems likely that much will exasperate because we are wary of that which does not make use of
familiar continuities. We like the "story" of usual thought,
and we are apt to distrust what so unembarrassedly wants
to throw that all away. But Kerouac says:

Like running a stick thru water
The use and effect
Of tellin people that
                their house
                is burning . . .

(126th Chorus)

So I write about heaven
Smoke for the scene,
Wanta bring everyone
Straight to the dream.

If you could only hold
        What you know
As you know it forever,
        instead-a
Moving from griefy to griefy,
        lament to lament,
Groan, and have to come out
        and smile once again . . .

(196th Chorus)

Perhaps the "big words" will be missed, or more, the manner which contains them — and the forms of wiseness and security which that manner of investment secures. It is not that simple to find a language whose emphases will be common perhaps. I mean that Kerouac may well distract and irritate more than he will teach. But the attempt is useful, with its clutch of old songs and childwise word-play, jogging the mind to a simplicity, making the old wiseness foolish, the old foolishness wise.

Irving Layton also distrusts the deceptive distances in manner which the more academic poet is apt to fall heir to, that remove from the terms (if not the situations) of a common existence with other men and women, in a common place. For example, in his preface to *A Red Carpet for the Sun* he makes very clear the position he has chosen for himself:

> ... What I've written — besides my joy in being alive to write about them — has been about this singular busi-ness of human evil; the tension between Hebrew and pagan, between the ideal and the real. The disorder and glory of passion. The modern tragedy of the depersonal-ization of men and women. About a hideously com-mercial civilization spawning hideously deformed mon-strosities.

With that intent there can be little misunderstanding of his commitment, and the poems themselves (here happily collected into one substantial volume from twelve others which came before it) make clear the range possible to this kind of sincerity. Layton is, all at once, the most tender of men, and the most purposefully satiric. He uses the pro-vincialism of his situation (Canada) to keep himself awake to the alternatives, and, being a Jew, he holds to a tradition of intelligence and compassion. Most simply, he writes in this way:

The Madonna of the Magnificat

I shall wander all night and not see
    as much happiness as this infant gives
to his plain sisters who are adoring him
and his mother cradling and covering
    him with her love.

She has borrowed the white moon from the sky
    to pillow his golden curls
and at her magical cry the dark roofs
the length of the street lie down
    like quiet animals.

The night will wear out and disappear
    like soiled water through the city's drains
but now it is full of noise and blessed neighbours
and all the tenement windows fly open
    the birds.

A world so made possible (in the mind of a man who will not give in to its pain) must be true beyond all contradiction.

What to say, then, of all those other worlds, equally the intelligences (or lack thereof) which have created them? It becomes less and less a "world" one may witness as an "objective" phenomenon. Nor does this seem a recent problem if Wyndham Lewis can write in 1927, "The material world that the human intellect has created is still there, of course; but as it is a creation of our minds, it will no doubt be found that we can even physically disintegrate it." That we can now do without question. Yet that hardly proves a relief.

Judson Crews has, for some time now, lived outside of the common areas of recognition, surviving by his persistence and by, as well, the respect those who have read his

work with care have come to give. He asks for nothing and
lives sparely in his work, a place for survival, where the
test of a life is that which is possible in it, terrors of image,
dream sensualities, hard thought, all given place. The twists
of language (which his titles most quickly describe, e.g.,
"Sated in Lucid Devine," "Bale Thaw") define this same
character of test, of meaning, curiously, of statement against
statement, word against word. The problem of meaning itself is defined by him in this way:

Of the Self Exceeded

The page itself was part of the meaning
and the man reading was part

The sky above is part of the meaning
and the bird drifting like a feather

Because the page is as perfect as meaning
and the sky is as perfect as air

The mind is startled in face of perfection
it hides from the limitless air

The bird is perfection of air, of air
but the mind is lost short of meaning

Both books (*The Heart in Naked Hunger, The Feel of
Sun & Air upon Her Body*) have this hardihood of thought;
and both as well use the device of occasional photographs,
of nudes, of flat building fronts, of many untoward things,
let us say, to shock the mind awake with a somewhat wry
invitation.

I find my own relief in such "worlds" as Crews and Layton
have worked to make actual, admitting that such a feeling
is a feeling — yet either man is openly concerned to make
a way common to all, despite the seeming difficulty of
Crews' images at times or Layton's insistence on values
which must (fairly enough) discriminate. It is the size of
the area involved by them which proves distinctive, and it

is not that they make a world apart from that given me —
which could only prove a competition. In one sense, we are
all "nature" poets these days, and whoever can show a
nature of world still possible, to men as well as "me," ought
to be commended.

[*Poetry*, June 1961]

The Fascinating Bore*

EARLY IN HIS book *The White Goddess*, Robert Graves provides this description:

> The Goddess is a lovely, slender woman with a hooked nose, deathly pale face, lips as red as rowan-berries, startlingly blue eyes and long fair hair; she will suddenly transform herself into sow, mare, bitch, vixen, she-ass, weasel, serpent, owl, she-wolf, tigress, mermaid or loathsome hag . . .

He continues, "The test of a poet's vision, one might say, is the accuracy of his portrayal of the White Goddess and of the island over which she rules. . . ."

This same figure is made use of in Mario Praz's study, *The Romantic Agony*, as a characteristic presence in Romantic literature, and it is in the work of Swinburne he believes "this type of Fatal Woman found its most complete form." Unlike Graves, however, who is himself involved in this same tradition, Praz depends much upon the sexual terms of such reference in Swinburne and the other writers with whom he deals. The question of Swinburne's algolagnia — the association of sexual fulfillment with pain — is the key to Praz's own use of the work itself. For example, he summarizes Swinburne's "formula" as follows:

*Swinburne: *Poems,* selected, with an introduction, by Bonamy Dobrée; Swinburne: *A Selection,* edited, with an introduction, by Edith Sitwell.

... man, in his work, aspires to be 'the powerless victim of the furious rage of a beautiful woman [here quoting from Swinburne's *The Whippingham Papers*]'; his attitude is passive, his love a martyrdom, his pleasure pain. As for the woman ... , she is always the same type of unrestrained, imperious, cruel beauty.

Whether or not such emphasis proves fair at last, it makes unequivocally clear the source of energy in Swinburne's early, and I think greatest, work. He himself, in the curious innocence of his nature, found it impossible to accept finally — or he could not use it as could Baudelaire, for whom he felt great admiration. In her introduction to *Swinburne: A Selection,* Edith Sitwell quotes from a letter of Swinburne's to his friend and mentor, Lady Trevelyan, who had warned him he was being attacked "on the score of his personal morality":

I cannot express the horror and astonishment, the unutterable indignation and loathing, with which I have been struck on hearing that anyone could be vile enough to tax me, I do not say with doing, but with saying anything of the kind to which you refer. ...

It does not seem to me possible to answer as simply as does Edith Sitwell, "I cannot believe this extremely brave man was a hypocrite." Nor does it seem otherwise possible to settle the question as does Bonamy Dobrée, the other editor here involved:

One need not close one's eyes to these things in Swinburne; indeed to do so would be foolish. Most men and women have in them vestiges of such destructive impulses, which normal beings turn into more beneficent channels, or suppress, but which Swinburne had no wish to hide. Such things need not concern the reader who seeks in poetry for imaginative release, for support

of the more directive energies, for relations he can
contemplate and ramify; they belong, rather, to the
realm of psychiatry, and, so far as this Introduction is
concerned, will be left there.

It is a little ironic that Swinburne found just that "imaginative release" and the "support of the more directive energies" which Dobrée notes in the writing of the very poems
which raise these questions. And there the reader must follow him, or else lose contact with all that ambivalence of
experience for which the poems serve as means. Had it not
been for the complexity of Swinburne's sexual nature, his
work would be only a thin exercise of technical virtuosity
few in fact have so acquired, yet which, by itself, serves
little. It was his genius that in these poems he could so resolve, with such art as he had, "such destructive impulses."

Even in Swinburne's sense of liberty, "what his poetry
sings out loudly," as Dobrée puts it, there is much equally
equivocal. Those familiar with the writings of de Sade —
"that illustrious and ill-requited benefactor of humanity,"
Swinburne calls him in a letter to Monckton Milnes — will
recognize the basis for Swinburne's own antitheism. For
example, here is a brief instance of de Sade's argument in
Dialogue entre un Prête et un Moribond.

PRIEST: Who can comprehend the vast and infinite de-
signs of God upon man, and who can understand all we
see?

DYING MAN: The man who simplifies things, my friend,
and especially the man who does not increase the causes
the better to muddle the effects. What do you want with
a second difficulty when you cannot explain the first?
And since it is possible that Nature quite unaided has
done all that you attribute to your God, why do you
want to look for a master for her?

Swinburne makes use of a like argument in "Hymn to Proserpine":

Wilt thou take all, Galilean? but these thou shalt not take,
The laurel, the palms and the paean, the breasts of the
[nymphs in the brake;
Breasts more soft than a dove's, that tremble with tenderer
[breath;
And all the wings of the Loves, and all the joy before
[death . . .
More than these wilt thou give, things fairer than all
[these things?
O daughter of earth, of my mother, her crown and blos-
[som of birth,

        ❀   ❀   ❀

I am also, I also, thy brother; I go as I came unto earth.

Atalanta in Calydon, described by Edith Sitwell as "indisputably Swinburne's greatest work," was also his first published book. Our knowledge of it is now usually confined to the choruses, "When the hounds of spring are on winter's traces . . . ," and "Before the beginning of years . . . ," and perhaps others like these. We cannot read it as the great release from Victorian limits it then seemed. Although Browning, with some acuracy, felt it a "fuzz of words," Ruskin thought it, symptomatically enough, "The grandest thing ever done by a youth, though he is a demonic youth . . ." The play is, whatever else, a beautifully maintained control of means upon a classical theme, of no great depth of thinking — on Swinburne's part at least, since de Sade is again the clue to its logic of argument. But if sounds alone can engage us — and Edith Sitwell provides much provocative comment on this score — then we should be satisfied with this:

And I too as thou sayest have seen great things;
Seen otherwhere, but chiefly when the sail

First caught between stretched ropes the roaring west,
And all our oars smote eastward, and the wind
First flung round faces of seafaring men
White splendid snow-flakes of the sundering foam,
And the first furrow in virginal green sea
Followed the plunging ploughshare of hewn pine . . .

Yet the most incisive of Swinburne's poems remain those
in which he underwent the "test of a poet's vision," in
Graves' sense — or when his concern with the terms of his
algolagnia is unmistakable, as here:

As one who hidden in deep sedge and reeds
Smells the rare scent made where a panther feeds,
   And tracking ever slotwise the warm smell
Is snapped upon by the sweet mouth and bleeds,

His head far down the hot sweet throat of her —
So one tracks love, whose breath is deadlier . . .

("Laus Veneris")

The major part of Edith Sitwell's selection comes from
Poems and Ballads (1866), and includes the whole of *Atalanta in Calydon* (1865). Dobrée ranges more out of necessity, since the Penguin selection intends to represent the
whole body of Swinburne's writing. After Swinburne's
"rescue" by Watts-Dunton (with whom he shared a house-
hold for the thirty years until his death in 1909), there is
little of interest in his poems. Perhaps it was the confinement from his excesses that quieted his earlier energy. It
was Watts-Dunton's assertion that, "From this moment
(1879) Swinburne's connection with Bohemian London
ceased entirely." But much had in fairness stopped before
that, it would seem. *Songs Before Sunrise* (1871), written in
hero-worship of the Italian political exile, Mazzini, shows
increased diffuseness and verbosity despite the occasional
interest of a poem like "Hertha" or "Hymn of Man." Still

both these last become a tedium of accumulation and patterned manner. The intensity is gone.

It is doubtful to me that Swinburne can now be of much use to us. We have come, or have tried to, so far from the manners of that period, moving toward (as Grierson notes in his monograph on Swinburne) an increased use of spoken rhythms. This is why, perhaps, Swinburne's poems must seem so interminably artificial a contrivance so very often. Or perhaps it is, as Robert Duncan suggests, that Swinburne's "pleasurable pain/painful pleasure specialty may have something to do with his aesthetic in the actual poem — going on almost unbearably as he does. The fascinating bore in discourse is a sadist in that way."

[*Poetry*, August 1962]

"Think what's got away..." *

ONE TENDS TO value any kind of statement for what one can take from it as a content, or a state of feeling some way about something, a viable association between what the statement has "said" and what terms of response it can gain in who hears it. We learn young that the way in which some thing is said, the tone of voice, the literal words used, and all the relations implied in the context of their use — all these say "things" too. It is equally a commonplace that in a poem such content may have, finally, a greater value for the reader than the literal facts the poem is otherwise making clear.

The work of Brother Antoninus begins, first of all, with a very emphatic content, characterized by him as follows: "A poem, like a dream, is a 'whole' to the extent that it registers the mystery of the psychic complex which produced it." *The Hazards of Holiness* is a collection of specific tests, of "scalps torn dripping from the skulls of interior adversaries," which last way of speaking will not outrage those who are willing to admit that a "Dark Night of the Soul" may exist for a man who attempts to find himself in relation to God. Again as Brother Antoninus says, "These are the

*Brother Antoninus: *The Hazards of Holiness;* William Stafford: *Traveling through the Dark;* Anthony Ostroff: *Imperatives;* Robert Sward: *Uncle Dog;* Richard Emil Braun: *Children Passing;* Frederic Will: *A Wedge of Words;* Raymond Souster: *A Local Pride;* Charles Bukowski: *Run with the Hunted;* Thomas McGrath: *Letter to an Imaginary Friend;* Lorine Niedecker: *My Friend Tree.*

terrible wrestlings his verse begins to register; and this is the
harrowing ambiguity, so fraught with terror and mystery
and meaning, that cross-riddles this demon-haunted realm."

Such a way of speaking will have, of course, an immediate
impact, and it will either be one of respect and sympathy
for the man who has so endured, to speak, or it will be perhaps a questioning of such an invention of agony in a world
so substantially tormented. Either response will here depend on the reader's own relation to the literal facts dealt
with, the faith in God which is the issue. But, in either case,
there can be without such question a simple response to
the ways the words are working, as here:

> Christ-cut: the cedar
> Bleeds where I gashed it.
>
> Lance-wound under the narrow rib.
>
> Eve's orifice: the agony of Abel
> Enacted out on the Tree.
>
> Blood gushed
> From the gash . . .

The heavy, harshly stressed alliteration is sign of the
intent, and it is, at times, a rhetoric that is present apart from
demands of specific content; I find this most the case, for
example, in the more dramatic poems, as "Saints" and the
two parts of the title poem. I do not like — and it is my taste
which qualifies: "Herodias, that corrosive female wrath, /
Black grasp of the invidious breed, / Blanched, swore
blooded reprisal . . ." But I cannot avoid nor deny the force
of this language, despite my own characterization of it as
often melodramatic, that is, an enlargement of occasion
purely willed. What the poems effect is a language, itself a
formality, a distinct way of engaging feeling, a testing of
tones of response and recognition. They speak in one voice

because their occasion — despite the variation of subject —
is always the same, the search for substantial faith.

The poems of William Stafford are, in some contrast, much
quieter in tone. But, despite the frequent colloquialisms, an
equally conscious rhetoric seems to me at work. For example, it is present I think in this kind of balance of manners:
"no acrobat of salvation, / I couldn't help seeing...." Stafford familiarizes his reality, makes it often subject to a "we,"
generalizing in that way the personal insight. The primary
tones of his work are those of nostalgia, of a wry wit, often,
which can make peace with the complexities of times and
places. He says "that some kind of organization / is the
right way to live." The danger is simply that things will become cozy ("The earth says have a place.."), and that each
thing will be humanized to an impression of it merely.
When the irony can outwit this tendency, then an active
intelligence comes clear. In the following poem I am put
off by the personifications of the first verse, but, in fairness,
they do underline what becomes the point of the second:

Found in a Storm

A storm that needed a mountain
met it where we were:
we woke up in a gale
that was reasoning with our tent,
and all the persuaded snow
streaked along, guessing the ground.

We turned from that curtain, down.
But sometime we will turn
back to the curtain and go
by plan through an unplanned storm,
disappearing into the cold,
meanings in search of a world.

Formalization of intelligence, or whatever to call it —
that is, the manner which wants to invest subject with its
own wit before there is any subject — can become a great
problem. At present there seems still a "style of the period"
which got its authority from the work of the New Critics,
and which still lingers, heavily, dspite the fact that it grows
increasingly out of fashion. All fashion is a distraction, and
perhaps old modes, in this respect, are really more pleasant
than new ones. But I must object, just that I lived through
it, to the manner in which Anthony Ostroff writes. Here is
the first poem in his book:

> *Matinal: The Stockyards*
>
> Wooly wooly
>
> The bright brick shines
>
> The sheep's feet peck there
> All in a line
>
> And lines in lines
> Moves out on the wet
>
> Brick in the light
>
> The sheep forget

This is not the primary tone of the book, or, rather, the
way in which the poems are usually organized or directed.
The book is really a collection of literary manners, exercises,
in conventional styles of our day. There is a "Dirge" ("Where
are the lips, the breast, the thigh / That were such poetry . . .") a "Folk Song" ("Sing deathily, deathily, deathily
sing./The crops are to seed and the seeds are rotting . . ."),
and other usual visits to the country, elegies, "littlest sister,"
and so on. The technical means seem competent, although
stiffly present — again, the will "to write" "a poem" is dominant. And the intelligence is so battered in the process of

getting it all, just so, together, that very little otherwise gets said. It is taste, as ever, balking, but I cannot react any longer to tricks like this one: "The library thinks of itself I think ..." I question that anyone is thinking at all.

Problems coming in pairs, Robert Sward joins Anthony Ostroff to drive the point home. What are literary "manners" and how can we be rid of them, so that poetry can become again an active investment of all the range of language and all the reality which can be found there? Sward's humor is a good sign, but why destroy the poem with banality:

> Hello wife, hello world, hello God,
> I love you; hello certain monsters ...

And why insist, so often, that the range of experience dealt with has to be an itsy-bitsy business of tiny tots and their ironic elders? The assumption that all childhood memories — or these curious recollections that now pass as such — are intrinsically valuable baffles me. In Sward's book there are also letters to a psychiatrist, take-offs on advertisements, odd animals (and again I wish these could be let rest), and other arch inventions. I like best those poems in which he does invent, wildly and wittily ("Beach Scenes — and Other Scenes" for one), but here also the wiseguy manner grows tiresome.

It is curious, if terrifying, to see how deeply a literary manner can cut into resources that must, at some level, be holding the whole unwieldy coherence together. Richard Emil Braun has a complicated and interesting mind, but he wants to say everything in one breath, not so much grandly as conclusively:

> The bodies of the children
> whose characters I am hired to strengthen are grotesque:
> faces eruptive, extremities
> disproportionate, voices stridulous.

The ensemble, ugly with cruel, abrupt
    asynchronous growth cripples their minds
which I am paid to fortify by means of Caesar ...

And I can sympathize with what's going on in his head,
so to speak, having taught Latin to such children in the
southwest. But what happens, then, to the poem — is what I
question. I am not, I hope, being sentimental. In any case,
he tends to "subjectivize" the poem's content to that point
where no possibility of what's outside him remains volatile,
free in its own term, even when he "speaks" in the guise of
the several voices he chooses, as in "Late Promenades."

When the literal thought of the poem has energy, then
a sharper gauge of means seems to occur. There is not that
working up of a subject so dulling in Ostroff, or so glib in
Sward. Frederic Will writes in a traditionally developed
manner, but he feels perceptions in a poem specifically:

Across the Street

Those berries on fire from fire:
I shall repair
Losses of passion here.

Memling would have held the instant
Sure in a cardinal's hat
Taking it down in sight.

I am less sure.
What will not cool from the word,
Ashed in the very instant?
Lost, when heard?

The last line gives pause, certainly, for reflection. I wish
something freer, quicker, might have been found for the
statement of the second two lines; Memling is also a distraction, though that is clearly my opinion. I don't like the
"Ashed ..." in the next to the last line. But the poem is in-

teresting, it says something beyond a manner; and no
matter what I may cavil at, I hear it.

In a like sense one hears this poem by Raymond Souster:

Morning Certainly

Coming back from away out, a darkness,
there is light at the window
my clothes are on the chair, as if waiting,
there is even
someone in bed with me.

After so much self-consciousness and preening, I like the
flatness, the very openness of this language. It is simply
said, but I had never thought of it that way, and I am left,
quietly, with the perception.

But it isn't all that quickly an issue of a volcabulary because Charles Bukowski uses very open speech, and common
sentiments and references. But not the same thing comes of
it; ". . . hooray say the roses, today is blamesday / and we are
red as blood . . ." does not think in the way that Souster's
poem thinks. Souster also at times drops to a level of response
that he knows too well, feels even too comfortably, despite
the pain of the reference. The starved, the poor, the bewildered, the dragged, sullen reality of usual life does not
want, nor not want, to be a poem. The work is still to be
done.

Even a life is no continuity, it happens here and there,
now — then it was or will be. *Letter to an Imaginary World*
by Thomas McGrath is very moving in the world it makes
tangible in its opening sections, the harsh farm world of a
young boy:

. . . I couldn't quit. I came out of sleep at four
Dazed and dreaming and ate my food on the run,
And ran to the barn . . .

Then it tends to become programmatic, crossed by defined
purposes, as are even the terms of love it meets with early
Approximations of reality take the place of literal orders,
or, more fairly, the reader is given attitudes rather than
precise contexts: "Now in the chill streets/I hear the
hunting, and the long thunder of money. . . .'"

How can such life be told? In his introduction to Lorine
Niedecker's *My Friend Tree* Edward Dorn makes a useful
comment: "What is in will come out, it does not always work
the other way. . . ." And he ends by saying: "I like these
poems because first they attach an undistractable clarity to
the word, and then because they are unabashed enough to
weld that word to a freely sought, beautifully random instance — that instance being the only thing place and its
content can be. . . ." I cannot believe that there is anything,
finally, to be proven. All we see, we see. By nature, then, and
of course unfairly, I will stick with Miss Niedecker, who
writes:

> Remember my little granite pail?
> The handle of it was blue.
> Think what's got away in my life!
> Was enough to carry me thru.

> > [*Poetry*, April 1963]

More on Kearns

DEAR WEBB:

I dislike, finally, explaining another man's explanation, particularly one that seems to me as basically clear as Lionel Kearns'. What he's trying to do — in my mind — is break up the visual reference of lines on a page, etc., and to get on with some sense of *beat* or stress (the analogy is the same reference in music) that will find an order for the poem's formal organization consequent to the poem's literal character as an *utterance,* i.e., a unit of speech. In conversation recently Duncan was remarking the comment of linguists, that American tends to organize itself in 'clusters,' one beat given to each such grouping, etc. At that same time David Bromige (also from Vancouver as it happens, but now in Berkeley) called our attention to a letter from Williams to Eberhart, in the former's *Selected Letters,* p. 325, dated May 23, 1954. It is well worth reading, in relation to Kearns' sense of notation, e.g., "Count a single beat to each [line]. You may not agree with my ear, but that is the way I count the line . . ." What Kearns has done, is to indicate the position of that 'beat' in its relation to the line unit. I hope no one will be distracted by the visual appearance of that line running vertically through the poems — it is, to my mind, simply there to indicate the regularity of interval, and to show, visually, how the 'notes' or syllables of the line may occur in relation to it.

Now no one can be 'helped' completely. Kearns' seriousness and his care with this question are not to be misled

with any false issue of a 'school' or the usual hogwash
attending something 'new.' As he himself can make clear,
this recognition he's documented and used in the presen-
tation of these poems has been managed by a variety of
poets at a variety of times — for the reason that, the speech
we have so argues, etc. So, again, I don't want to 'help'
anyone understand Kearns' premise more than to say what
I have. And/or I wish everyone might be, at last, as deliberately conscious on their own time as he has been on
his. My best to you —

ROBERT CREELEY

[*Outsider*, No. 3, 1963]

Frederick Eckman: The Epistemology of Loss

THE TITLE of this book gives an accurate sense of its content, and, as well, the manner of its feeling. It is an "epistemology" wryly considered, for the most part, and also one which moves from the feeling of knowing something to the ironic situation here of what is known, and how it is known — and finally, to that sense of 'what for,' which provokes the rhetoric of:

>   ... Mother of silences,
> Invoke the blind rosebush below, whose round
> And scarlet sounds ring fence-notes heaven-high,
> That is the singing echo of swift wings
> We choke not, chance not, fling not away
> Our leaf and passport through this atmosphere;
> But glide in cloudy echelon of rose,
> Beyond the heat-streaked doppelgänger Now...
>   (from "July: A Devotional")

It is an actual nightmare which is felt, unrelieved, or if at all so, then simply as that 'relief' the intelligence may suppose when it has reduced the person it inhabits to something "Cold with terror, rigid as a beast/held in some pit or trap . . ." There is a persistent sense of an animal rage, and bafflement — a frustrated physical anger that wants to strike out against that which has hurt it. But there is also the continuingly ironic emphasis on the uselessness of such acts — as here, in a poem called "Hurry, Hurry":

271

> Say: "Heart is a black stallion,
> evil as midnight. His eyes
> glint fire, his hooves can murder.
> He thunders across the world."
> Say & say. Meanwhile the heart
> spurts out its fury, embers
> to cold ash, calmly nibbles
> gray grass in a gray meadow.

The book has, however, another way of speaking to my own mind even more moving — in which a quiet is left to "say" more than does the violence of what I have quoted. It is not simply that this tone is more malleable, or that it lets the reader develop his own assumptions — but that it comes so directly from what it involves, a literal pain which can only say what it literally feels. "Omega":

> What is there
> to be said
> when everything
> has been said?
> *Words? Words*
> *are nothing!*
> This from you
> in another spring,
> & once more the
> flowering Judas
> betrays us, o the
> sprawling wisteria
> purples across our
> crumbling wall.
> The flowers, they
> too will decay.
> No, you are not
> right, but neither
> (o my lost love!)
> are you wrong.

If — as Pound once wrote — "Nothing counts but the quality of the emotion . . . ," one has in this poem a measure of that possibility.

[*Elizabeth*, March 1965]

Five

Waiting for Godot

WAITING FOR ANYONE is a usual problem these days, particularly in America. It is, for one example, the army's, "Hurry up and wait." Or when will you be through with the bathroom. Or when — anything.

But to deal with this, as one says, in a play is not at all simple. Granted the obvious difficulty of having nothing happen, in fact of having nothing happen what happens — how not to release the audience just by that, i.e., how far can one go with this? A friend tells me of a problem she had been given as a dancer, wherein she was to effect movements which would, in turn, effect an intolerable boredom. First the audience would shift a bit, then writhe more openly, until, at last, something would snap. And that would be the point.

It's point enough, frankly. As it is, we live on the edge of it all too often, and one can say that Beckett is aware of this — of a deep, deep pointlessness, which maims people far more than they are willing to acknowledge. Certainly far more than they are able to repair. His play, then, is an abstraction of this awareness. Two men, indiscriminate, waiting for a third, who will prove something not only for them, but equally of them. It will effect something. Otherwise they have been there for they are by no means sure how long. Other things happen — activity of a kind — but what does this mean?

VLADIMIR: We can still part, if you think it would be
    better.
ESTRAGON: It's not worth while now.
    Silence
VLADIMIR: No, it's not worth while now.
    Silence
ESTRAGON: Well, shall we go?
VLADIMIR: Yes, let's go.
    They do not move.
        Curtain

There are three other 'characters' in the play (Lucky, a
liberal slave; Pozzo, the landowner who 'owns' him; and A
Boy, the absent Godot's perpetual messenger), but they are
frosting of a kind. And literally enough, the play is that
which I have just quoted. Some parts are better than other
parts but they are all the same thing. It is a play of 'the
same thing,' taken as far as Beckett has thought practicable.

It's here, in this question of practicability, that one can, I
think, argue at least the obvious difficulties. One is, for
example, how effect variations upon this *monotony*, which
will appear to relieve it, but which will, in fact, only contribute to it. It is the particular tightrope on which the play
must balance. To let this monotony slack — that's no good;
but without some relief, the man watching (remembering
that he has both chosen and paid to watch) shudders and
leaves. So Beckett chooses to make it a 'ballet' of sorts, by
which I mean, a very formal and mannered interplay.

ESTRAGON: A relaxation.
VLADIMIR: A recreation.
ESTRAGON: A relaxation.
VLADIMIR: Try.
ESTRAGON: You'll help me?
VLADIMIR: I will of course.

ESTRAGON: We don't manage too badly, eh Didi, be-
    tween the two of us?
VLADIMIR: Yes, yes. Come on, we'll try the left first.
ESTRAGON: We always find something, eh Didi, to give
    us the impression we exist?

But it stays a *spectacle* — and that in itself is too much a
relief from it. I think Beckett has, finally, solved the dilemma
elsewhere, i.e., in a story called "The End" (printed in
Merlin, Vol. II, No. 3). The hero of this is an old man from
anywhere one cares to think of, for him. Let out of a hospital,
sanatorium, or whatever, he begins to stagger. "I am greatly
obliged to you for these clothes, I said, and for this money,
is there a law which prevents you from throwing me out
naked and penniless?" He turns to begging. "There are those
to be sure, who stoop, but generally speaking, people who
give alms much prefer to do so without having to stoop.
What they prefer above all is to espy the wretch from afar,
get ready their penny, drop it in their stride, with an innocent air, and hear the God bless you dying in the distance.
Personally, I never said that, nor anything like it, but I did
make a noise with my mouth. So I got a kind of board, and
tied it to my neck and waist. It jutted out just at the right
height, pocket height, and is edge was far enough from my
person for the mite to be bestowed without fear of con-
tagion."

One day I was present at a strange scene. Normally I
did not see much. I did not hear much either. But on
this particular day the intrusion was too marked. For
some time I had thought I heard an unwonted sound.
I did not investigate the cause. For I said to myself, It's
going to stop. But as it did not stop I had no choice but
to find out the cause, and so be rid of it. Its cause was a
man perched on the roof of a car, haranguing the
passers-by, of whom many stopped, the better to see

and hear. That at least was the way I looked at it. He
was bellowing so loud that snatches of his oration
reached my ears: injustice ... union ... brothers ...
Marx ... capital ... bread ... love ... right to live. It
was all Greek to me. The car was drawn up against the
curb, just in front of me, and I saw the orator, from behind. All of a sudden he turned around towards me, as
to a specimen. Look at this down and out, he vocifer-
ated, this leftover. If he doesn't go down on four paws,
it's for fear of being impounded. Old, lousy, rotten, in
the garbage heap. And there are a thousand like him,
worse than him, ten thousand, twenty thousand. A
voice. Thirty thousand. In your plutocratic Sodom, resumed the orator, every day of your life you pass them
by, and when you have won at the races you fling them
a farthing. Do you ever think? The voice, No. No, indeed, resumed the orator, you find that normal, the
way of the world. A penny, tuppence. The voice.
Thruppence. It never enters your head, resumed the
orator, that your charity is a crime, that you are sub-
scribing to enslavement, stultification and organized
murder. Take a good look at this living corpse. You
may tell me it's his own fault. The voice, After you.
Then he bent down towards me and flung me a phrase
I did not understand. I had perfected my board. It
now consisted of two boards hinged together, which
enabled me, when my work was done, to fold it and
carry it under my arm. So I took off the rag, as I always
did when my work was done, pocketed the few coins
remaining on the board, untied the board, folded it and
put it under my arm. Do you hear me, you crucified
bastard! the orator cried. Then I went away, although
it was still light ...

[*Black Mountain Review*, Winter 1954]

D. H. Lawrence:
Studies in Classic American Literature

It's AN ODD FEELING now to read a book like Cooper's *Deer-slayer*. There is hardly much left of that place, and I won-der how far one would have to look, in the United States, to find timber still standing in its first growth. It must have been a fantastic world. We are, of course, the heirs to it.

So Lawrence says: "... it seems to me that the things in Cooper that make one so savage, when one compares them with actuality, are perhaps, when one considers them as presentations of a deep subjective desire, real in their way, and almost prophetic." Beyond the prose, heavy as it now seems, a man like Natty Bumppo is familiar enough: "This is Natty, the white forerunner. A killer."

Cooper was one root, or evidence, of the 'classic' Ameri-can literature which Lawrence, and few others, had eyes to see. Even a present reclamation of Hawthorne will not judge, clearly enough, that the "prettiest of all sensations [is] the sensation of UNDERSTANDING."

> *The Scarlet Letter* gives the show away.
> You have the pure-pure young parson Dimmesdale.
> You have the beautiful Puritan Hester at his feet.
> And the first thing she does is to seduce him.
> And the first thing he does is to be seduced.
> And the second thing they do is to hug their sin in
> secret, and gloat over it, and try to understand.
> Which is the myth of New England.

Deerslayer refused to be seduced by Judith Hutter. At least the Sodom apple of sin didn't fetch him.

But Dimmesdale was seduced gloatingly. O, luscious Sin! He was such a pure young man. That he had to make a fool of purity. The American psyche.

For Lawrence *The Scarlet Letter* was ". . . perhaps, the most colossal satire ever penned." It is not a comfortable implication for any of us, but there it is.

You have the pure-pure young parson Dimmesdale. You have the beautiful Puritan Hester at his feet.

Not one of Lawrence's implications can give us very much peace, if that, in fact, is what we are after. The "great grey poet" (and/or Whitman) is given the roughest ride ever accorded him. And yet it is incredibly right, all of it. The "I AM HE THAT ACHES WITH AMOROUS LOVE . . ." is a bore of immense proportions — or no one ever indulged himself so emphatically at such length. But Crane's Whitman is also seen, again clearly, without innuendo or tenuousness: "Now Whitman was a great moralist. He was a great leader. He was a great changer of the blood in the veins of men." That is fact.

And Franklin: "Benjamin had no concern, really, with the immortal soul. He was too busy with social man." Crevecoeur: "NATURE. I wish I could write it larger than that N A T U R E."

Franklin is the real practical prototype of the American. Crevecoeur is the emotional. To the European, the American is first and foremost a dollar fiend. We tend to forget the emotional heritage of Hector St. John de Crevecoeur. We tend to disbelieve, for example, in Woodrow Wilson's wrung heart and wet hanky. Yet surely these are real enough. Aren't they?

At a time when so much 'revaluation' and 'revisiting' are the practice, Lawrence can serve the very actual function of showing how it might be done. We have valued, foolishly, the perspective of time alone. And lost the very thing we claim to have gained, namely, understanding of *any* of these men Lawrence cites for a classic American literature. For one example, Melville. God knows there has been enough talk around and about him to satisfy any of his admirers. But — how many come up with such a simple statement as this: "Meville knew. He knew his race was doomed. His white soul, doomed. His great white epoch, doomed. Himself, doomed. The idealist, doomed. The spirit, doomed."

To have a literature Lawrence adjudged it necessary to have a soul. And so we have laughed at him — how funny. How funny is it now?

"The old American literature. Franklin, Cooper, Hawthorne & Co.? All that mass of words! all so unreal!" cries the live American.

Heaven knows what we mean by reality.

[*Origin*, Summer 1954]

"By God, Pomeroy, you here!"
A NOTE ON FRANCIS PARKMAN

THE PROBLEM OF 'history' is a peculiar one for the American, involving as it does, "where do we come from," or better, how shall we come from where we came. It is just that apparently nonsensical statement of the dilemma, which may relieve it. And there are other clues, if you will, like: skyscrapers could not have been built if it weren't for the Indians, since they are the only men in America having the nerve-set for balance at such heights. Too, what would the United States be like, if it had a king? To relieve the President for actually administrative duties, as opposed to egg-rolling, etc.

It all relates, like it or not, to a backdoor which stays shut for us, faced as we are with no past which we will recognize but that of Europe. This we will not accept, and turn in upon ourselves, to be 'better' — which is a horror, in its effects, a kind of restless continual battle to override the English, or the French, or whoever it may be we choose for the moment as our predecessors.

Parkman, Edward Dahlberg has said, had the mind of a twelve-year-old child; and *The Oregon Trail,* for him, reads like any Rover Boys story. We are so grown-up, it seems, that stories have lost all point, and in our maturity, anecdote, that which stays in the mouth and heart — however 'romantically' — is a trivial way of passing time, of killing it. Dahlberg himself is by no means so quick about these things, and has used such material with sometimes admirable ingenuity. He is as concerned as any man, to find a place to live in. In any case, it comes to, where can we begin, and Parkman, I think, is our only 'historian' in the deep tradition of the tongue.

But all that can stay beside the point for the moment. Francis Parkman's *Works* (in twelve volumes) are as follows: *Pioneers of France in the New World, The Jesuits in North America, La Salle and the Discovery of the Great West, The Old Regime in Canada, Count Frontenac and New France under Louis XIV, A Half Century of Conflict, Montcalm and Wolfe, The Conspiracy of Pontiac and the Indian War after the Conquest of Canada,* and *The Oregon Trail.* The first book in the series has this for a dedication:

> To The Memory
> Of
> THEODORE PARKMAN, ROBERT GOULD SHAW, And HENRY
> WARE HALL
> Slain In Battle
> This Volume Is Dedicated By Their Kinsman
> The Author

You may take that as the *tone,* the ground-sense, of all Parkman's writings, not in point of the 'battle' so much as the 'kin.' Parkman was a New Englander, he wrote roughly between the dates, 1847-1892. and in his Preface to *A Half Century of Conflict* he says:

> This book ... fills the gap between Part V., "Count Frontenac," and Part VII., "Montcalm and Wolfe": so that the series now forms a continuous history of the efforts of France to occupy and control this continent ...
> The collection was begun forty-five years ago, and its formation has been exceedingly slow, having been re-

tarded by difficulties which seemed insurmountable,* and for years were so in fact.

The last complete edition of the books was published in 1898-1899, by Macmillan & Company, and since that time *The Oregon Trail* has been the only one to remain in print.

Parkman's idea as to how to write 'history' is happily simple, and is most concerned, I think, with getting it straight. This comes itself, if you will, from a tradition wherein a man can simply look you in the eye and say, I don't think so. People from Maine are apt to be good liars, but that is almost from an excess of virtue and a cold climate. But from the beginning Massachusetts and those outlying places of a like nature took such responsibilities as 'history' with a very great seriousness, and Parkman comes, very much, from there.

His materials were not to his liking in many instances. For example, only La Salle could have distrusted Jesuits more than he does. But he is honest with, at times, wit, and always with a determined patience. He is quick to judge how deeply the Jesuit character held to its own determination, and how much these men were not only prepared to suffer, but did. "France aimed to subdue, not by the sword, but by the cross; not to overhelm and crush the nations she

---

*The difficulties in question were poor health and, particularly, bad eyesight. In the introduction to *Pioneers of France in the New World* he mentions these difficulties more explicitly: "During the past eighteen years, the state of his [the author's] health has exacted throughout an extreme caution in regard to mental application, reducing it at best within narrow and precarious limits, and often precluding it. Indeed, for two periods, each of several years, any attempt at bookish occupation would have been merely suicidal. A condition of sight arising from kindred sources has also retarded the work, since it has never permitted reading or writing continuously for much more than five minutes, and often has not permitted them at all." (January 1, 1865.)

invaded, but to convert, civilize, and embrace them among her children."

... Who can define the Jesuits? The story of their missions is marvellous as a tale of chivalry, or legends of the lives of the saints. For many years, it was the history of New France and of the wild communities of her desert empire.

To the north, then, Jesuits, a rank breed of 'gentleman,' and a race of fur-traders, the *coureurs de bois* — of which last Parkman writes:

... At least, he is picturesque, and with his red-skin companion serves to animate forest scenery. Perhaps he could sometimes feel, without knowing that he felt them, the charms of the savage nature that had adopted him.

Then follows a description of these 'haunts' — "deep recesses where, veiled in foliage, some wild shy rivulet steals with timid music, etc., etc." Typical of Parkman is the footnote he adds to this, in justifiable irritation:

An adverse French critic gives his opinion that the sketch of the primeval wilderness on the preceding page is drawn from fancy, and not from observation. It is, however, copied in every particular, without exception, from a virgin forest in a deep moist valley by the upper waters of the little river Pemigewasset in northern New Hampshire, where I spent a summer afternoon a few days before the passage was written.

It is, of course, impossible to outline all of the work in question, but think of it as, first, the *place*. Spanish to the South (Ponce de León, Pamphilo de Narvaez, Hernando de Soto), to the North the French (Cartier, Pontgravé, Champlain) — and then, of course, New England. There is noth-

ing really more to it than that, except 'history,' what then
followed. And like it or not, it was hardly a process of much
clarity, certainly not to those whose fortunes (much more
than their lives) were the issue. As far as I know, Parkman
is the first American historian (and perhaps the last?) to
pay such careful attention to the *ground*. For example:

> It has been a matter of debate on which side of the
> Niagara the first vessel on the Upper Lakes was built
> [the *Griffin,* which La Salle and his followers built in
> the spring of 1679]. A close study of Hennepin and a
> careful examination of the localities, have convinced
> me that the spot was that indicated above [Cayuga
> Creek, which enters the Niagara "two leagues above
> the cataract"]. Hennepin repeatedly alludes to a large
> detached rock, rising out of the water at the foot of the
> rapids above Lewiston, on the west side of the river.
> This rock may be seen immediately under the western
> end of the Lewiston suspension-bridge, etc., etc.

However irrelevant this may seem, it is by a like care that
all 'history' is written, and from a like 'place.' To analyse
comes, finally, to a presumption that no man careful of his
materials cares to show. It is simple to talk about something,
as if it were a convenience for the mind — whereas the mind
is 'history' long before it knows that this particular problem
exists.

Be that as it may, Parkman is careful to leave 'history' in
the two places where it can endure; and one is, I think, in
its own 'present,' i.e., where the rock has since washed away,
where the foundations of the fort still show, and the other,
in the letters, sayings, stories, and so on, that maintain
'history' much more actually than the supposed 'records'
and commentaries.

Though his most complete success is La Salle — by which I mean, the fact of this man, given plainly, and with care — for myself, it is also in the countless anecdotes and (finally) flavors of a place I of course am too 'old' to know as he must have, because *The Oregon Trail* was written from a journal no man can ever keep again. For me, he returns 'history' to the only place which it has, in an actual continuity — hardly ours because we are its issue, but because we can perhaps recognize that we are. (At this point, surely, all the worry about 'europeanism' and so forth must become beside the point.) He stays at that one sure root, anecdote. "So they say." Men, if you will, are raised from the dead by just this:

> On board one of the transports was Seth Pomeroy, gun-smith at Northampton, and now major of Williard's Massachusetts regiment. He had a turn for soldiering, and fought, ten years later, in the battle of Lake George. Again, twenty years later still, when Northampton was astir with rumors of war from Boston, he borrowed a neighbour's horse, rode a hundred miles, reached Cambridge on the morning of the battle of Bunker Hill, left his borrowed horse out of the way of harm, walked over Charlestown Neck, then swept by the fire of the ships-of-war, and reached the scene of action as the British were forming for the attack. When Israel Put-nam, his comrade in the last war, saw from the rebel breastwork the old man striding, gun in hand, up the hill, he shouted, "By God, Pomeroy, you here! A can-non-shot would waken you out of your grave!"

Parkman continues:

> But Pomeroy, with other landsmen, crowded in the small and malodorous fishing-vessels that were made to serve as transports, was now in the gripe of the most

unheroic of maladies. "A terrible northeast storm" had
fallen upon them, and, he says, "we lay rolling in the
seas, with our sails furled, among prodigious waves."
"Sick, day and night," writes the miserable gunsmith,
"so bad that I have not words to set it forth."

It is never a question of 'making it real,' but rather of allowing it, whatever it is, to *stay* real. Perhaps this is simply a
matter of wit, of necessity — but this character, of telling
'history,' has the proper quality of effacing even the man
who records it, until it becomes all 'story,' and so, all true.
It's hard to take any of it out of its place — because there are
no morals to be conveyed, unless the whole substance which
contains them is also to be recognized. When Parkman
separates, becomes the 19th-century Democrat, then he is
also 'history' — also a good story. But, at his best, he leaves it
as it was, and so is:

Among the numerous war-parties which were now
ravaging the borders, none was more destructive than a
band, about sixty in number, which ascended the Kana-
wha, and pursued its desolating course among the settle-
ments about the sources of that river. They passed
valley after valley, sometimes attacking the inhabitants
by surprise, and sometimes murdering them under the
mask of friendship, until they came to the little settle-
ment of Greenbriar, where nearly a hundred of the
people were assembled at the fortified house of Archibald Glendenning. Seeing two or three of the Indians
approach, whom they recognized as former acquain-
tances, they suffered them to enter without distrust;
but the new-comers were soon joined by others, until
the entire party were gathered in and around the buildings. Some suspicion was now awakened; and, in order
to propitiate the dangerous guests, they were presented

with the carcass of an elk lately brought in by the
hunters. They immediately cut it up, and began to feast
upon it. The backwoodsmen, with their families, were
assembled in one large room; and finding themselves
mingled among the Indians, and embarrassed by the
presence of the women and children, they remained
indecisive and irresolute. Meanwhile, an old woman
who sat in a corner of the room, and who had lately
received some slight accidental injury, asked one of
the warriors if he could cure the wound. He replied
that he thought he could, and, to make good his words,
killed her with his tomahawk. This was the signal for a
scene of general butchery. A few persons made their
escape; the rest were killed or captured.

Parkman believed himself to be engaged in something,
perhaps, more notable; in one of his prefaces (*Pioneers of
France in the New World*), he says "The springs of American civilization, unlike those of the older world, lie revealed
in the clear light of History." That was a very hopeful sur-
mise. But Archibald Glendenning's wife escaped — having
first been captured "with her infant child" and forced to
march, "guarded before and behind by the Indians."

As they defiled along a narrow path which led through
a gap in the mountains, she handed the child to the
woman behind her, and, leaving it to its fate, slipped
into the bushes and escaped. Being well acquainted
with the woods, she succeeded, before nightfall,
in reaching the spot where the ruins of her dwelling
had not ceased to burn. Here she sought out the body
of her husband and covered it with fence-rails, to
protect it from the wolves. When her task was complete,
and when night closed around her, the bold spirit
which had hitherto borne her up suddenly gave way.

The recollection of the horrors she had witnessed, the presence of the dead, the darkness, the solitude, and the gloom of the surrounding forest, wrought upon her till her terror rose to an ecstasy; and she remained until daybreak, crouched among the bushes, haunted by the threatening apparition of an armed man, who, to her heated imagination, seemed constantly approaching to murder her.

[*Black Mountain Review*, Winter 1954]

Louis-Ferdinand Céline: Guignol's Band
& *John Hawkes:* The Goose on the Grave

GUIGNOL'S BAND lies so vulnerable to attack, like they say, that only a man with a penchant for beating carpets can really take much pleasure in working it over. But it can serve as occasion for several comments, among them, 1) that following the war a number of American 'violence' novels were published in French translation, and 2) that the reason for this was due, at least partially, to the fact that French writing had at that time no 'vocabulary' for that character of apparently gratuitous violence which they had just experienced.

So there is something strangely an insult in the publication of this particular novel in America, i.e., it is much too much like sending out some drugstore cowboy to help with the branding and all that. Because Céline is very much the dude, spit and froth as he will. And the basis of his novel, an implied attack on the conditions that make for a man like this "young French veteran now turned spiv" and his milieu, is both too late (the first World War) and too general in outline (these are types, not people). More than that, the novel's manner stays very static: "I got to know Clodo well later on. It's true that he was obliging, eager, you might say even zealous, only he'd falter for a moment, he was vague with words, had to tell him right away what you wanted, to put it on the line . . . had to know how to handle him . . ." I don't think Céline has considered the necessary mess involved in writing a novel in which it is impossible to give a damn about *any* of the characters. If this is the point (and /or Life's Forgotten Men, etc.), then he makes his statement of it the weakest yet on record. Which is a considerable come-down for the author of *Journey to the End of the Night.*

John Hawkes' *The Goose on the Grave* gives us a little of the same dilemma, backwards, since the title novel (one of two) proves he can cut the Italians, at least as we have had them in English translation. Hence the Italian campo, given Hawkes, becomes:

> The eyes were upon the body in the clay beyond them. Only Adeppi glanced up to see the crow flying. The silent figure turned in the white mud. Dragging itself, slowly animated, hardly visible, bones of the fingers resting upon the rot of the helmet filled with mud, its bare head lifted and was unable to catch breath in the rain.

Hawkes has a genius for the singularly unpleasant, and his use of it seems sometimes too simple, by which I mean, to no evident purpose but that of being unpleasant, etc. But it would be a literal distortion to put him off with that. Whereas Céline's fantasy has gone old-maidish, Hawkes' world rides in with a deep and careful terror, best used and best seen, I think, in the first of the two novels, *The Owl.* Admittedly, it is a dream-structure, a *place* which is more real, as one says, in its capacity to suggest than in the literal elements of which it is composed. And the hangman is the Hangman, Il Gufo, the Owl. People fade, eyes divorce from faces, peering out, a field tilts, men whisper. There are great heights, and wind.

> The prisoner, delivered into altitude where there was time and silence to devour him, was the hangman's. The

fortress which kept him safe was cleft in two parts on
the pinnacle of the city, high tower and low tower, and
from either battlement there was an iron-edged view
of the world, its cliff, the tilted slopes at the bottom,
the sunrise and sunset, and, not so far off, the border
itself of a definite black and white. To the east it was
possible to find a thin white horizon, the sea. If any in
Sasso Fetore saw out there a Venetian sail, they pre-
tended it was a dream.

Disaster has only to declare its form; its premises, barren-
ness, despair, have already been accomplished. In that way
the novel is an 'allegory,' and much of Hawkes' writing, even
most of it, has been that. In this book, authority in its absolute form, the Hangman, moves with an inexorable rigidity
— like those movie shots of locusts covering a field. Except
that this is one man, rather one face, two hands, one mind,
etc. The town, the women, the men, the Prisoner — actually
they take the forms of characters, virtues and vices (though
hardly that unshaded) which are met in the old morality
plays. But Hawkes puts these things against the final character of a landscape, his own mind, I think, in point of the
moods it takes on.

[*Black Mountain Review*, Autumn 1954]

Witter Bynner: Journey with Genius

WITTER BYNNER comes late to that distinguished group who *knew* D. H. Lawrence as opposed to those who have read him. His book is based on a slighter acquaintance than that, say, of Aldington, but the thirty odd years which have since passed allow him considerable cud. And he was also the 'American' in the beginning of *The Plumed Serpent* — which probably seemed motive enough.

Perhaps it is time, in any case, to say to hell with all such as Witter Bynner, and to grant him, certainly, his friendship but also to insist it was apparently misused. At least the account of it makes very dull reading now.

As it is, we have another champion of Frieda — and why, always, do these men go so female in their causes? Aldington wailed of ragged undies, and the beast who let his wife go so clothed. Bynner proclaims a conspiracy, to wit, his sage advice that she fight back and the almost nauseous insistence that she then did, all because *he* said to.

It is in this character that Bynner becomes precisely the has-been, the would-be, in short, the fake which a good many good-tempered men must have been putting up with for years. I recently read a review of his on the biographers of Willa Cather (also a 'friend'), and that was more amiable. But nonetheless Bynner is still one who *knew* others, and it is a dreary, dreary occupation.

The loss here is that the bulk of the comment on Lawrence is always this personalism and/or the attempt so much

296

more ragged than any underwear, to hang on to a man who had all this complexity of effect. And who was, it seems, not very simple to forget.

But all such statement is a bore. It gives us at best, as Bynner does, a kind of lover's album of a few faded flowers — because both Aldington and Bynner did aspire, as did Murray, Carswell, 'E. T.' even, who was I think the most justified. But there it is, books about a man as opposed to those books he himself wrote. Or much more important, an actual levy on what Lawrence himself was after — simply things like his pick-up on Frobenius, on American writing, on the political set of Europe, and so forth.

And that *is* what matters. In England he is still for the most part sunk in the old social fix. By which I mean, people still worry that he was a miner's son. But that is only counterpart to Bynner's remarkable insight, viz., that he spoke like 'all' British men-of-letters, with a 'high' voice, etc. Or that he took his wife swimming at the far end of the beach, because he was embarrassed by his own body. Or that he got angry, unreasonably angry, and had little boys put in jail.

No matter the middle chapters — with their ridiculous headings — this is what Bynner is talking about. And this is the extent of his contribution. He wants, I think, to posit a 'while I was doing this, Lawrence was doing that,' and that of course is the end of him. There is no equivalence between them, either as men, as poets, or as anything else. And this is clear, very clear, from what each have written — the *work*. It is much too late now for Bynner to work, to do what another man was doing all the time.

[*Black Mountain Review*, Summer 1954]

Ramon Sender: Two Novels

THERE ARE MANY QUESTIONS on which any piece of writing can take off — not glibly, or one hopes not, but because these 'questions' stay the one 'given,' in a context otherwise constantly in process of reformation. So — what does one believe in? Is the real real because one admits it? Tastes it. Feels it. Knows it? Or because it is?

> We are ringed with filters attenuating all the impressions pouring in on us from outside ... Those filters which are acting through all the forms of our sensibility constantly guard us against attack by light, sound forms. But the best of these filters is the mind. We have minds not primarily to understand but rather not to understand too much. What horrible or transcendent truths repair to our understanding and remain outside? Against what terrible revelations or evidence does our mind protect us?

This is quoted from the first of a series of 'mottos,' placed at the beginning of each chapter, which form an anterior 'novel' to the one otherwise occurring.* The writing, or rather what the writing resolves as, is a continuing displacement of a man already beyond the character of a 'natural' reality in that 1) it is a question as to whether or not he is dead, yet he has not found death, so he is not; and 2) the book is placed on a boat, i.e., it is the geography of

*Ramon Sender: *The Sphere.*

298

no geography but that which human disposition can arrive at.

More aptly, it is the journey to death, to a death realized, which is impossible — but which is *necessary*, when all calls to life have become so rotted, and ambiguous, that nothing remains outside the mind, not enough. Or, as Lawrence says it:

Oh build your ship of death, oh build it!
for you will need it.
For the voyage of oblivion awaits you.

Sender says: "I am closer to my death than yesterday . . ." The progression of the novel is through circumstances, trails perhaps, or again and again questions — of the body: "And Saila came back to his mental constructions: 'I've told myself time and again that love is a "reintegration" and that it is both necessary and impossible . . .'" Of the mind: "There is a perfection upon which we all rest when we wish: reality." Of that complex, belief: "Faith was born before miracle."

And all of this comment decrys, despairs, and distorts — what is being said, by this book. The form it takes, the 'mottos' juxtaposed against the 'action' and/or the literal events which form its sequence, are, also, the 'how it is, as it is,' which the mind, damned (is it), feels itself so obliged to repair to. To repair, to in fact be, also, present to — as 'it' happens. So in this instance Sender records in one man, Saila, this complex, this man with his hands, on the woman, yet un-on, or un-relieved. For example:

With her look she asked him: "Still? In the situation we are in? What for?" But Saila said to himself: "When every road has been blocked to us there remains the absurd feminine, the great chaos over which we can place our hand in order to feel the infinite accessible."

For the moment — there is no injustice, I hope, in *using* this novel as a means to suggest the world, the literal time, which encompasses it, and also, which it hopes to encompass. A wise man asks only questions. Because the answers to them, granted they have in fact been asked, lie in the man to whom they are asked. Sender is unlike, or rather differs from, most writers of so-called 'fiction' in that he is not so eager to persuade as to demonstrate (first to himself) the complexity of the *idea* of the world which he has been brought, of necessity, to consider — whether or not that 'world' is in fact of a real kind, or, more literally, is the real world. We know — as we say in that now familiar tone of reassurance — that a world does exist, beyond our minds; yet we do not.

The person, child of experience — the return of reflection upon action — holds to a lineal or superficial idea of everything. It is born, grows and develops with that primitive tumour of the ganglia we call the brain.

*   *   *

And what is spirit? Is it flight? I sense that force which impels everything to disintegration, reflecting perhaps the very centrifugal impulsion of the planet. Gravity prevents or conditions our disintegration. The feeling of escape which disintegration communicates to everything we ourselves find in the tendency of our spirit first to self-sufficiency, and then to departure and detachment from self. This possibility of separation from, and even action against, the very self we recognize as a 'need to flee.' But at the very moment this need seems most imperious, a curious thing happens. That is, we return to the ganglia, and instead of fleeing, strengthen the unity of being; a reciprocal movement — it might be said — between the notion of essential being and the feeling of elemental being.

This is a resolution — a 'melting,' a 'separating into parts.'
Yet — "Mirliflor looked at him confused: 'You, you Spaniards . . .' he said, unable to finish."

2

The world of Sender's most recent novel* is one assembled,
stumbled upon — as a man will stumble — again of necessity.
We cannot call Ramiro "the affable hangman" until we have
also stumbled, willynilly, into or upon, that thread of
occasional purpose by which a man directs himself, given
eyes and mouth, hands and legs, and a mind, and also a
heart. Diotima tells Socrates, in Plato's *Symposium*, that:

> On the day that Aphrodite was born the gods were
> feasting, among them Contrivance, the son of Inven-
> tion; and after dinner, seeing that a party was in pro-
> gress, Poverty came to beg and stood at the door. Now
> Contrivance was drunk with nectar — wine, I may say,
> had not yet been discovered — and went out into the
> garden of Zeus, and was overcome by sleep. So Poverty,
> thinking to alleviate her wretched condition by bearing
> a child to Contrivance, lay with him and conceived
> Love. Since Love was begotten on Aphrodite's birth-
> day, and since he has also an innate passion for the
> beautiful, and so for the beauty of Aphrodite herself,
> he became her follower and servant. Again, having
> Contrivance for his father and Poverty for his mother,
> he bears the following character. He is always poor,
> and, far from being sensitive and beautiful, as most
> people imagine, he is hard and weather-beaten, shoe-
> less and homeless, always sleeping out for want of a
> bed, on the ground, on doorsteps, and in the street. So
> far he takes after his mother and lives in want. But,
> being also his father's son, he schemes to get for himself

*Ramon Sender: *The Affable Hangman*.

whatever is beautiful and good; he is bold and forward
and strenuous, always devising tricks like a cunning
huntsman; he yearns after knowledge and is full of
resource and is a lover of wisdom all his life, a skilful
magician, an alchemist, a true sophist. He is neither
mortal nor immortal; but on one and the same day he
will live and flourish (when things go well for him),
and also meet his death; and then come to life again
through the vigour that he inherits from his father.
What he wins he always loses, and is neither rich nor
poor, neither wise nor ignorant.

An account of Love is, loosely enough, what later com-
mentators have called the 'picaresque novel,' i.e., a story of
a man who travels much, who becomes involved in untoward events for singular reasons, and who 'distills' (as the
book-jacket in the case of Sender's novel puts it) an 'idio-
syncratic' philosophy.

Yet Ramiro is a hangman: "he felt real gratitude toward
me [the story's narrator] because I had offered him my
hand, knowing that he was a hangman . . ."; and Love would
do no less.

But why does a man become a hangman — these days?
Or, better, how is it that a man — in whom love moves, or
else he is not — arrives at that 'authority' which allows, as
Ramiro's instructor does: "It is not that one is ashamed of
one's work. Someone has to do it, and nowadays they don't
mistreat the *pobreto* — poor wretch — as before, but dis-
patch him neatly and rapidly . . ." And is not this, also, a
rather *familiar* 'man's world'?

Faced with a loyalty to this or that idea, he finds himself
on either 'side,' on the one hand witness of the killing of
men and women with whom he has sided, and, later, on the
side of those who have killed them, at another like incident,

where men are forced to jump into a well and then sticks of dynamite are thrown in after them.

On the way back Ramiro was thinking: "This is more cruel than what they did to Chino and Curro Cruz and the peasants of Benalup. And the Duke, the priests of my town, the mayor, the judges know it or take it for granted. Everyone knows it and no one does anything about it." They returned in silence. It suddenly occurred to Ramiro that it had been a good thing for him to make himself responsible for all that. To accept the responsibility that everyone shunned. With his presence he was already responsible. He wanted to be even more so. The word responsibility rang out inside him in an urgent way and with tremendous force. It was an obsession.

Sender's method, in this book, is a constantly shifting character of 'reality,' i.e., of fable, of naturalistic detail — of the supposed 'real' put against the hyper- or also-real. And in the narrative occur other 'stories,' for example, of Lucia, who is in love with her sister's husband, whom she denounces, whereupon he is killed. Ramiro thinks:

"I would like to make myself responsible for all the crimes in the world," he muttered to himself. "But how?" Then he remembered Lucia naked amidst the snow and he found her appealing. He liked not only her body but the disorder of her mind. He really believed that she had denounced Joaquina's husband and yet he regarded her as innocent. "She got into the game," he said to himself, "and had to do what she did, and now she is paying for it."

When Ramiro was a little boy, his mother "told tales that made [him] cry with pain, and then she would tell everybody how tender-hearted [he] was . . ." What is the man who will witness, and thereby 'do' what all others imply,

but will not do — as, for example, we all know that this or
that has to be done, yet wait for someone to do it. Is that
why we have armies, etc. At the close of the book Ramiro
and the narrator are sitting in a cafe, talking. Noise is heard,
outside. A fiesta of some kind seems to be starting.

"But why all this?" I [the narrator] repeated, sens-
ing an immense scandal in it all.

"I don't know. In any case it concerns me alone. Don't
you worry, it's only because of me. It apparently has
nothing to do with you."

He was more afraid than I. He looked at the cars lined
up, at the patient crowd, and said very nervously:

"There is no doubt about it. It is the end. This is the
end. Or the beginning. Who knows?"

People are all around the cafe, the building; the two men
are 'prisoners,' and then going out, Ramiro asks "questions
to the right and left of him, but no one seemed to give a
satisfactory answer."

The procession was formed. The bands continued play-
ing. Ramiro started marching under the canopy . . .

So that is the end of it. Thinking of the first book, *The
Sphere* — why will we not believe, or try to, until the mind
itself *is* broken, breaks back, forcing the world to declare
itself. Finally? Or at least 'occasionally.' And of the second,
The Affable Hangman — the sacrifice we make is a witness,
of course, to that act; and is our authority for it.

[*Black Mountain Review*, Summer 1955]

On Love

ONE HAS BEEN TRYING, for weeks, to compose oneself in terms of, or rather in relation to, a given instance. For example:

> Your letter came in a moment when my heart was limping. A star had come and I couldn't receive it for I was repenting pride. And though you were expressing the world you know in Plato's *Symposium*, the nature of love, Socrates' conversation with Diotima, "and that one's disappointment finally becomes expectant...," I knew the chatisement. I'd provided the mantle of my personal size... Love is the world and Logos the word but Life demands that Love know itself and when Love isn't in Grace it is testy and bitter...

I know this lady is a fine one, and was grateful for her reassurance. For an instant – I did not, I think, wish to laugh at either one of us, but how not to. I was afraid that I was I, and she was she. Writing is private, I thought. Later I read in Stein's *Everybody's Antobiography*:

> ... when you say what you do say [these were lectures] you say it in public but when you write it in private if you do not write it, that is what writing is, and in private you are you and in public you are in public and everybody knows that...

My heart has been limping, for months now. In that way, I tend to forget the lady, a little. Without glibness, Wyatt must have known it, very exactly, and he was then much

older: "They flee from me who sometimes did me seek."
For an instant, no matter more — there are these several
juxtapositions possible, e.g., H.D.'s saying, *I go where I love
and am loved* . . .; Williams', *what, shut grief in from us? We
who have perhaps nothing to lose?* And the, *myself forgetting
violence, and long betrayal* — of Robert Graves, the poem
which introduces the first edition of *The White Goddess*.

Should we roar with laughter — or what do we have to do,
with the moon, these days? Stendhal writes: "I am full of
admiration for the shrewdness and unerring judgment with
which women seem to me to grasp certain details; and yet
the next moment I find them praising some dullard to the
skies, allowing themselves to be moved to tears by a plati-
tude, or gravely treating some hollow affectation as a sign
of character. I cannot understand such folly. There must be
some general law beyond my ken governing these
matters . . ."

Robert Duncan, in a letter: "And I want them all as best
I can, and so do you, any man: want to be free to give
myself over to the sexual lure, to fall in love — and to learn
the art of place and person, of tone and definition that might
render the experience to itself. But it's a cheat to bring the
accusation against ourselves or our lovers of selfishness in a
situation that is of the essence 'thotless.'

"And a mixd hell on wheels to try to come to *love* that
which has possessd us. Well, but then there is the figure of
an hysterical female figure on a rollercoaster crying 'I
simply love this.'"

2

Conversely, Wyndham Lewis' *Self Condemned* is a terrifying relation of more than 'one man's life'; it is a statement of
the impossible distance of an intimacy, too often, these days.
At the beginning:

As soon as she saw that he was occupied with his correspondence (and she was not detained by her own, which had been nothing but a few bills), she shook off the contretemps of the *Princess Casamassima* discussion — such a highbrow feature for their breakfast-table talk was almost without precedent — and returned to the setting of her own little traps. The terrific success of the night before, and René had been in perfect honeymoon form, must really be put to some good use. The moment had come, it seemed to her, to seize time by the forelock while his eyes were still gooey and his brain still drugged with the fumes of the Venusberg. Her eyes shining, her waist arched in and hips thrust out, she held up a page of her newspaper on which were displayed a bunch of late-spring coats, a bait for those who were so silly as to imagine that in warm weather fur coats grew cheaper.

"Now *that*," she exclaimed, arching her eyebrows, "is what, if you ever had a really *lavish* fit — *that* is the sort of thing I should get you to buy."

René looked up from his correspondence, momentarily stung almost to fury by the brazen naively mercenary calculations of the good Hester, with her garishly stock notion of what was a propitious moment...

This image is not a 'criticism' of anyone, or rather, I use it in no such context. Nor am I concerned with the 'reality' of either character or situation, except that they are here — some pages (weeks, months, countries) later:

..." Will you kindly tell me at once what my wife has done," demanded René.

"What did she do?" echoed the policeman. And René noticed the change of tense.

"She did nothing?" he asked; his lips trembled. "And if she has done nothing, why did you demand my presence here?" The aggressive tone provoked the reappearance of the unmodified jowl of the dogs of the Law.

"She did do *something*, Professor. She threw herself under a truck."

It continues: "... The poor hair was full of mud, which flattened it upon the skull. Her eye protruded: it was strange it should still have the strength to go peering on in the darkness."

René took a step forward towards the exhibit, but he fell headlong, striking his forehead upon the edge of the marble slab — the remains being arranged upon something like a fishmonger's display slab. As he fell it had been his object to seize the head and carry it away with him. To examine his legal right had been his last clear act of consciousness...

D. H. Lawrence writes: "... But if your wife should accomplish for herself the sweetness of her own soul's possession, then gently, delicately let the new mode assert itself, the new mode of relation between you, with something of spontaneous paradise in it, the apple of knowledge at last digested. But, my word, what belly-aches meanwhile. The apple is harder to digest than a lead gun-cartridge..."

[*Black Mountain Review*, Spring 1956]

The Journals of Jean Cocteau*

THE OCCASION OF Jean Cocteau's election to the French Academy (1955) has meant an increase of interest in his work in this country. Actually, this kind of interest most concerns publishers and their use of such events to provide "times" for concern with the writing of this or that man. This is a perfectly reasonable exploitation of a circumstance perhaps, but it can often lead to hasty thinking, editing, translating — and so on. The occasion forgotten, the book shows its gaps and awkwardnesses, and ends by disobliging the very man it assertedly hoped to honor.

The present book* is an "occasion" book. Mr. Fowlie's introduction is twenty-nine pages long almost in defense of his uneasiness. He was given a sizable task, clearly. I am by no means as familiar with the material as he must be; but I am aware that it must have been very difficult to select things out of it — it does not break open into pieces, but is a texture of attention, endlessly reforming. At times Mr. Fowlie can only shout his goodwill ("Membership in the Académie Francaise will hardly slow him [Cocteau] down!"). But his translation is readable, and given his word — "A fairly literal translation seemed often to serve Cocteau better than an effort to recast the original in order to find a style and phrasing more native to English..." — we will have to trust him, and also thank him, because no one has as yet done more, or as much.

*Edited and translated with an introduction by Wallace Fowlie.

This brings us, then, to Cocteau — not fatuously, please, because I have taken pains, or have tried to, to separate him from his translator, and particularly, from the "occasion" behind the translator — forever to be suspected. As Mr. Fowlie suggests (p. 3), Jean Cocteau is not a widely read writer, although many people know his name, and sense a half-glamour in it, for reasons they themselves continue to produce. He has, however, been recognized by his contemporaries for many years. The first sections of the book describe his relationships with Satie, Max Jacob, Stravinsky, Raymond Radiguet, Pablo Picasso, Maritain, Proust, Diaghilev, Apollinaire. In the American context, Ezra Pound mentions him several times in *Guide to Kulchur,* once as follows: "To establish some table of values as among men I have seen and talked with . . . Gaudier had and Cocteau has genius . . . By genius I mean an inevitable swiftness and rightness in a given field. The trouvaille. The direct simplicity in seizing the effective means."

What is his writing like, then? I would like to know too. I have seen three of his movies, including *Beauty and the Beast;* know nothing of his poetry; read *Opium* when younger with great care (and wonder — it was not at all what I expected, and was very strictly written); and began *Thomas the Imposter* (remembering the kaleidoscoping of short scene-images, with which it begins); and read with what French I had, *Journal d'un Inconnu,* what I could of it — excited to find the mind so capable of balance and continuance. Cocteau writes:

On Words

> I attach no importance to what people call style and that by which they think they recognize a writer. I want to be recognized by my ideas, or better, by my bearing. I make every effort to be heard as briefly as

possible. I have noticed, when a story does captivate the reader's mind, that he was reading too fast, and gliding down the slope. That is why, in the book, I skirt around the writing which forces me not to glide in a straight line, but to start over again, to reread the sentences in order not to lose the thread.

When I read a book, I marvel at the number of words I find in it and I dream of using them. I note them down. But in my work it is impossible. I limit myself to my own vocabulary. I cannot go beyond it, and it is so restricted that the work becomes a puzzle.

I wonder, at each line, whether I shall go on, whether the combination of the few words I use, always the same ones, will not end up by blocking the way and forcing me to silence. It would be beneficial for everyone, but words are like figures or letters in the alphabet. They are able to reorganize differently and perpetually at the bottom of the kaleidoscope.

I said I was jealous of the words of other writers. It is because they are not mine. Each writer has a bag of them, as in a lotto set, with which he has to win. Except for the style I dislike — Flaubert is the leading example — too rich in words — the style I like, Montaigne, Racine, Chateaubriand, Stendhal, does not spend too many words. It would take no time to count them . . .

The sections into which the book is divided show a preoccupation with personalities, not Cocteau's nor perhaps even Mr. Fowlie's, obliged as he was by the concerns evident. Sections I (Childhood and Early Influences) and III (Testimonials) contain the bulk of it; and Sections II (The Writer's Character) and VI (Aesthetics) seem the most purposefully free, and useful. But what use we are intent upon, is what we must of course decide.

A use of words is a definition of words. This is not new, but worth, like they say, the repeating, always. The structure of language is at stake, so to speak.

There is also the question of "authorities," concerning which Robert Duncan, an American poet who has read Cocteau's work with care, writes:

> What Joyce sees as "conscience" because he is guilt and and sin centered, Pound sees as sensibility or Ibsen sees as awareness or Dante sees as Grace. Cocteau in *Journal d'un Inconnu* voices an aspect of the problem. It is here in the terms of the economy of fame. The work, as it is realized, is a flowering; and like all flowerings — the author here no more intending than a plant intends — an attraction; its emanations draw and repel, its colors exhibit or conceal. No matter! a host arrives, or hosts depart, of all sorts. This clustering about an emanation is its fame in which sometimes the plant can survive; thru which at times the plant comes even to flourish or, as in the relation of certain plants thru their flowerings with bees, to depend; or it may perish. All artists draw a sap out of solitude. The work of art flowers forth, ripens, and falls away from a vitality drawn out of a privacy, a secret source of the artist in the fields of time and space . . .
>
> The relation of a poem to what the world calls events is similar. The "world" cannot view a poem as an event in itself, and seeks to translate as if the poem were referring to "real life." Yet for the poet, the reality of time and space which is realized in making, in a poem, is the real life. [From an unpublished Notebook.]

The attempt to wrench segments from any completed work (happily called a *book*), to reassort, re-*time*, reaffix, etc., — is not easily defensible. Most reasonably, it would be the act of the man who wrote the book or books. In this case, it is not. In twenty years there have been five books by Cocteau published in English; two were translated by the British poet and playwright, Ronald Duncan, one by the British novelist, Rosamond Lehmann. The fourth is a retranslation of the same novel translated by Miss Lehmann (no translator given), published in this country. And the fifth is the present book. I think we had better go back, and start over.

[*New Mexico Quarterly*, Winter 1956-57]

Evergreen Review, *No's. 1 and 2*

THE USE OF THE "little magazine" format in contemporary publishing is a result of the wide increase in paperback publications generally; and must, I think, be first recognized as a commercial device rather than a use relating directly to contemporary writing. In fact, the little magazine *per se* finds itself in difficult straits these days. Increased publishing costs, more highly developed means of distribution, lack of independent subsidies, and like factors have all tended to push out any actual parallels to the old *Dial, Transition,* or *The Little Review,* which might otherwise have appeared. The increased use of little magazines by universities has also resulted in a generally academic tone which reaches over into reviews without such connection, e.g. *The Hudson Review.* Writers for these periodicals have usually a well determined axe to grind — not certainly their fault, but again the result of anterior preoccupations: in this case, that universities have come to expect their employees to be active in such publication, particularly the members of their English departments. The subsequent search for occasions has led to any number of specious revivals, and the independently creative writer — to use a well-worn phrase — finds himself more beside the point than ever.

What is a little magazine? It used to be, most usually, the publication of a group of *writers,* however restrictive that might seem. It was not, in any case, the publication of a group of publishers or teachers. At times a sympathetic editor, such as Ford Madox Ford, could, with an *English Review*, publish both Lawrence and Pound, no matter what each thought of the other. *Transition* practiced an almost voracious eclecticism, but one clearly committed to writers, not pocketbooks. And there were as well magazines such as *Broom* with a more narrowly cohesive editorial commitment. The late *View*, for example, was dedicated to American surrealism, with Charles Henri Ford and Parker Tyler as mainstays. In contemporary writing only *Origin* (which has now stopped publication) seems to have been committed to a group — its nemesis perhaps, but also its use. The writers it published were given means to develop their own idiom, with the very significant security of knowing there was a place where they might appear free of obligating "limits" — which is a very important security indeed.

The *Evergreen Review* has, as yet, no "group" and it is perhaps not to be expected of an essentially commercial publication. Publishers, reasonably, use such magazines as this as a form of advance publicity; Gallimard in Paris has maintained a review of this kind for some years. But this use will explain in part the hodgepodge character of *Evergreen Review* No.1, despite single excellences such as James Purdy's "Cutting Edge." The contents include Sartre, Michaux, Baby Dodds, and Samuel Beckett — and these do not relate, nor is the eclecticism of such inclusion very interesting. Sartre's essay, "After Budapest" is not demonstrably an attitude with which the editors "agree" — or on which they stake their own political commitment — or by which they define a position they intend to maintain. It is, rather, an "example" — useful, but limiting, because it is an example of Sartre, not of an editorial program or policy.

This randomness is in some sense corrected in *Evergreen Review*, No. 2. Here a cohesiveness is obtained by giving over the issue to San Francisco writers; and Kenneth Rexroth leads off with a confused, but certainly explicit, "letter," maintaining the importance of *disaffiliation* to the writers involved. This of course implies liveliness and the like, but it also involves some error of generalization as does, equally, calling Jack Kerouac and Allen Ginsberg writers of this geographical "school," despite the impact they have had there. Michael Rumaker seems to me equally detachable. The more true members are, perhaps, Rexroth, Brother Antoninus, Duncan, Spicer, Broughton, and Josephine Miles — though these as well share many differences. There is, in any case, some danger in promoting geographical relationships; they are rarely significant, and add somewhat specious labels to writers who have troubles enough.

In both issues the problem seems coherence. The first relies primarily on an unabashed eclecticism, with the use of "names" to provide interest. This is a familiar practice. The second in turn makes use of a geographical "scene" (the publisher has printed on the cover SAN FRANCISCO SCENE in fact), and again the coherence is tentative, although somewhat more clear than in No. 1. But neither seems to me a very able substitute for a literal editorial policy or program, no matter the apparent limits of that commitment. It means of course that someone will be left out. It means, too, that several writers, or, in short, a group of writers will have precedence. But it means equally that something will be aimed at, and the editors will have arrived at the liberty of inviting writers to contribute to something more than a miscellany. There exist very clear "sides" in writing today, and they are not described by calling something "good writing." I should myself hate to see the *Evergreen Review* become, simply, another *New World Writing* — which can boast it prints writers of completely divergent opinion only because it has none itself.

I make use, however, of a writer's attitude in this review; and forget that it is not here the point. Readers will find much of interest in both issues despite my qualifications. "Baby Dodds' Story" in No. 1, for example, is a fine exhibition of a very free-wheeling prose; Michaux's tour "through the hallucinated hell of Mescalin" in the same issue is also a timely subject. And *Evergreen Review*, No. 2, is I think the most interestingly diverse and generally excellent instance of the "little magazine" in big publishing yet to be done. So, if I hope, it is mainly that it will become the occasion for writers it can now be claimed to be for readers. That will be the day.

[*New Mexico Quarterly*, Spring-Summer 1957]

Edward Dahlberg: The Sorrows of Priapus

MANNERS ARE CUSTOM insofar as they represent continually and generally reaffirmed notions of value. We shoot to kill. We think to act effectively. The world is nine-tenths to be found in the way one moves through it, be that with resistance, longing, good nature, or whatever other possibilities of attitude exist.

For a writer this problem of "manners" converts, partly, to that of "style" — of which Stendahl said, it is the man. In America there are no very actually customary writers such as the English have. From Melville on, those men who have managed a formal distinction have done so with great labor, and *Moby-Dick* sweats a composite language of completely singular kind. It would seem that the American writer has constantly to refind, and, equally, to redefine wherein lies the value of the words he uses. Awkwardly, and persistently, this is what they seem to me to have done: Whitman, James — utterly unlike otherwise — and in our own time, Pound, Williams, Crane, Faulkner et al. To the European our "stylists" at times seem outrageously selfconscious; they do not at all write in a way that anyone might have. But I think that is, again, a reaffirming of this question of "manners" which has nagged at our dress, our food, our attitudes, ever since we first came to this country. The only way is the one way, and that way is to be found by each man only, one by one. Perhaps we arrive at custom without any manners at all.

From the character of writing in his first book, *Bottom Dogs*, a novel published in the late twenties, to that now shown in *The Sorrows of Priapus*, Edward Dahlberg has come by no means unwittingly. *Bottom Dogs* is a flat, harsh work of realism; and for the last word, read the attitudes subsequent to Dreiser, the affective photographing of life sans relieving characteristics of sympathy. Why then this manner?

> Our annals are weak, and we know not our rivers; we cannot understand today which is Father Ra, the Egyptian sun, until we gather up yesterday, who is Osiris. These rivers are immense legends and would cure us of many ills, did we know them, for all nature is our corpus, and once we relinquish a part of the earth, we lose, in some way, the use of our hands, feet, loins, and spirit.

This is not a realism of any kind familiar to critics, though I would argue its concerns are ultimately just so oriented. For those familiar with *Bottom Dogs*, the language has certainly a new character of reference and tone. Yet the strong monosyllabic structure holds. Sentences stay closely based, running to compounds in passages of argument and explanation; but even there they end with even, flat statement, unmistakable contentual emphases.

The Sorrows of Priapus argues two main images: 1) a natural world, dominant in animal and plant, as corrective to that "understood," intellectually "purposed," defiant of natural authorities; and 2) a source-world, of New World histories, and custom, origin, whereby to secure continuance and understanding of a more primal sort. The last sentence in the book is: "Be primordial or decay." Which injunction — both to continually begin, and to begin with what you began with — can give some sense of the manner in point of content. The beginning note reads:

> This is fable and not natural history. The polestar of the writer is a legendary book, using geography, the beasts in the earth and in the sea, and voyages, as the source of maxims, mirth and an American myth . . .

The natural world is the "plural" world of the Greeks, and those around and before them. It is devoid of humanistic hierarchies; the trees are there as much as the man is, no matter he can chop them down. The second, the source-world, is that of the Maya, Aztec, geographers, the forms of land, and the rivers which mark them. In Dahlberg's use it breeds overtones, insistencies, of great strength:

> Memory is our day of water tutored by want. La Salle sought virgin Tartars, descendants of Prometheus. He returned to Frontenac, but he had not found the Alpha of the river . . .

But what does that first sentence mean? It means that we remember what we have, because we do not have it. It means that fate does not necessarily argue accomplishments.

> Water is death, but man must seek it. All our seeming wakings are the debris of evening waters; most dreams come from mean shallows, and are the digestive rot of secure bottoms; prophecies rise up from the marine depths ancient as the Flood. We are cartographers, unheeding the singing maggots, or bereft of the Angel.

Is it to gain an authority, the manners of authority, that Dahlberg has developed such a "style"? I argue that its purpose is as follows: to demand attention from men, for the content, the things with which it is concerned. The book is a compounded book, formed of many things; "many narratives have been employed . . ." The book is a legendary *imagining* — from *imitāri* to imitate, or some form lost "back there," in the same world; and derives its form from tales, and writings, of men who were there, and provides for us the image of a "new world" which has filtered down to us.

Finally, pedantically, manners comes from *manus*, hand; and custom, at least possibly, in part, from *suescere*: to have it for one's own. At least that can stand as an American reading of the work Edward Dahlberg has done.

[*New Mexico Quarterly*, Spring 1958]

"Her Service Is Perfect Freedom"

ROBERT GRAVES* presents an attractive figure; he is diverse, he is multifaceted as some might say, he writes clearly and with engaging emphases. Many of his books — like the occasions which prompted them — may well fall away; but some, equally, seem squarely fated to stick.

So, what to think of *The White Goddess?* Is she really for real — because that has, it seems, been the question. Perhaps it is our ingrained monogamy that has made most readings of this book, ironically enough, a frustrated rejection of its proposals. The subtitle gives an orientation, however; the book is "A historical grammar of poetic myth." By its "historical," the text will depend on what is known in and of time; by its "grammar," will offer a wherewithal to "know one's letters"; and, by "poetic myth," will depend on those evidences, tales of the tribe, which poets, the makers in language, have used as a basis for their work. This in hand, one may read as literally as he cares to; but he would do well to see that the book is an "argument" as much in its own form and methods, as it is in the literal details to which it refers.

In short, this book is much concerned with an image of how poets have worked in this world, and of the "magic"

*Robert Graves: *The White Goddess, Five Pens in Hand,* and *The Poems of Robert Graves* (chosen by himself); Lucius Apuleius: *The Golden Ass* and Gaius Suetonius Tranquillus: *The Twelve Caesars*— both translated by Robert Graves.

source by which they have survived. Poetic faith, Coleridge's plea for a "willing suspension of disbelief," the timeless acknowledgment of the *other*, such things may, or may not, depend upon the matrilinear institutions which Graves exhaustively premises. But his working premises of conjecture, of a formulative (basically) rather than an analytic ordering of the "what happened," are, I would argue, the only ones which will work in this area. He is right that the poet is a man peculiarly fated to move by such alphabets as he restores, and by such sidewise containment of knowledge as "The Battle of the Trees" demonstrates. Philosophically enough, the poet is here to prove nothing but the continuance of that which was given him on his arrival. The Muse, "the White Goddess . . . the Mother of All Living, the ancient power of fright and lust," etc., is both source and denial; seen as "generation" there is no other relevance possible. Because if you are a poet, you will know that presence of fate, against which you might, even effectually, interpose your own will — if you covet a quick death, and the loss of all you thought to honor. The principle of the animate, in language, is that "things" can become absorbed by their presence there, until their life, in that character, equally represents their force in other, more "literally" given, characters. This, in turn, can generate a power of reverence and recognition capable of continuance. The Goddess, whether characterized as the ultimately personal, or impersonal, wife, mother, queen, or simply the generically "unknown," is the most persistent *other* of our existence, eschewing male order, allowing us to live at last. The obedience of a poet's gratitude, for this, is the authority which you hear in his poems, and it is obedience to a presence which is, if you will, that which is not understood, ever; but which he characterizes as all that can happen in living, and seeks to form an emblem for, with words.

Otherwise poets, like other men, face the necessities of this life, in terms of the money needed to support themselves and their families. Graves has found his solution in making prose support his verse; and thinking of the diverse occupations which poets in this country have used to accomplish the same end, it appears happy for him that he has so managed. But the evidence indicates that this way has had its problems. *Five Pens in Hand,* a miscellany of his criticism, stories, etc., is reminiscent of the schoolman's "Publish or perish . . ." With few exceptions (e.g., *The White Goddess,* "Prologue to a Poetry Reading") nothing offers much purchase for the problem with which Graves has been elsewhere concerned. If nothing in the collection represents "any task or . . . any relationship . . . inconsistent with poetic principles . . . ," again "nothing" is the explanation, by being what is said. The book documents, painfully, what is necessary to manage self-support by writing; how persistently one must be entertaining (cf. "The Whitaker Negroes"); how able to rise to any occasion (cf. "Legitimate Criticism of Poetry"). The process is the more uncomfortable, since the ingenuous good nature back of it all will expose whatever the dictates of the situation ask for — a situation as endlessly of no use as the minds of the editors who create it.

Fairer purpose, better game, for this process is one which allows a firmer grip on such "occasions," as Graves' historical novels have previously shown. Two books, each in its own way, give quick example, i.e., his translations of Suetonius' *The Twelve Caesars,* and of Apuleius' *The Golden Ass.* In America we read Latin poorly, if at all; and translation is a thing on which we are more and more dependent. Graves' translation of Suetonius demonstrates a very certain "poetic" facility, an intuitive response to another man's mode of speaking; and the text is thereby restored to wit and precision, which are things often lost in the translation of Latin. Equally, his transformation of *The Golden Ass* from a somewhat bawdy "classic" to a whimsically moving, full-fledged "religious experience" is token of "poetic" insight, notable here since the vision of the Goddess (pp. 268-271) in other hands might have proved full of doubt or awkward acknowledgment.

But it would be better to forget all of these books, to keep hold only of *The White Goddess*, an act of poetic faith if ever there was one — when you read Graves' poems. Coming from such a Hydra-handed intelligence, they are nonetheless small, lyric, and often commonplace in their concerns. When one thinks of the sheer bulk of prose written in order to support their creation, one is staggered; but that too is like the day, which passeth away. The point is, it does not really matter how you write a poem, so long as you write it.

A poet's "handwriting," whereby he may be known, Graves has termed the rhythms peculiar to his work; to which I would add, it is also the rhythm of his thought, of the ways in which he sees the "out there," and the "in." Graves' forms are primarily traditional, which fact may blur them for a careless reader; but he both uses and informs them in a manner unlike our own current "traditionalists." By which I mean that he is at home in them, thinks with them, and shapes the content of his obligation to their pattern with a good grace:

The Door

When she came suddenly in
It seemed the door could never close again,
Nor even did she close it — she, she —
The room lay open to a visiting sea
Which no door could restrain.

> Yet when at last she smiled, tilting her head
> To take leave of me,
> Where she had smiled, instead
> There was a dark door closing endlessly,
> The waves receded.

A constant acquaintance with any woman will take humor;
it is the only footnote possible. No poet ever quite dares to
make such reference to the Goddess, but a deep humor
grows also from that association. This element is a constant
in Graves' poems; "Questions in a Wood," "Woman and
Tree," and many more, some funny outright, and some much
more quietly, give evidence of that one male prerogative he
has used for sustenance. Others, at last with bitterness, strike
flatly on despair:

> Counting the beats,
> Counting the slow heart beats,
> The bleeding to death of time in slow heart beats,
> Wakeful they lie . . .
>
> ("Counting the Beats")

Despair or not, like it or not, the faith which Graves defends
comes of belief, and is a renewal. You die many times to
acknowledge one birth.

                                        [*Poetry*, March 1959]

A New Testament

Some years ago I had the opportunity to publish a section of this novel* in the *Black Mountain Review* (No. 7). I felt then (and continue to feel), that it was an extraordinary piece of work. At that time I also saw the book in manuscript in a form substantially different from the one which Olympia Press published in 1959. It had a more discursive manner, being in fact three books, one of which had been published in the United States as *Junky* (under the pseudonym, William Lee) and the other two having the titles *Queer* and *In Search of Yage.*

These books, then, made a trilogy progressing into the observation of a despair, with all possible terms of degradation, of commitment to sensation as an alternative logic to organizational 'goodness' or 'purpose.' The present book does that too, but in a form so much more telling in itself that it is immediately remarkable in that way also. For example, this book has no 'historical' logic of any significance. It follows a more real apprehension of life, as significant (or insignificant, the same) memory of detail, of frustrate invention upon the mock taboos of society, of humour used to weigh possibility, of echoing loneliness and repetition. This novel pictures society by coming from it — just as the image of The Rube comes from the cover of a *Saturday Evening Post*, with the catfish in hand, and reoccurs as innocence con-

*William Burroughs: *The Naked Lunch*.

verted to use out of the pressure of needs the society itself
has taught. The dirty words, so to speak, which the book
contains are not the simple 'shit,' 'fuck,' 'cock,' and so on,
that society has made use of from time immemorial — or
rather they are here played upon for what they are, for any
of us, the power of fantasy, of an ultimately successful
touching, carrying with it all the fearful load of suggestion
that any ad for a brassiere can demonstrate. It is that 'fuck'
here *is* fuck, not the guffawing punch-line to a giggling joke,
but horror, ultimate in its *free* term. If we had the money
(say it), what wouldn't we do . . . The inventions Burroughs plays upon the organizational man, the *square* gone
rigid with logically coherent *method,* the sunken man or
woman with the 'condition' ("You think I am innarested to
hear about your horrible old condition? I am not innarested
at all."), the forms of authority or societal control taken to
satiric limits of fantasy so naked it cannot remember the way
any longer to another term or situation:

Old violet brown photos that curl and crack like mud in
the sun: Panama City . . . Bill Gains putting down the
paregoric con on a chinese druggist.
  "I've got these racing dogs . . . pedigree grey-
hounds . . . All sick with the dysentery . . . tropical climate . . . the shits . . you sabe shit? . . . *my Whippets are
Dying* . . ." He screamed. . . . His eyes lit up with blue
fire. . . . The flame went out . . . smell of burning
metal . . . "Administer with an eye dropper. . . . Wouldn't
you? . . . Menstrual cramps . . . my wife . . . Kotex . . .
Aged mother . . . Piles . . . raw . . . bleeding. . . ." He
nodded out against the counter. . . . The druggest took
a tooth-pick out of his mouth and looked at the end of it
and shook his head. . . .

'Wouldn't you?' Which, and why? The vacuum that is the
condition, the nightmare without sound except that it *is* —

and waits, patiently enough. Which control do you choose?

Burroughs says: "There is only one thing a writer can write about: *what is in front of his senses at the moment of writing* ... I am a recording instrument ... I do not presume to impose 'story' 'plot' 'continuity' ... Insofar as I succeed in *Direct* recording of certain areas of psychic process I may have limited function ... I am not an entertainer."

The terms of this book are responsible in that they make the *responsive* areas of intelligence and sensation their logic — beyond any hierarchy of social purpose, good men and bad, evil seen as a side issue (beside the side issue of the nominal 'good'). Its form is an increasingly narrow range of recall, of stories told and retold, in shortening phase, so that they end as an echo of a page, paragraph, sentence, phrase, word: *Wouldn't you?*

There is no way to explain need except to state it. You can solve what you will as you will. We assume that to prevent such issues as Burroughs derives content from, we need only cut them out, away from ourselves. So much of the world has been tidied up in this manner that it is probable that very few people either want to, or can, recognize the anguish their own faces make clear. But Burroughs has written from all the evidence of his own body and mind their testament as well as his own.

(Note written for Grove Press who plan to publish *Naked Lunch* this year.)

[*Outburst*, No. 1, 1961]

A Note for Thread *and Fielding Dawson*

I HAVE LONG been impressed by Fielding Dawson's abilities as a writer. His consciousness is *in* his writing and that is, for me, a rare and useful fact. Speaking of stories, he said once that unless they *take a turn on their own,* they can come to nothing. He meant, simply, if one write only what one intends, as some presumption always to be respected, then intentions are really all one ever comes to — good or bad. There must be a further place where all the assumptions of significance are lost, and some much more *present* instant of integrity can occur. Such location has its obvious dangers, and yet I do not see, personally, how they are not to be risked. It is foolish to define as 'control' an ultimately rigid formula of effects — 'gimmicks' as they are called in the States, the cheap clichés of a tired so-called 'industry.' Control here means the recognition of a moment to moment term of possibility, which is *not* static, but rather so volatile in its nature it demands all possible articulation of attention — to give shape to smoke in air.

1964

Introduction to Thongs *by Alex Trocchi*

AT TIMES world (consciousness) seems containment absolute
in all systems. As — "All Systems GO . . ." Expanding consciousness is burst out — as pressures "grow" in paradoxic
isometric tensions. Patterns are, so to speak, points of the
sphere — "points define a periphery." *Blow your mind . . .*
The truth is that all *is* — a living center.

For the Puritans — William Carlos Williams called them
tight, *small* seeds of distrust and endurance — the experience
of the *outside* is primary, and the edges of their world, in
either "direction," are the terminals, the terms. Charge
them, as you might a battery, and the organization, or
organism, tenses and extends — the phenomenon of increase. It was the peculiar stroking of this life by the experience of space in the 17th century that affects the world
in continuing forms — which the Puritans distrust and
attempt to contain. Morphology — the *logos* of forms — in
McLuhan becomes a "How-to" manual, and *sells* information in the modes it would qualify. It "shows" you so that
you'll "know where you are."

Complex, then, of sexual possibilities: input, output —
modulations in the terminal experiences. This way and
that — leading to William Burroughs' Cut City — mind tapes,
genetic taping — the great mart, distributes the world in
substance.

"Puritan" — sexual possibility an inverse ratio to the degree of self-responsibility. "Is this trip necessary?" *Must* (a

familiar expression to this "way of life") I do this, is it
really necessary? Modes of people having this life-order
seem to range from self-shrinking, convenient-to-others-
commitment, *self*-imprisoned paranoids to harsh direct
noninvolved absolutists, whose actions *never* respond to
what they experience.

Hurt me — so that I may feel *pleasure*. Each agency of
thought in this situation effects the same condition — from
the Old Testament to Samuel Beckett's *How It Is*. Pain is
the measure of possible value, the primary in all cases.

Stendhal questioned, is pleasure the absence of pain? But
the Marquis de Sade proposed with a logic not unlike
Freud's, that pain was perhaps the most *formal* means
society had evolved for the experience of itself. In *Thongs*,
as in the other novels he has written in this genre, Trocchi
defines the *isolation* of persons in sexual rapport, and the
facts of life as unrelieved in all possible senses. The two
human conditions most evident seem the intellectual and
the animal. There is no "love" felt as a convenience of
possibilities for "other" relationships. Gertrude insists upon
a Platonic experience of identity: "The triumph is in the
rising beyond the painful into Pain. Once that leap out of
the self has been made, it is an anticlimax to go back..."
Insofar as other persons of the novel betray a sympathizing
attraction to each other, or want, as Gertrude says, "to go
back," they fall away, as Harry or the Prince in the closing
section. Only Miguel is possessed of a like intensity:

> I am alone. The Prince is alone. Miguel is alone. The
> Prince lies. He tries to tell me that I am not alone. Mi-
> guel tells the truth. He tells me that I am.

> Miguel my love, be my executioner!

So ends the book. I leave these notes as they are in hope that the reader will find his own occasion to think of what "Puritanism" is, and to consider — with a little of that lovely wit Trocchi is so possessed of — just what it is, and has been, *to love.*

July 28, 1967

Six

Divers Sentiments

LOOKING through old manuscripts, I find the following, from a little known *Journal de M. Laubiès* written upon the occasion of his arrival in Paris.

Ils me chargeoient incessament de mille brocards & de mille injures; je me suis veu en tel estat, que pour ne les aigrir, je passois les jours entiers sans ouvrir la bouche . . .

Hence, perhaps, the kindness of Laubiès to critics, even to myself. Painting these days is the discharge of a rare duty, and the public has of course its usual right of comment — to wit: *La Nature n'a pas les bras assez longs, etc.*

This was the death of romanticism, or better, of those poor men at the turn of the century, with their *eaux d'essences*, and their hope of competition with appearance — which any woman might have undeceived them concerning. What followed led finally to that peculiar situation:

1. *C'est le naturel des artisans de se plaindre et de gronder.*
2. *La diversité des gages les fait murmurer, etc.*

And/or the jungle of Paris. Against that any man stands a little, at least, helpless. And Laubiès' work has been judged accordingly. I heard recently that his paintings had been much influenced by a visit to Mallorca. The colors, of course, became those of that delightful retreat — although the truth of the matter was, very simply, that he found himself running low on everything but red, brown and death's head (purple?), and so he made out the best he could. There was also an old lady (*"Ils me répétaient sans cesse: Nous te brûlerons; nous te mangerons; je te mangerai un pied; et moi, une main, etc."*) who wished to hang her tomatoes in the studio in which he was working, and one morning arrived at a little before seven to throw both paintings and Laubiès out.

May I suggest, then, that painting is one thing to a public — and quite another to a man so engaged? I don't think there is any reason to take it much beyond that. It is neither the business of the one nor of the other, to think very much about what each, in turn, think. I am tired, as I suppose many others are, of reading of deep, deep symbolism and mutterings of a soul, and so on. These are all, at last, much too far from that very thing we might otherwise notice — the work itself.

At least some such attention might be reasonable. As it is, and no matter "true or false," some sufferings merit acknowledgment:

. . . ny le froid, ny le chaud, ny l'incommodité des chiens, ny coucher à l'air, ny dormir sur un lit de terre, ny la posture qu'il faut toujours tenir dans leurs cabanes, se rammassan en peloton, ou se couchans, ou s'asseans sans siège & sans mattelas, ny la faim, ny la soif, ny la pauvreté & saleté de leur boucan, ny la maladie . . .

Much that we see, we forget.

[Galerie Fachetti, 1953 or 1954]

René Laubiès: An Introduction

A MAN DOESN'T have to develop theories to look at anything, all he has to do is open his eyes and look. Or call that the rational minimum for an attitude toward some character of painting which may not have a formal category, or some settled opinion concerning it, which can be appropriated for a guide.

Such guides are in fact deceptive. What the eye sees is also deceptive, but in a more useful sense. Say, for example, that you come into a room, drop your coat on a chair, switch on a light — and there, on the wall, is the shadow of a monster — perhaps. Obviously it is a shadow, and what else could it be. Just as the man who looks like Harry is not Harry, unless he is Harry. But this can wait.

A picture is first a picture, the application of paint or ink or whatever to a given surface — which act shall effect a thing in itself significant, an autonomy. And it may of course be that there has been something seen, a visual impression, which the man painting wishes to record, literally, without distortion, that is, without more change of that impression than his media, and the limits of himself, enforce. So representational painting, as we know it, has partially at least the necessity to overcome, by virtue of technique and media, a disturbance of the object, of the thing, so that its use is in the fact of its transference, from there to here or wherever it is, to the picture — so at last the picture is the thing, without need of further reference.

It is here that nonfigurative art becomes relevant, insofar as it can be, in inception, without reference of this usual kind. But that is a vagary, and one which has caused much confusion. Forms are — there are no 'dead' forms; form is the declaration of life. And not at all generally, because what we call life is utterly specific, and must be — to be itself. But the nonfigurative painter does not begin with the bowl of apples, however much he may see it. Or if he does begin there, his process is different from that of the man who would paint it as 'real.' He eats the apple, and then paints the picture. That is the sense of it. So it is a different engagement, a different sense of intent.

But often, wandering through a gallery of contemporary work, one looks up at the walls, and is bored. It is nothing, the painting is not 'real.' A clutter of unspecific forms, without trees or sunsets, proves little.

And this is how it can fail, insofar as such 'forms' may have nothing to declare of themselves — except that they are 'A Painting,' which is very hopeful. Otherwise it could and does happen — no argument can withstand it — that at times we are all of us shaken by forms perhaps unidentified but intimately involved with us, and unmistakeably. Can we anticipate that? Or is it ridiculous for me to see the shadow as a thing, a very real thing, which frightens me? Laubiès knows this very deeply, and anticipates it.

It is his art, if you will, to begin here, at this point of things as yet unrecognized, without more reference than themselves. It is his purpose to effect these things as form, as a painting, simply there. So that we are involved unmistakably — like a sound perhaps, which no 'language' has yet found 'words' for, may affect us nonetheless.

[*Black Mountain Review*, Spring 1954]

A Note on Franz Kline

THERE ARE women who will undress only in the dark, and men who will only surprise them there. One imagines such a context uneasily, having no wish either to be rude or presumptious. Darkness, in effect, is the ground for light, which seems an old and also sturdy principle. There is nothing quite so abrupt and even pleasant as rape — ask any woman. Think of the masses of misunderstanding that come from a betrayal of this. Make a list. Picasso? Much a way of being *about* something, minus night, etc. There are some men for whom it seems never to get dark. As, for example, for Klee it never quite seems to be sun, etc.

But, more interesting, think of it, a woman undressing in broad sunlight, black. What if light were black — is there black light? If there is black light, what is black. In other words, argue to the next man you meet that we are living in a place where everything has the quality of a photographic negative. Take hold of his coat, point to anything. See what happens.

With Kline's work, if the blacks were white, and vice versa, it would make a difference, certainly. It has to be black on white, because there he is, New York, etc. He has no wish to fight senses and all. But he is a savagely exact laugher, call it. I don't know literally if he depends on rape for a means to cohabitation, but I would myself argue that he is a lonely man. Men rarely laugh this precisely, without such a thing for a control. What is 'funnier' than forms

which will not go away. If you say this to someone, they
will laugh at you, but all the time, right behind them, there
is a skyscraper! It's incredible how they can notice it, if
they do, and still talk to anyone.

So what is form, if it comes to that. That question I once
tried to answer in relation (as they say) to the theater. I
was convinced that a man, formally, is no more and
certainly no less than a chair. Fool that I was, I took two
chairs, placed them either side of me, and sat down on the
floor. The answer was, from these friends: Who would
go to the theater to see a man be a chair? What would Kline
have said, if anything. Is this thing on the page opposite
looking at you too? Why do you think that's an eye. Does
any round enclosed shape seem to you an eye.

There is no 'answer' to anything. A painter (possibly a
musician) can assert this more effectually, more relevantly,
than any other 'artist.' He can be present all at one time,
which no writer can quite be — because he has to 'go on.' If
no one sees a painter, or, rather, what he is doing — finally,
not 'doing' — doesn't he still have *things*. At least no man
can point at a painting and say it's nothing, he'll be lucky
if it doesn't come down off the wall and club him to death
for such an impertinence.

God knows we finally enjoy, deeply *enjoy*, wit, the grace,
the care, of any thing — how it is. Kline's audience (no
doubt in Paradise) will be a group of finely laughing women,
plus what men won't be jealous.

[*Black Mountain Review*, Winter 1954]

Philip Guston: A Note

FOR A SENSE OF IT, say — I tried to be careful, but the form
would not have it. My care was the form I had given to it.
How to care, that one does care? *Care*, it seems, comes
from several words, among them the Anglo-Saxon *caru*,
cearu (anxiety) and the Old Saxon *kara* (sorrow). Is it
moving with care through care, that it comes to? I care,
certainly.

I think — in that denseness of anxieties, and sorrows, like
a nightmare world, of forms which are all exact and there,
yet *not* the forms? What *are* the forms, one says. It is not
possible that one should not arrive at them. Somehow not
to be accidental, not even enough or too much 'accidental.'
No one understands, but some know. It is a very articulate
determination which can, at last, "... take care/by the
throat & throttle it ..." with such care.

[*Black Mountain Review*, Spring 1956]

Harry Callahan: A Note

WHAT THE EYE is given to see, as image, in any sense, is a curious occasion. What is it, that they point to, for us to see? The new house with the dirt for lawn, the new tooth, the hat that does not fit, etc. And in the eye at last convolutions of precisely the despair, of no new house (not enough), of the tooth of no one at all, hat I never wore. I hate it all — pictures! What can I do with them, except ache to be there — ? Or to get away as fast as possible, turning the page.

So that the subtlety (inmense) of Callahan's photographs, must, of necessity, be already another thing: not 'pointer,' or reminiscence, or even 'experiment,' but fact. In them there is no movement to any image beyond the one, given. We will never see the face of the boy, nor of the woman, nor will (to remark it), the white pigeon light. It will always be (flat) winter with trees, trampled grass, window curtains and reflections, and paint. These are (as seen) images also of an isolation; that must in fact be almost another 'given,' to not drive the forms home to pasture, to 'where else,' in short. There is no quicker eye to see, nor mind, equally, to seize upon the instant, of chance. All of which (words) here go flaccid against the dry, clear 'eye' of it all.

[*Black Mountain Review*, Autumn 1957]

A Note

"The Question Answer'd"

What is it women do in men require?
The lineaments of gratified desire.
What is it women do in men require?
The lineaments of gratified desire.

— WILLIAM BLAKE

AND ALL THE WORLD lies in between, so to speak. Here is a paradox, and pathetic joke, that that which is most given to men and women, as a common occasion, should be also that least shared by them. We make a cult of the beautiful woman because we will never know her, if men, or be her, if women. We would rather look at the coldly suggestive than feel, in any part of our bodies, the substantial fact of our own warmth.

But these are drawings of another order than that which we are accustomed to in that they let us look. It was perhaps the primary heroism of Peeping Tom that let him look at Lady Godiva, no matter the occasion. The man who shuts his eyes at the sight of a lovely woman is a fool, and the woman who is blind to what sight she might be is also a fool. Finally, I like the comfortableness of these drawings, I like love so seen in its place. It is always there.

[Alice Garver: *Togetherness* (Albuquerque: 1962)]

John Chamberlain

THERE IS A HANDLE to the world that is looked for, a way of taking it in hand. But not as something familiar, nor as some reference to something else. Senses of Chamberlain's sculptures that want to return them to "crushed automobiles" seem to me as absurd as trying to put mother back together again. Surely what has happened is something too.

Things, then, are large or small objects, having the fact of space in whatever dimension becomes them. Space — such as we are given to conceive — is already the dimension of our own. We measure by what we are, as things, in what relations are possible to us. The small man sees the door as large, the large man as small, etc. But what things move more complexly in how they are, come forward insistently, disobliging all such scale, and will be other than big or small — as if we stood finally on our hands, and the so-called bottom disappeared at our feet.

"A new world is only a new mind," says Williams, and equally a new world is not only but wholly a new thing. Our sense of history looks for conformities of acts and effects, and in that respect does us poor service in the arts. Skills are accumulated but the effects of those skills have at each moment to be recognized. There are such things now present that the sciences have no vocabulary wherewith to describe them. They are confronted as facts of literal presence.

You will not live long if you look always for what was there, assuming the world to be no more than the time track of your particularities. A sudden crash, a disfigurement, the loss of anything not simply a pencil or some wish, and all becomes a present so huge it falls on you, crushing you more than that automobile you thought so neatly to remember. It was there, but now you are contained in a thing already changing, bringing you into its terms — and your house shrinks, far off, and things are bright and twisted.

But what things are is, again, more complex, and more distinct than some incidental violence done you. In that sense they used to say, stand back — but these things neither invite nor reject. It is the virtue of a mountain not to care — or not, at least, in such words as we use. Here as well to be liked is not an issue.

One wants a world wherein all that is possible occurs, neither as *good* or *bad* — however terrifying. It must happen. These things have come from such time that no one remembers it, and from such space they assert their own. It is all here.

[*Recent American Sculpture* (New York: The Jewish Museum, 1964)]

Frank Stella: A Way to Go

ONE OF THE most insistent gains of abstract expressionism is
that it gets rid of the frame as limiting factor. It regains the
canvas as surface — or literally imposes as significant surface anything on which the painting occurs. Instead of
making the canvas, as it were, a view box or screen where
something is then to happen, painters of this group forced
the sense of limiting edge to give place to what was happening in the painting itself. Equally, accumulated senses of
composition — for example, the Renaissance use of perspective as a vanishing point — were largely displaced. The
senses of balance, of 'tops' and 'bottoms' in relation to
'weight,' were also revised. It would now seem inevitable
that, in contrast to a nonfigurative painting that wants only
to disguise the nature of its figuration, painting of this kind
was most absorbed in that activity momently confronted as
it, quite literally, occurred. What could be seen then and
there was dominant, and if all the forms so discovered had
counterparts in other visual contexts, they were nonetheless
decisively found in the primary act of painting.

One aspect of this insistence is that painting loses its
historical sense of *picture,* insofar as our sense of a picture
seems to imply something which is referential. It is very
hard to think of a picture without wondering, of what. So,
again, abstract expressionism rids painting of having to be
pictures of things, symbols, mirrors of some otherwhere
present reality.

348

But what follows directly from these painters, both as mystique and example, is more confused. As Robert Duncan has usefully made clear, abstract expressionism has to do with energy embodied in the painting (*felt*) rather than energy referred to (*seen*). This fact makes the energy implicit in the character of the brush stroke, of the forms which it asserts by its activity, a dominant qualification of the painting itself. It explains Pollock's situation when he says, "When I am *in* my painting I'm not aware of what I'm doing . . . I try to let it come through . . ."

It is impossible to qualify what, then, will be significant about such 'being in the painting' except by looking at what comes of it. However, a sense of painting that wants to make itself significant by a random occasion of such energies — or looks for accidental discoveries of 'balance' — leads finally to an implicit chaos, which, in turn, yields only to taste and fashion. In other words, what follows from abstract expressionism, in direct imitation, too often depends upon an arbitrary process of discrimination, one that wants the thing to look like it looks like nothing.

It is interesting that it should be in what seems the antithetically disciplined formalism of Frank Stella, and those akin to him as Neil Williams and Larry Poons, that the gains of abstract expressionism are most used. For example, the interest in the materials possible to painting is continued, whereas the contemporary Action painters depend on those defined by the older men. Equally, the sense of the canvas, or whatever surface is used, is for Stella and the others noted a major preoccupation. Most relevant, the painting is not a reference to another reality — not even another painter's reality — but remains unequivocally its own occasion.

There are several senses of Frank Stella's work that seem to me useful. John Chamberlain speaks of him as having painted one line without stopping for the past ten years. What he finds interesting is that Stella has found in that apparent repetition the possibility of maintaining that line's activity. He is after it, like they say, and will not let go.

Neil Williams, on the other hand, told me of Stella's first use of Motherwell-like forms. As he said, there is this early parallel, but that then something began to happen. The forms became more formal, and in turn led to a linear context, so that — in Klee's vocabulary — the planar effect yielded to linear. But there must be a simpler way to put it. Suppose, for instance, one first sees a set of things as mass, e.g., bulky hills, large clouds, things occupying substantial senses of space. But then, as one goes on looking, that way we have of relating any such group of things, as occupying places together, leads us to senses of their position, in such relationship. The hill's top is roughly the apex of a triangle which points to the cloud, itself an awkward rectangle — and so on, because all that I am trying to note here, is that *lines* are an adamant assumption in any reference to space. Therefore, it is simple enough to recognize how the movement from preoccupation with shapes, or mass, to line occurs. It is not really the out-line, or the 'edge' of the mass, that is the point here — but rather, that what one calls a shape is primarily an activity of line.

So then, as Williams spoke of it, there begins to be an increasing interest in the linear relation of forms — of how they develop into (for the example he gave) a sequence of rectangles moving from right to left, parallel, but each in turn of less length than that to its right, but with a common balance in their point of possible intersection supposing a line drawn through the middle of the canvas on the horizontal axis — and, again, so on, because this is to say, much more simply, that these rectangles begin to assert the lines of a triangle, and that those lines, in turn, begin to determine the possibility of what 'forms' they can take.

Suppose a square, or rather, make one, as Stella now does, and taking the canvas as its possibility, a square canvas in turn, what is implicit in the linear fact of that square that can continue to happen throughout the area which the canvas offers? What is a square, in fact, that it can be drawn with line, or that a line can draw one? And, having drawn one, is a second square enclosing it another line or — despite the apparent fact that it happens in another place, and of another size — the same one?

These are curious questions, and worth the emphasis simply that a first impression of Stella's work may lead one to think that color, and more specifically, the bands of color which he uses to locate line (itself to my knowledge never painted, but left as the surface of the canvas itself), are the significant activity. This same factor leads, at times, to senses of depth or volume which lend the painting the possible effect of an optical illusion. It may be that this aspect is relevant — akin to Op painting more generally — but I have, finally, the impression that it is rather how the line follows through such a variable, that is the point. In "Sharpeville" (1962) there can be a sense of 'looking in,' although it seems soon embarrassed by my own feeling that the *line* of the squares is always on the same plane.

Squares, as a formal possibility for the line, lead to a number of variations. However, these terms seem left as constant: first, the bands, or intervening colored areas between the lines, are left equal in width — so that whatever occurs as qualification of that space is managed by color; and, secondly, the diagonals are insistent, very often implicitly as those lines which would pass through the angle of each square to meet at center, and also explicitly, as in

"Meknes" (1964). The effect of this last is to emphasize the four triangles which the diagonals define.

Two forms are therefore present, which now move to a complex of relationships. These in turn seem to me to follow two distinct patterns, which are difficult to describe — but briefly, they seem as follows. Either the squares occur as they do in "Line Up" (1962), so that one of the diagonals will originate from a point the width of one band in from the edge of the canvas; or else they begin as a development from a central point, itself the intersection of the diagonals from the edges of the squared canvas, as in "Sharpeville." The situation of the triangles is modified in each case in a distinct manner. Either they seem to set up alternative positions and/or to displace the presence of the squares (as in "Line Up") — or else lead to an intensification of them (as in "Sharpeville" and others of like kind). Then there are further possibilities in the 'double image' of "Jasper's Dilemma" (1962), with its negativized, tonal parallels in the right-hand square balanced against the 'positive' of the left.

At this point the fact of the square canvas is itself a concern I think, in the sense that although it is a limit, the structure of the painting works to include that fact in the activity of the painting. I mean, simply, that the sense of backwall, or edge, is played against, and used at times to return one to the intensity of the center. But what is happening in the painting forces further qualifications; and the forms which are there become increasingly active, clearly, and are demonstrating other possibilities in turn.

The triangle, and the angles involved by it, lead the line to qualify not only the context of shape within the painting, but as well its actual circumstance in the actual shape of the canvas. There are a number of variations which lead to this — increasing play on the activity of the diagonals for one thing — in "Fez (2)" (1964) —, so that they are shifted to pass through the center at a point midway on each side of the painting, making in that way four squares within it, and the sequence of expanding squares, familiar from the earlier work, is here shifted on its axis to make an increased emphasis on the triangular, chevron-like pattern the squares effect as they move to the outer edge. The bands of color, limited to an orange and green, alternate from one to the other as they meet at each diagonal, and the whole effect of the painting is an expanding pressure against that limit of edge, but one which also, paradoxically, returns to a balance as these bands grow shorter, approaching each of the outside angles of the canvas.

The frustration is really that it is a little specious to write of something which is so active when seen. Speaking now of what happens when the line begins to define the shape of the canvas itself, is even more so. But it is nonetheless what one has to do, simply that so much is so loosely assumed. The sense that 'function defines form' is familiar enough to people who have used hammers, or any so-called tool that has a specific thing to do. But that information does stay, oddly, an abstraction in that people reasonably don't want to be bothered when doing something, with how it happens they have something to do it with, etc. If one speaks of lines having similar possibilities, even necessities, it seems all the more vague. But there are so many simple instances. One, for example, that has always fascinated me, is that of moving the center white line, on a road, so that it goes off the road, and all the cars smash up in the ditch. Or take the friend who got a job once painting the stripe down the center of a village street, past a bar he was drawn to as he painted toward it, and finally the line hit the sidewalk — and the street likewise. Because where the line goes is where it is, and what locates itself with reference to that line goes too.

Line begins to have this unequivocal presence in "Haines City" (1964) in that the shape of the canvas is directly the form given it by the activity of the line, and the form it defines. The diagonals are, again, a center for this activity, but now the parts of the canvas which cannot be used are removed. In other words, not only has the activity broken free of the physical situation of a canvas within a frame — as abstract expressionism managed to do, insisting that the coherence of what was happening in the painting was quite enough — it has managed to affect all that context of surface qua 'picture' to such an extent that only such surface as is actively engaged by the painting will be admitted as a physical object. It has done this with line.

Last fall I was able to see Stella's show at Kasmin in London, and it was an extraordinary experience — for these reasons. First, line in these paintings not only determines the context of the canvas' shape; it further allows no other possible sense of such shape to begin with. It is moving on a ground that can only be felt as its activity. It does another thing as well. I was there with a friend, and as I was sitting on that bench seen in the illustration, she walked in front of the painting on the far wall. It was as if she reoccurred, momently, i.e., her own size shifted and changed with reference to the lines she moved in front of — the painting was as much a defining *object* as she was.

But the lines, in any case, were going elsewhere, and it is not only the point, that they had this effect. Nor that they created 'architectural' effects (as she said) and seemed to make a volume. I think the fact that they had gained their own articulation, that they found shape as they moved — rather than as 'it' might — is the primary one.

What Stella himself secured seems to me a large possibility indeed. In his show at the Ferus Gallery in February relationships of triangular forms reoccur, and the shape of the canvas follows them, with a quiet, intense wit and care. After the more variable 'open' shapes of the Kasmin show, he comes to these with a line so sure he has only to follow it.

[*Lugano Review,* No. 1, 1965]

Feedback: "Contemporary Voices in the Arts" *

THE WHOLE THING BEGAN characteristically enough. I'd got to the Mohawk terminal at La Guardia, and met the others — Billy Kluver, John Cage, Merce Cunningham, Stan Vanderbeek, Jack Tworkov, and Len Lye. Some were hungry, so went off to find something to eat quickly, leaving Len, myself, and a young friend of Stan's to find some place to be comfortable till the plane was ready to go. Len led us into a rather formal restaurant where a waitress immediately gave us large menus and waited for our orders. We simply wanted to talk and so Len with a lovely avoidance kept the whole scene in confusion. We sat there with all this *function* around us somehow unable to catch up with the fact we were not really there to have dinner nor to do anything but that which we were obviously doing.

There is a lag in the situation of the eye's response to projected film image, for example, which Stan reported as about one-tenth of a second, that lets the eye see a continuous image rather than the literal fact of the static frame-by-frame that is the case. Just so in the proposal of the restaurant, the assumption of a *necessary order* let the three of us use it in quite another manner, and we were thus able to enjoy the lag of their adjustment to the fact that we were there to do nothing more than sit comfortably and talk.

*Early in 1967 a group of seven artists toured several universities in New York State as part of the New York State Council on the Arts' program "Contemporary Voices in the Arts."

At one point — at Albany State — Billy and John were continuing a conversation with students that had started in an almost impossibly dead ballroom, just that no one could hear anything said even a few feet from them, and now we were all sitting in an anonymous classroom. John had been speaking of what he felt to be the necessity of testing all assumptions of cause and effect. As answer to a student who asked him how that might be done, he said, simply try to make use of any situation in a way that the assumptions proposing it have not dealt with. If you get a grant, say, proposing you study cloud formations, see if you can use it for a trip to Europe, or whatever might interest you in that sense specifically.

We were an odd company without question. Often I felt an awkward distance in my own occasion from that which was clearly the possibility of the others, and I envied the articulation and particularity of Stan's nonverbal 'language.' Reading poems, as I'd known it, with the discreet placement of the audience, the fixed focus, the single term of the reader's voice and image, all seemed to make an impossibly static circumstance. Consequently I never made use of it during any of the eight evenings we had together. Instead I tried to project voice into the simultaneity of the multiple occurrences much as Stan was in fact doing with his battery of projectors and view-o-graphs. I was very curious to discover what *kinds* of hearing were actual in such a multiplicity of event. When some people at Union said they hadn't been able to hear anything back of the first few rows, I couldn't really care, just that I'd heard, as I knew those first few rows had, a fantastic blast of sound into which entered *images* of voices as actual as William Carlos Williams saying, in a suddenly vacant quiet, "Be patient that I address you in a poem . . ." to be bumped abruptly by what-

ever it was did then occur. The world of my own head,
selfishly enough, was changing significantly.

Since there were seven of us, and, in the two weeks of
the tour, seven places to be visited, we decided that each
one of us in turn would take an evening. He could, if he
chose, make use of the others as he saw fit. Since Harpur
had an active dance program, Merce was given direction of
that evening, and the rest of us were placed at various points
on the stage, which was segmented in at least five sections,
all of which could be raised or lowered independently.
David Vaughan, the tour manager, was back of the stage
operating the control panel without being able to see us,
so that we went up and down with a lovely randomness.
Back of us Merce drew the form of the space into a sequence
of extraordinary articulations. There were various mic-
rophones placed about which we could use as we wished,
either to note senses of dance or to say whatever we wished.
Billy read a quietly didactic sequence of proposals with an
icy blue-white spot on him. Len, always impatient with any
located place, was walking around somewhat like a carnival
barker, trying to get hold of the audience directly and ad-
monishing them to admit the fact of their own feelings. I
felt like Gagarin, saying something like, I'm a bird, I'm a
bird! John was making great gnomic sense, but Jack was
somehow most articulate of all. He sat there, saying literally
nothing, as the section of stage under him raised and lowered the chair he was sitting in, as Stan's images floated all
around him and off the walls and ceilings surrounding. The
intensity of his attention to the *newness* of this experience
was so evident it became more than any of us could say.

Immediately when we had first met, we decided any
formal *panel* procedure would be specious. As John said, if
we began by talking about where we thought the arts were
going, then we'd be stuck with where we thought they had

come from – and that was patently an endless dialogue. In the discussions that did often follow the specific activities of the evenings, there were inevitably both faculty and students who felt themselves defrauded by our conduct. I remember one professor in particular at R.P.I. who said he felt us pathetic, coming as we did with what were acceptably defined abilities in the various arts he assumed us to represent, to engage an audience in what he could only recognize as a primitive randomness. John answered him sharply, pointing out that he was imposing a decision of taste and habit upon a situation that was literally a process of exploration. There were no assumptions there to be insisted upon other than the one which might feel possibility to be more interesting than the limits of habit.

Much that was said continues to be very active for me. For example, in an afternoon conversation with students, John said: "Distinguish between that 'old' music you speak of which has to do with *conceptions* and their *communication*, and this new music, which has to do with *perception* and the arousing of it in us. You don't have to fear from this new music that something is bad about your liking your own music."

He made use of a simple diagram on the board: conceptions/fixed – perceptions/fluid. He suggested: Likes and dislikes are associated with the ego not on its dream side but on its daytime side in connection with what it receives through the senses. Now if you divide your sense perceptions into what you like and dislike, you might just be cheating yourself. As far as we know for sure, you're only alive once. Your sense perceptions are in good working order. They will not necessarily remain in good working order. Beethoven, for instance, growing deaf ... While your ears are in good working order, and while your eyes are in good working order, it seems to me that you would want,

rather than shutting your eyes and ears to available experience, rather to open them . . .

Stan put frequent emphasis on the very evident fact of
process as condition of contemporary environment, noting
that colleges and universities, as airports, were always being
built, rarely completed. Again, it was in the exploration of
this situation that we found a common vocabulary. Billy
Kluver made a unique contribution to the company in that,
being an engineer, process is an unequivocal attention for
him, happily apart from a conceptual 'aesthetics.' At R.P.I.
he and Robbie Robinson, another engineer from Bell who
had participated in the "Nine Evenings," created a sound
system that permitted the audience to tune FM radios to
particular 'broadcasts' of live activity, so that one had
'campfire' situations of various groups in the audience so
tuned in as all the other activity went on around them. He
had wanted a kind of trade fair environment, with each of
us in 'booth' locations that the audience might move freely
around, again tuning in what interested them. But once
there, the limits of the equipment and the auditorium, with
its fixed seats, which he had to work with, caused a modi-
fication — proving again that what happens is more relevant
than what doesn't.

Toward the end a kind of feedback gained in the continuity began to be a problem, I felt. Inevitably we gained
a sophistication in dealing with the kinds of questions we
were asked. Yet the habits, in that sense, of the audience
were the most continual limit. It is interesting to remember
how the idea of the last evening, the "TV Dinner" eaten
literally at the Y in New York, came about. We were in
Albany, having dinner, guests of Mr. Hightower, and Jack
said, why don't we do this — and immediately John was
thinking of contact mikes, Stan of the possibility of closed
circuit TV, Billy of the obvious engineering problems, and

Len of his lovely fish. When the actual evening came, I found I'd learned one very useful thing — to trust the fact of any literal condition I am in. But the fairly discreet rage of the audience — neither students nor faculty this time, and very sophisticated indeed as to its judgments — was something else, and the screaming feedback, and the projected pleasure of that meal and ourselves eating it, seems to have met with active qualifications.

I don't think I've ever eaten a better piece of meat, and the company was especially pleasant. There was a very happy air of being together again. At one point apparently the Y's stage manager came up to Robinson and said, "You've got to do something, the crowd is getting very restless." Robinson continued with his own preoccupations. They were literally more interesting.

[*Arts Magazine,* Summer 1967]

"Mehr licht..."

Not so very long ago it was characteristic to associate film with dramatic or with narrative art. We *saw* the images, so to speak, but we tended to place them as a story, a continuity necessarily involved with a message that either a novel or a play might otherwise convey. Something flashing, or stuttering in a myriad of colors, might alter our attention, but it was at best, we thought, an effect used in support of the actual purpose: to get on with the story itself.

In contrast to this presumption, a film by Stan Brakhage wants to push us out, to force us, in fact, to *see* as the activity of light itself permits us to. One mutual friend may object that he is "ruining our eyes" but I would emphasize that it is in the defense of those eyes, and their possibility, that his work takes on its most real and singular character. Therefore I interrupt myself and these notes to look again at a beautifully simple and precise instance, *Mothlight*. What do I see?

> pulsing —
> > kinetic — flicker
>
> tones brown, green
> > details of [moth] wing, other parts —
>
> occurring between light source — and
> > the light now on the wall —
> > scale — as detail of "size"
>
> the presence (present-s as he would say)
> of what occurs *in* the light.

> And I find myself seeing the "blank" film
> at the end as particularized now — dust bits,
> scratches, something *in* the light.

My understanding is that this film was made by placing fragments of mothwings and parts between strips of scotch-tape — and of making from that a print capable of projection. To see, in short, what is in the light — as dust motes in the air might be so seen.

His early films are, effectually, "psychodramas" but his work moves intensively, and quickly, into the literality of light as the eye is given to experience it. A significant film of this experience is *Anticipation of the Night*, which he has spoken of as follows:

> The daylight shadow of a man in its movement evokes lights in the night. A rose bowl held in hand reflects both sun and moon like illumination. The opening of a doorway onto trees anticipates the twilight into the night. A child is born on the lawn, born of water with its promissory rainbow, and the wild rose. It becomes the source of all light. Lights of the night become young children playing a circular game. The moon moves over a pillared temple to which all lights return. There is seen the sleep of innocents in their animal dreams, becoming the amusement, their circular game, becoming the morning. The trees change color and lose their leaves for the morn, they become the complexity of branches in which the shadow man hangs himself . . .

What I find relevant here is the apparent melding of a vocabulary involved with symbolic action ("a circular game") and with the phenomenal character of light itself ("anticipates the twilight into the night").

His notes for beginning film-makers are relevant in that he proposes one take film into a light-free room and there expose it to specific activity of light — for example, the flare of a match or the beam of a penlight. Equally, he suggests scratching on black filmstrip, so that this qualification of light may be experienced. He wants to emphasize that what the film will evoke or more accurately make manifest is the *activity* of light as the eye is given to experience it by means of its action on the "light sensitive" film.

Consider how explicit the activity of light is to film in all senses. We see the movie by virtue of the fact that light is being projected from a source, through a material variously prepared (e.g., by camera, painting, scratching, direct exposure, alternate chemical action, etc.) — and here of course the point is that light may be used not only to "create" the initial condition of the film, but is itself "created" and/or brought to reveal the multiple condition of its nature by its passage through the film.

In fact, it is *light* and the *eye* which experiences it that seem to me the two insistent terms of Brakhage's activity as a film-maker. I know that he has also deep concern with "what things mean" and with basic human relationships — but light, in all its modality, as "seeing sees it," is much more to my own mind his insistent preoccupation. So it is that perhaps the most ambitious of his masterworks is called *The Art of Vision.* No doubt he thinks as well of that kind of vision which is called "visionary" and he without question possesses it. Yet I love that teasing, nonsense wisdom of, "Where was Moses when the lights went out . . ." It must be part of all that says, "Let there be light . . ." — or that calls one into the light, asks that light be shed on this, lightens the load well as the heart.

Not long ago I sat with friends watching a number of the 8mm films which comprise the lovely *Songs* sequence, and because we were in the living room of an adobe house, and senses of earth in that way all around us, and because there were the occasional lights of passing cars, like firelight flickering on the walls — I felt an oldtime invocation of *possibility*. Pound says, "Damn your taste! I'd like if possible to sharpen your perceptions after which your taste can take care of itself . . ." John Cage has spoken of that previous music, as he might put it, which had to do with concept and its demonstration, and of that music he himself has had so much to do with, which concerns perceptions and their arousal. The center of what we were seeing was the very possibility of sight itself. We saw the light.

To return then . . .   I have been looking at a recent issue of *Scientific American* (September 1968) devoted to "Light," and much of it I can't follow. Still much of it and/or what its subject concerns is familiar to me because of conversations with Brakhage. For example — that what we see as color is due to the failure of the material from which light is being reflected to absorb that color. But more to the point here: the experience offered by his films is initial, and has to do with the primary fact of sight, as light creates it.

October 29, 1968
[*Arts Canada*, December 1968]